Culture& Civilization

Culture&Civilization

Irving Louis Horowitz, editor

VOLUME FOUR:
RELIGION IN THE SHADOWS
OF MODERNITY

Transaction Publishers
New Brunswick (U.S.A.) and London (U.K.)

Culture & Civilization
Volume Four

Contents

Editor's Introduction   xi

Religions

1.   Christian Sources of Western Civilization   1
     A. L. Kroeber

2.   The Catholic Church and Sexual Abuse   13
     William Donohue

3.   Economic Structure and the Life of the Jews   35
     Simon Kuznets

Civilizations

4.   Why is Africa Poor?   40
     Greg Mills

5.   Freedom and Exchange in Communist Cuba   51
     Yoani Sánchez

6.   Regime Change and Democracy in China   69
     Liu Xiaobo

7.   Shifting Balances between Business and   85
     Government in the United States
     Murray Weidenbaum

United Nations
Publications

Basic Facts about the United Nations

Release Date: June, 2011
ISBN 13: 9789211012354
Publisher: United Nations, Department of Public Information

Civil Society, Conflicts and the Politicization of Human Rights

Release Date: July, 2011
ISBN 13: 9789280811995
Publisher: United Nations University

Progress of the World's Women 2011-2012: In Pursuit of Justice

Release Date: July, 2011
ISBN 13: 9781936291335
Publisher: United Nations Development Fund for Women

State of the World Population 2010: From Conflict and Crisis to Renewal - Generations of Change

Release Date: June, 2011
ISBN 13: 9780897149747
Publisher: United Nations Population Fund

30: UNAIDS Outlook Report 2011

Release Date: August, 2011
ISBN 13: 9789291738915
Publisher: United Nations, United Nations Office in Geneva

World Youth Report: Youth and Climate Change

Release Date: April, 2011
ISBN 13: 9789211303032
Publisher: United Nations, Department of Economic and Social Affairs

Cultures

8.   The Democratic Warrior and his Social Identity   99
     Andreas Herberg-Rothe

9.   Reconstruction of Liberal Education   126
     Daniel Bell

10. The Anti-leadership Vaccine   134
     John W. Gardner

11. The Social Context of Medicine   144
     John Charles

History of Ideas

12. Crane Brinton, the New History, Retrospective   164
     Sociology, and *The Jacobins*
     Howard Schneiderman

13. Herbert Spencer and the Science of Ethics   179
     Jonathan H. Turner

14. Hannah Arendt as Radical Conservative   195
     Irving Louis Horowitz

15. Max Gluckman, *The Politics of Law and Ritual*   211
     in Tribal Society
     Sally Falk Moore

Editor's Introduction to Volume Four of *Culture & Civilization*

THIS IS THE FOURTH ANNUAL publication of *Culture & Civilization*. There is a librarian's folktale that if a serial publication survives beyond its third year, it somehow merits recognition—or at least a purchase from the slender library budget. Whether such a view is myth or fact, it is clear enough that the general purposes of a publication begin to be filled out and specific targets of attention take on greater clarity—for editors, contributors, and readers alike.

In the case of this publication it amounts to something of a literary shadow imitating what in music is known as theme and variation. The theme in our case remains the driving force: to provide a paradigm for explaining precisely what it means to speak of the larger picture, something beyond the psychological but not so far removed from ordinary life that it veers over into the metaphysical. This is a thin line that every musical composition must walk. It is also the delicate line that editors must walk.

In this instance, the emergence of religion as a fact of quotidian life has been established beyond a shadow of doubt by debates on the meaning of religious belief in an advanced technological age—something far beyond the nineteenth century imagery of the "warfare" between science and religion. This is more so by the stunning emergence on the world scene of militant Muslim beliefs in a period of relative quiescent religious belief or, at least, dormant church attendance throughout parts of Europe where dominant religions such as Christianity received their burgeoning growth if not their beginnings.

If the theme remains culture and civilization, then the variation in this issue is religion and post-modern societies. The piece by William Donohue is both as old as the Roman Catholic Church and the vows of probity and chastity it insists for its clerical personnel (male and female), and as new as present day headlines on issues of child abuse, pederasty, and infidelities of all sorts. Two additional pieces are underground classics: the previously unpublished essay by the great economist Simon Kuznets on the "Economic Structure and the Life of the Jews," and the rather breathtaking essay by the anthropologist A.L. Kroeber, who actually risks talking about the "Christian Sources of Western Civilization."

The anomaly of authoritarianism and development is taken up in a brilliant piece by Greg Mills on "Why is Africa Poor?", the courageous and humor spiked remarks by Yoani Sánchez on freedom and exchange in Cuba, and Liu Xiaobo's statement on regime change without economic system change in China. The cultural segment examines democratic processes and the social contexts of education, medicine, and identity as such. The final segment on the History of Ideas continues a pattern of review-essay writing on famous figures, providing a retrospective of the general views of special figures ranging from Crane Brinton, Herbert Spencer, Max Gluckman, and Hannah Arendt who do not quite go quietly into the silent night of academic fossils with strong political agendas.

The volume as a whole has an easy feel. It does not get trapped either in past reminiscences or present remorse; it projects a sense of the future that well avoids hysteria. In this, one might say that the fourth volume is old-fashioned, but with a sharp edge that speaks in a critical voice to the dilemmas of the present world order.

1

Christian Sources of Western Civilization

A. L. Kroeber

OUR OWN CIVILIZATION, the Western, grew up largely on the European part of the soil previously occupied by the Roman half of the Hellenic or Greco-Roman or Classical civilization, but with some extensions beyond the former Roman frontier, as in Germany. The time of its beginning may be set somewhere between 500 and 900 A.D.

Toynbee says before 700. One might shade this more narrowly to 650, as the date perhaps marking most closely the nadir of barbarization intervening between the past Classical and the coming Western civilization. Spengler says 900, or sometimes tenth century, in referring to the birth of the Western culture; but with a gestation or "prodromal" period since 500.

In favor of the recognition of such an embryonic stage there are the following facts. By 500 all of the Roman west was in barbarian power and political control, and the old Classical culture was in clear disintegration there; but nothing was yet apparent that was qualitatively suggestive of the future European civilization. However, around 900 or soon after, as Spengler observes, the main modern nationalities of Western Europe emerged: that is, they attained consciousness of themselves as nationalities. The first historical appearance of the French and German languages, as distinct from Latin and from Germanic vernaculars, is in a tenth century record of the Strasbourg oaths which the grandsons of Charlemagne gave each other in 842. Spengler's prodromal phase of 500-900 has the merit of doing something, conceptually, with Charlemagne's empire and the so-called Carolingian cultural renaissance. This Carolingian renaissance obviously underlay all Western civilization chronologically; and yet it left so little impression on this civilization as to be puzzling. If it was a revival, how could it have so little permanent effect? Was it therefore perhaps an abortive endeavor rather than an actual revival? In fact, in the century after Charlemagne, everything Carolingian disintegrated[1]—the empire with its internationalism as well as much of the meager little rebirth of culture. By contrast, the basic alignments that emerged during the following tenth century—whether national, social, or cultural alignments—have persisted until today under all the enrichments and modifications that have been added to them.

It has always been a question of what the Carolingian empire and unification of western Christian Europe—and this was the only political unification that Europe ever attained!—what Charlemagne's empire really meant, on long-range view. Apparently its significance lay in its declaration of autonomy. Charles the Great's empire declared the westerly Greco-Roman civilization definitely dead, and the West now independent of the Byzantine survival of easterly Greco-Roman civilization. Hence the suddenly overt tensions between West and East within the Christian Church at this period.[2] But the West was still too poor in material wealth and in cultural content to develop a real civilization under Charlemagne. So it had to begin over again, and much less pretentiously, a century or more later when the Carolingian empire had not only fallen to pieces, but had been definitely superseded by the emerged nationalistic consciousness.

Western civilization has throughout remained multinational, "polyphonic and orchestral," as it then began in the 900's. It is of very real significance that Charlemagne's unification has never yet been successfully imitated in Europe, though Spaniards, French and Germans[3] successively have tried; and Russians are apparently still trying. Precedent is therefore against the Russians, if they belong to the Western civilization. Whereas if they represent an essentially separate civilization, as Danilevsky contended, there is no precedent for or against their prospects. In that case, the "youth" of Russian culture may mean either that it possesses greater vigor and strength than the older Western civilizations, or that it is characterized by greater immaturity and fumbling.

The basic multinationalism of Western civilization is also evident from the fact that it had hardly begun to crystallize out when, within a generation of the year 1000, there were added to the French and German consciousnesses a further series of emerging nationalities: Polish,[4] Hungarian, Scandinavian, and English,[5] which have persisted.[6]

We may therefore conclude that at some time between 500 and 650 or 700 the essential detachment of western Europe from Greco-Roman civilization became effective; that from 650-700 on this autonomy began to come into the consciousness of western societies and that these tended to assume first political cohesion and then national scope; and that around 900 or 950 the framework of the new culture began to fill, however humbly at first, with cultural content of its own creation. By 1100, with the Crusades, the youthful Western society had already become aggressive against the societies of the Byzantine and Arab Islamic civilizations—impracticably aggressive as regards permanent expansion, it is true, but nevertheless actually successful for a time.

> Western civilization is at the moment the dominant one in the world. Its ending has been repeatedly forecast.

This Western civilization is at the moment the dominant one in the world. Its ending has been repeatedly forecast: as follows. By Danilevsky, it was forecast to happen soon, whenever Russia shall become consolidated; because the West is already overripe. By Spengler, the prediction is for about 2200, Caesarism and the "civilization" phase having been entered on around 1800. By Toynbee, the end threatens and is indicated by numerous warning symptoms. This end may possibly happen soon, but it is by no means inevitable, because ultimate resources are moral and religious, and are therefore beyond real predictability. For my part, I refrain from long-range prophecy. It is tempting but usually unprofitable, practically as well as intellectually: its emotional repercussions tend to be high, its probability values low.

The course of this Western civilization of ours is remarkable for the strong degree of difference of content between its two main phases, which are usually called the Mediaeval and the Modern. The first, which culminated in the twelve hundreds and really ended soon after 1300, is characterized by the power and success of the Church. It was in the High Mediaevalism of the West that Christianity reached the crowning success of its career. Christianity at that time achieved an organization and domination of society that were not only extraordinarily effective but were culturally productive and concordant. Mediaeval philosophy, architecture, and art are thoroughly religious and at the same time embody secular values of a high order. Other branches of Christianity—Greek, Slavic, and Nestorian—were equally sincere and fervid, but they failed to produce even rudiments of anything comparable either aesthetically or intellectually.

Around 1300 and the ensuing decades the tight High Mediaeval Christian frame began to be unable to contain any longer the cultural creativity that was swelling within it. The earlier satisfaction afforded by mere existence within this frame and the essential indifference or hostility to everything outside it now commenced to disappear. Knowledge of what lay beyond, knowledge of the past, and secular knowledge became more and more sought. Religious feeling weakened, at least relatively. The Church as an organization fell into troubles: there happened the attempt of Anagni, the Popes at Avignon, the Great Papal Schism, the Hussite Revolt, and the Councils that failed to result in reforms. Systematic scholastic philosophy virtually died as knowledge increased by leaps and bounds—knowledge of the world as well as inventions and technologies: gunpowder, printing, oil painting, seaworthy ships, spectacles, clocks, playing cards, Arabic numerals and algebra, casting of iron and other metallurgical processes. Not one of these had anything to do with religion or furthered religion, but they all enriched the civilization and the life under it. The Gothic arts continued for a time, on momentum. But they showed definite symptoms of decadence: flamboyancy, perpendicularity; or they were applied secularly to guild halls and tomb monuments, not to cathedrals. The Mediaeval profane vernacular literatures, lyrical and narrative, now became arid, allegorizing, or extravagant. Even the political structure shook.

The monarchies receded from such mild strength as they had attained in the thirteenth century. Towns grew in wealth and strength but also in embroilments; feudalism was losing its hold, but no substitute for it had forged into consciousness. Politically, the two centuries were centrifugal and disruptive; in Spain and Germany as in France and England royal power receded.

Only northern Italy now marched forward to an affirmation and realization of cultural achievements; while in France, the Low Countries, Germany, and more or less in all the rest of Europe, culture, though growing, was at the same time floundering and sliding as a result of the progressive weakening of the traditional Mediaeval patterns. This was the period of the north Italian city-states; of growth, of commerce, and industry, as well as of applied science—spectacles, chimneys, "Arabic" arithmetic and calculation. It was also the time of great Italian literature, painting, architecture, sculpture, then of the foundation of great Italian music—in short, the Renaissance. The beginnings are around 1300, with Dante and Giotto as the symbols—both still Mediaeval in their thinking and feeling, but also initiators of a long line of illustrious personalities whose surge did not begin to enter full culmination until 1500 and was two centuries more in subsiding. This stretch of Italian greatness was achieved wholly without national political unity or military triumphs. It was briefer and more localized than the Mediaeval phase, and thus is perhaps more usefully construed as an interphase transition than as a phase in its own right.

Around 1550 or 1600—perhaps 1575 will serve fairly as a precise definition, though nothing of this sort occurs without gradation—the second main movement in the European symphony began to be played when the other West European countries drew abreast of Italy in wealth, refinement of manners, the arts, and the sciences, after having politically consolidated themselves into organized nation-states. This consolidation gave them a massive weight which before long put them culturally ahead, as regards to productivity, of the free but fragmented Italian cities, or of the "duchies" into which most of these had been transformed or absorbed. Portugal, Spain, Holland, England, and France successively achieved this new phase of activity. Meanwhile, with the Reformation, a degree of ideological and emotional autonomy from Italian supremacy was also attained by the northerly nations. This autonomy aided the northern nations, such as Germany, that remained nationalistically or culturally backward, to lay a foundation for greater accomplishment in a subsequent century.

Still later, after about 1750, industrialism, enormously rapid accumulation of wealth, experimental science, democracy and liberalism developed especially in the northwesterly countries, and gave this corner of the continent an increasing precedence of strength, prestige, and influence, in which America came to share and predominate. Now, this shift is fully familiar; also, like everything that touches us immediately, it is difficult to appraise in historical perspective. A complete understanding of this shift, if it could be attained, would no doubt be full of implications as to the future of our Western civilization—as to its "fate." But that is just what we are not considering at the moment when we are trying to define the *known* boundaries and organization of our civilization, not to guess or argue its future.

Western Civilization has throughout been multinational and Christian. After a gestational period of some centuries, it entered a first full phase of about four hundred years in which all higher achievements were meshed into religion. This was the time of culmination of not only the church as an ecclesiastical institution but of Christianity as an ideology and affective nexus. There followed a two or two-and-a-half century period of transition in which many or most of the patterns of this first phase were increasingly loosened and softened, while a set of modified or new patterns gradually formed which were to characterize the subsequent second or Modern phase. Creative cultural leadership in both phases was Transalpine, mostly centering in or near France; in the intervening transition time the leadership and influence were strikingly Cisalpine.[7]

Italy as a segment of Western civilization thus culminated while the remainder of the West was formally uncreative due to being in metamorphosis. But, as the northern and western countries got their second phase patterns organized, by about 1575, Italy receded in innovation and influence. Italy's peculiar role within the civilization seems bound up first with its having been the political and prestige center of the last phase of the preceding Greco-Roman civilization, with consequent tendency to retain remnants or remembrances of that civilization. Second, Italian particularity seems connected with having, perhaps on account of its retentions, resisted with a measure of success full acceptance of the High Mediaeval patterns with their barbarian Transalpine provenience and "Gothic" feudal and non-Classical quality. And third, as these patterns were nevertheless at last partly accepted in Italy, but, by a sophisticated population which had never wholly left its towns, they blended with the vestiges and occasional recoveries[8] of the former civilization on the same soil, and above all with the now unleashed creative energies of the people. This put Italy transiently into the van of Western civilization. At about the time when the impulses of this spurt were waning, the Transalpine peoples had begun to formulate their new patterns—such as a dissenting cast of anticlerical Christianity, geographical discovery and expansion, centralized monarchy of power, and noticeable accumulation of wealth. Blending these with what they took over from High Renaissance Italy in patterns of manners and art—as Italy had previously accepted some of their Mediaevalism—these northern and western nations attained to the full second phase of Western civilization. This phase in turn, from about 1750-1800 on, spread toward the margins of Europe—Germany, Scandinavia, the Slavic areas—and into the Americas.

> The course of a large multinational civilization may be more complex than a smooth rise, culmination, and decline.

If this characterization of the salient physiognomy of Western culture history is essentially correct, it has certain implications of a general and theoretical nature. Such general implications may be more important than even successful close-up predictions would be. The implications may in fact be what in the end will contribute most to our capacity to predict reliably. What this formulation shows is that the course of a large multinational civilization may be more complex than a smooth rise, culmination, and decline; that it may come in successive surges or pulses—what we have called phases. It is further plain, so far as the preceding formulation is sound, that the intervals between the pulses may be, at least over most of the area of the civilization, periods of pattern dissolution, preparatory to pattern reconstruction. Consequently, even if the mid-twentieth century suffered from a breakdown of its cultural patterns—as is so often alleged and perhaps with most force and reason as regards the arts—the question still remains open whether such a breakdown is part of the final death of our civilization, as is sometimes feared or asserted; or if, on the contrary, it is merely symptomatic of an inter-pulse reconstruction. In the former case, Spengler's prophecies and Toynbee's fears would be right; in the latter, the present time would be only a sort of counterpart of what Transalpine Europe—most of Europe—was undergoing during the Italian Renaissance.

This question cannot be answered off-handedly in the context of the moment; and even less properly ought a too sure answer be given to it at any time. The points to be summarized at this stage of our argument are essentially these. First, it is clear that civilizations are not simple, natural units that are easy to distinguish, or that segregate themselves out from the continuum of history on mere inspection. Second, the duration limits of any one civilization, the points of its beginning and ending, may also be far from easy to define. Instead of being something one begins with as evident, a determination of the limits may be a problem in itself. If Toynbee can recognize China I and II and India I and II, why can we not recognize Western I and II?—with perhaps a Western III about to follow? Especially so since it is customary to accept without qualms Egypt *a, b, c, d,* even though not quite separate Egypts I, II, III, and IV. For all that has yet been shown one way or the other, the future may have in store not only Western III but perhaps even IV. In that event, our troubles of today would prove, when the full record shall be in, to be the reconstructive or the growing pains of the transition between phase II that ended say with the nineteenth century and a phase III that will perhaps reach its full beginning in the twenty-first.

Offhand, indeed, Western I and Western II—Mediaeval and Modern Europe—would seem probably to differ more in their patterns than China I from China II. That is, Tang-Ming China would appear a less altered continuation of Shang-Han China, in spite of its addition of the new religion of Buddhism, than Modern Europe is a continuation of Mediaeval Europe even though Christianity was maintained through both. To be sure, what is foreign and remote always seems more uniform and more continuous than the familiar. Accordingly a careful judicial weighing after intimate acquaintance with both sets of civilizations—if anyone possesses an equally sensitive acquaintance—might conceivably reverse the impression and leave us with the finding that Europe did indeed constitute a single though double-phase civilization, but that China was better construed as two successive civilizations, as Toynbee has it. Yet who could today press with honest assurance for the greater historic truth of either of the two alternatives? The problem is one of estimating the relative degree of difference between complex value-systems. For those interested in such judgments, it is intellectually fair and profitable to form impressions and opinions, but not to assert them beyond tentativeness. All we can really do at present is to ask ourselves questions of this kind, perhaps adding hesitant suggestions of answers. When a number of equipped minds shall have weighed the relevant evidence for perhaps some decades, their findings will carry real weight.

But, as long as we are essentially only asking, we can even now push our questioning farther. If we grant Toynbee's China I and II, and India I and II, and Mesopotamia I and II;[9] and if we are ready to concede at any rate the possibility that the unity of Western civilization may properly be dissolved into Europe I and II; then why should not the taken-for-granted unit which Toynbee calls "Hellenic" civilization and Spengler "Classical"—why should this not be broken into its Greek and Roman components—in parallel terminology, Greco-Roman I and II?

For that matter, genuine consideration could be given this taxonomy:

> Aegean =Northeast Mediterranean civilization I
> Greek = Northeast Mediterranean civilization II
> Roman = Northeast Mediterranean civilization III
> Byzantine = Northeast Mediterranean civilization IV

The four would be phases of one localized continuum of civilization that lasted no longer than the continuity of China or India or Mesopotamia or Egypt.[10]

It is evident, I hope, that we are in the stage of seeing problems such as these, indeed of having them forced on the attention; even though our verdicts remain as undogmatic as possible.

In the face of these larger problems, let us then leave the question of when Western civilization will end, or whether it has already begun to end, and of how many stages, phases, or movements it will have consisted when it has terminated—let us leave these problematical matters to the future to which they belong. We can summarize our findings on the completed segments of Western civilization somewhat like this:

500/700—900+/-. Prodromal stage. Pre-national; Christianity still developing its root system; cultural patterns unformed.

900+/-—1325+/-. First phase, Mediaeval. Nationalities present but little organized politically; culmination of Christianity; other culture, so far as well-patterned, saturated with Christianity.

1325+/- —1575+/-. Transition, Renaissance in Italy; loosening and re-constitution of culture patterns in Transalpine Europe.

1575+/- —?. Second phase, Modern. Nationalities politically organized; culture patterns founded on those of First phase but reformulated secularly, and of wider range.

? (1900?)—?. Commencing disintegration of whole civilization? Or second transition to a third phase?

Notes

1. The weakness accompanying the Carolingian disintegration is pregnantly illustrated by the fact that the peak period of Viking raiding and spoliation of the continent fell between 830 and 900.

2. The tensions and rift are instanced by the Pope's crowning of Charlemagne as Caesar in 800; by Charlemagne's intervention in the *filioque* doctrinal dispute in 809; by the council of [Constantinople, 869-870] and the quarrel of Photius with the Popes [Nicholas I and Leo VI]; [and] by the contest of the eastern and western churches for the adhesion of Bulgaria.

3. Reference is to Hitler, not to the mediaeval Holy Roman Empire, which was always an unrealized dream nostalgic for a form. Even the Italians, whom in a sense this mediaeval pseudo-empire exalted, were for the most part opposed to it.

4. Russia also attained its first national organization around 1000, but is not included here because this early state still lay wholly outside the Roman Catholic and Western sphere of influence.

5. Decision would have to be made as between Canute the Dane, 1014-35, or Alfred, with the latter construed as preceding 1000 because of English geographical nearness to the Frankish-North French center.

6.   There is a brief tabular collocation in my Configurations, 726.
7.   Except for a definite trickle down the Rhine into the Low Countries.
8.   This incidental or secondary element of rediscovery or revivification is what has given the Italian cultural surge the name of Renaissance. It was of course far more a birth than a rebirth; but there is some minor ingredient of the latter, as there is of persistence from Greco-Roman civilization.
9.   Spengler simplifies the situation by recognizing only the "I" of China, India, and Mesopotamia, approximately, and refusing to discuss the "11's" as being merely frozen "civilizations," fellaheen petrifactions without living culture. But of course this is equivalent to recognizing the "117s." It is not their existence that Spengler denies-only their reaching a certain threshold of cultural worth.
10.   This interpretation has been developed in Configurations, 687-695, 1944.

A. L. Kroeber (1876-1960) was professor of anthropology at the University of California at Berkeley and director of what is now called the Phoebe A. Hearst Museum of Anthropology. He was best known for making connections between the field of archaeology and culture and is credited with developing the concepts of culture area, cultural configuration, and cultural fatigue. He is the author of numerous books including *The Religion of the Indians of California* and *Indian Myths of South Central California*.

VIRGINIA

After Apartheid
Reinventing South Africa?
Edited by Ian Shapiro
and Kahreen Tebeau

$40.00 | CLOTH

Major scholars chronicle South Africa's achievements and challenges since the transition to democracy in 1994.

Imagining Mount Athos
Visions of a Holy Place, from Homer to World War II
Veronica della Dora

$35.00 | CLOTH

"Beautifully written, scrupulously researched, fully illustrated, this is a visionary work, remarkable in its insight."—Metropolitan Kallistos (Ware) of Diokleia

The Reason of the Gift
Jean-Luc Marion
Translated by Stephen E. Lewis

$29.50 | CLOTH | RICHARD LECTURES

"A set of typically rigorous, informative, challenging, and illuminating essays by one of the world's leading philosophers."—Thomas Carlson, University of California, Santa Barbara

The Science of Religion in Britain, 1860–1915
Marjorie Wheeler-Barclay

$45.00 | CLOTH | VICTORIAN LITERATURE AND CULTURE SERIES

"*The Science of Religion in Britain, 1860–1915* is a major contribution to the history of ideas, the history of religion, and British history. It is a considerable achievement."
— Jeffrey Cox, University of Iowa

2

The Catholic Church and Sexual Abuse

William Donohue

IN THE AFTERMATH of the media blitz in 2002 exposing sexual abuse by Catholic priests, the United States Conference of Catholic Bishops (USCCB) created a National Review Board and an Office of Child and Youth Protection to deal with this problem. The Review Board subsequently commissioned researchers from the John Jay College of Criminal Justice to study what happened. In 2004, the first study, *The Nature and Scope of Sexual Abuse of Minors by Catholic Priests and Deacons, 1950-2002*, was published. Now it has released its latest study on the causes and context of abuse.

The initial study pinpointed the timeline when the abuse crisis was at its peak, roughly from the mid-1960s to the mid-1980s, and provided rich data on a host of important variables. What it did not do was account for why this happened. This is the subject of the *Causes and Context* report. Unlike the initial study, this one is fraught with controversy. One reason for this lays with the nature of the inquiry: studies on the causes of social problems generally leave more room for interpretative quarrels with the data than is true of reports of a more descriptive nature. Another reason, more serious, is the reluctance of social scientists to state conclusions that are highly controversial and that run against the grain of the conventional wisdom in the academy. All of this will be addressed, but first a look at what this second study sought to uncover.

The volume presents the context in which sexual abuse of minors by priests took hold. It is followed by a historical analysis of the problem. The third section explores the thorny issue of accounting for causes, the fourth deals with the way the Catholic Church responded to this matter, and the next analyzes the rise and decline of sexual abuse. The last chapter records the conclusions and recommendations of the authors. A wealth of material is presented, including a good overview of the relevant social science literature on the subject.

The crisis peaked in the 1970s and occurred at a time of increased levels of deviant behavior in society. The authors cite the role played by the sexual revolution in shaping the environment, and for this they have been attacked by those on the left. The *New York Times*, for instance, opines that this amounts to "sociological rationalization," saying it sounds very much like a "blame Woodstock" explanation.

> The cultural winds of promiscuity that hit the larger society in the 1960s and 1970s came smashing through the windows of the Catholic Church.

This is unfair. The authors were asked to put the abuse crisis in context, and it would have been delinquent of them not to cite the social and cultural milieu in which the problem emerged. Moreover, an explanation is not a justification. It should be clear by now that the cultural winds of promiscuity that hit the larger society in the 1960s and 1970s came smashing through the windows of the Catholic Church; it is not an insular institution. Mentioning this is not only defensible, it is good social science.

Celibacy as a cause is quickly dismissed because it cannot explain the rise and decline of the scandal. In a later section, the report astutely notes that "celibacy has been constant in the Catholic Church since the eleventh century and could not account for the rise and subsequent decline in abuse cases from the 1960s through the 1980s." The logic is sound.

Importantly, pedophilia is discounted: less than 5 percent of the abusive priests fit the diagnosis of pedophilia, thus, "it is inaccurate to refer to abusers as 'pedophile priests.'" Later we learn that the authors set the age of puberty at eleven, though it must be said that the American Academy of Pediatrics uses the age of ten, and other reputable health sources say that the onset of puberty begins at the age of nine. This warrants attention for good reason: the higher the age when puberty is said to begin, the lower the proportion of postpubescent sex that will be recorded. All of this figures into the discussion of pedophilia v. homosexuality.

Early on in the volume we get a glimpse of the controversy to come. "The majority of priests who were given residential treatment following an allegation of sexual abuse of a minor also reported sexual behavior with adult partners." Now we know from the first John Jay study (and the data are cited several times in this one), that 81 percent of the victims were male, and that almost as many were postpubescent. If we can extrapolate from this, it suggests that acts of abuse were not only mostly of a homosexual nature (pedophilia being largely ruled out), but that the abusive priests also had sexual relations; the partners, as will become evident, were mostly of the same sex. Yet the study contends that sexually active homosexual priests were not more likely to abuse minors. This apparent anomaly will also be addressed in detail.

An interesting piece of evidence shows that prior to 1985, it was the parents of the abused who reported the molestation. Ten years later, most of the reports stemmed from adults who claimed they were abused a decade or two earlier. Now it's the lawyers who are bringing suit, almost all of which are about alleged incidents that took place decades ago. The delay in bringing about the accusations become even more curious when one factors in something the authors of this study do not address: the increase in false accusations being made these days.

Comparative Data and Tainted Sources

The authors give credit to the Catholic Church for being the only institution in society to do a comprehensive report on the sexual abuse of minors. This complicates comparisons, of course. They attribute much of the progress to "human formation" courses in the seminaries. Whatever the reason, we soon learn something of great moment. It is said that the "incidence of child sexual abuse has declined in both the Catholic Church and in society generally, though the rate of decline is greater in the Catholic Church in the same time period." This cannot be said enough, especially given the unfair stereotyping of priests and bishops.

Though comparisons with other organizations are hard to make, there are good data with the public schools. Charol Shakeshaft is rightfully cited for her yeoman work on sexual abuse of students by educators. It would have been helpful to report what the Virginia Commonwealth University professor has said about sexual abuse by public school employees as compared to priests. She estimates that "the physical sexual abuse of students in schools is likely more than 100 times the abuse by priests." No one has been able to dispute her conclusion.

It was troubling to read the authors giving credibility to advocacy groups that are reflexively opposed to anything the bishops do. For example, there is no organization in the nation that has been more unfair to the bishops than the Survivors Network of those Abused by Priests (SNAP). Their animus is so consuming that when the Vatican issued worldwide guidelines on the proper way to handle abuse cases, SNAP issued a broadside against the proposals *the day before they were released.*

> **Incidence of child sexual abuse has declined in both the Catholic Church and in society generally.**

The report misrepresents this professed enemy of the Catholic Church as "a national movement of support for victims of sexual abuse by any church leader and, more recently, all victims of sexual abuse by any person in a position of authority." This is nonsense: almost all of its work is directed at the Catholic Church.

The same is true of Voice of the Faithful. Voice is a dissident Catholic group that has worked overtime to condemn practically every decision by the bishops. Just recently, the Catholic League exposed how Voice developed a fraudulent "survey" that sought to paint the priests of the Philadelphia Archdiocese in the worst possible manner. In the report, the authors mention a Voice "survey" of twenty priests who are at odds with their bishop. They actually admit that the "survey" was "distributed to a selection of priests known for their explicit action in support of victims and/or acknowledged for their support by the Voice of the Faithful (VOTF) organization." Seasoned social scientists should know better than to cite such ideologically tainted data.

Citing BishopAccountability.org as a credible source is also problematic. This website, which tallies accusations against priests, admits that it "does not confirm the veracity of any actual allegation." Not surprisingly, *it attacked the John Jay report the day before it was issued.* Why? Because the authors cited data from the Catholic Church.

Bishops Respond

The bishops have commonly been criticized for not sufficiently responding to the problem of abusive priests. As it turns out, the report does much to question the validity of this charge. It provides plenty of evidence that when this issue became well known in the mid-1980s, several initiatives were forthcoming.

"In a public statement made in 1988," it says, "the General Counsel of the NCCB [now the USCCB] defined 'affirmative activities' for dioceses to undertake as a proactive response to the issue of sexual abuse of minors by Catholic clergy. These activities included the education of diocesan personnel about the prevention of abuse of children, the development of policies to guide responses to a report of abuse, and the importance of working to mitigate the harm to victims and families."

In 1992, the aforementioned recommendations were codified and became known as the Five Principles. The next year saw the release of a report on priestly sexual abuse and the formation of the Ad Hoc Committee of Sexual Abuse. Over the next few years, this committee issued reports on treatment centers for abusive priests. However, the Vatican, unlike the American bishops, was slow to respond. As the report notes, when Archbishop Pio Laghi learned of what was going on in the 1980s, he was "shocked, perplexed, and mystified by the entire phenomenon." Yes, many in the Vatican hierarchy were slow to understand the breadth and depth of the problem.

While the bishops were taking this issue seriously, much of what they tried to do, we now know, was in vain. To be exact, they were being briefed in the late 1980s and the early 1990s about the wrong problem, and were similarly misled about the right remedy. It must be stressed that this is my own conclusion. But it is reached by reliance on the data contained in the report.

In the section dedicated to the organizational response to abuse, the report says that the bishops were offered several presentations by clinical psychologists about pedophilia at their meetings. But we now know that pedophilia was never the problem. It is not hard to surmise that to do so would be to raise questions about the role which homosexuality played.

In the same section, it makes it plain that therapy was being sold to the bishops as the right remedy. "Prior to 1984," it says, "the common assumption of those who the bishops consulted was that clergy sexual misbehavior was both psychologically curable and could be spiritually remedied by recourse to prayer." It also says that *after* 1985, "prompt psychological treatment for the priest was seen as the best course of action and became the primary intervention."

> Many in the Vatican hierarchy were slow to understand the breadth and depth of the problem of priestly sexual abuse.

Well, it is painfully obvious by now that the psychologists oversold their competence. It is not hard to surmise that the reason why the authors of the book do not flag this matter has something to do with their reluctance to indict their own profession.

Both of these issues are critical. If pedophilia was not the driving problem, then it seems that both the psychologists and the bishops wasted a lot of time considering it. Similarly, if therapy was mostly a failure, then informing the bishops that the abusers were successfully treated was doubly troubling: it was precisely this advice that led many bishops to reassign these supposedly rehabilitated priests; after they were transferred to a different parish, some of them offended again.

Regarding the utility of therapy, the report notes that "the use of treatment declines in the 1990s, and this decline reflects concerns about relapse and re-offense." This deserves commentary. If the decline in treatment coincided with a decline in the incidence of abuse, it suggests the failure of psychologists to treat the molesters. This doesn't mean that the psychologists were ill-trained; it means that the problem exceeded their ability to deal with it successfully. We don't blame doctors for not curing cancer, but all of us have a right to know the limitations of their expertise.

Another way the authors let those in the behavioral and social sciences off the hook, as well as abusive priests, is to claim that professional literature did not quite come to grips with the problem of the sexual abuse of minors until recent times. Victimization, they say, was "little understood" at the time when the abuse crisis peaked, and there was "little developing knowledge around the concepts of sexual violation, victimization, and the like." Furthermore, "priests may have been uncomfortable with their actions but would not have viewed them as criminal or harmful."

It strains credulity to maintain that sexual predators had to await the findings of social scientists before recognizing that what they were doing was wrong. According to this logic, in the 1950s, when the public, including priests, were really in the dark about the consequences of sexual abuse, there should have been more of it than in subsequent decades. But no one believes this to be true.

More to the point, are we to believe that priests, of all people, did not know that sexual abuse was wrong? Did they never hear of the Sixth Commandment?

A more accurate rendering is afforded by Religious Sister of Mercy Sister Sharon Euart, a canon lawyer. She observes that "the Church's canon law has made provision for sexual abuse of minors to be a grave offense since the Middle Ages." In other words, the medieval Catholic Church did not have to await the findings of behavioral and social scientists—which would not be published for hundreds of years—to know that sexual abuse was a sin. The problem in the Church, as the "Murphy Report" on abusive priests in Ireland said, was that "the Church authorities failed to implement most of their own canon law rules on dealing with child sex abuse." Had they done so, in the U.S. as well, matters would have been different.

The Role of Homosexuality

Despite many strengths, the report is seriously marred by its ideological reluctance to deal forthrightly with the role of homosexuality. We live in a time when the rights of homosexuals are ascendant, and talk of a negative nature is not only greeted with suspicion, it is silenced. This is especially true in higher education. It does not exaggerate to say that any professor who is associated with a study that implicates homosexuality as a factor in sexual abuse is setting himself up for trouble. This is unfortunate because unless we come to grips with this issue, our understanding of how this problem emerged will never progress.

Let it be said at the outset that it is not my position that homosexuality causes predatory behavior. Indeed, this argument is absurd. As I have said many times, while it is true that most gay priests are not molesters, most of the molesters have been gay. Nothing in the report changes my mind, and indeed there is much in it that fortifies my position.

Social scientists eschew singling out any one variable as the cause of human behavior, and that is why discussions of unicausality make no sense. Behavior is typically the product of multiple variables, which is why multivariate analysis is the norm. This does not mean, however, that all variables carry equal explanatory weight; they most certainly do not. All it means is that to attribute behavior to one causative agent is not credible.

> While it is true that most gay priests are not molesters, most of the molesters have been gay.

By way of example, consider the following. We know that the Irish are overrepresented among alcoholics. The data shows that African Americans are overrepresented in the prison population. The Chinese are overrepresented among smokers. Italians are overrepresented among organized crime families. And so on. But no one seriously maintains that inclusion in any one of these racial or ethnic groups determines the negative traits associated with them. On the other hand, where overrepresentation (or underrepresentation) exists, it does so for a reason. It is the job of the social scientist to follow the evidence, and not be driven by ideological concerns.

Certainly, in the priesthood, homosexuals have been overrepresented among abusers. Unfortunately, there are indications that the authors of the report are skittish about being identified with this position, despite their own data. For example, in its discussion of sexual abuse in the Boy Scouts, the report mentions that this organization "has been criticized" by "various civil rights organizations" for "prohibiting homosexual Scout leaders." This normative comment is revealing: by duly noting the criticism from elite circles, it tells us something about the concerns of the social scientists.

There are other giveaways as well. "Interestingly," the report says, "an increase in the number of male victims occurred during the peak years of the abuse crisis." Shortly thereafter, we learn that "interestingly, the use of alcohol and drugs by abusive priests increased significantly during the peak years of abuse (1970s and 1980s), but only for male victims." What is most interesting about these two remarks is that the authors appear almost surprised by what they found.

From my perspective, it would have made more sense to say "unsurprisingly" than "interestingly." Here's why. Four related events emerged at the peak of the crisis that account for what happened:

1. There was an exodus of heterosexual priests after Vatican II, a large percentage of whom got married;

2. The effect of this exodus was to leave behind a greater proportion of homosexual priests;

3. A tolerance for sexual expression in the seminaries was evident at this time, leading many previously celibate homosexual priests to act out; and,

4. There was a surge of homosexuals into the seminaries. It was the interaction of these four factors, I would argue, that accounts for the increase in male victims at the height of the sexual abuse crisis.

Similarly, they are struck by the fact that alcohol and drug use would increase at the same time the abuse crisis was peaking. But is this hardly surprising: from everything we know about molesters, substance abuse often accompanies sexual abuse.

In the concluding section of the report, it says, "the clinical data do not support the hypothesis that priests with a homosexual identity or those who committed same-sex sexual behavior with adults are significantly more likely to sexually abuse children than those with a heterosexual orientation or behavior."

How the authors came to this conclusion when it plainly admits that "81 percent of the victims [between 1950 and 2002] were male," and that 78 percent were postpubescent, is not only unclear, it is downright perplexing. It gets even more perplexing when we consider that the report takes the issue of pedophilia off the table. So if the abusers weren't pedophiles, and the victims were mostly adolescent males, wouldn't that make the victimizers homosexuals? What else could we possibly be talking about if not homosexuality?

The report says, "As generally understood now, homosexual behavior is the commission of a sexual act with someone of the same sex, in contrast to a heterosexual act, or sexual behavior engaged in by persons of different sexes." But has this not always been true? Why the need to state the obvious? More important, what accounts for their reluctance to state that most of the victims were abused by homosexuals?

We next learn something that weighs greatly on the social scientists. "What is not well understood is that it is possible for a person to participate in a same-sex act without assuming or recognizing an identity as a homosexual." Yes, it is entirely possible for a homosexual not to recognize that he is a homosexual. So what? Isn't it behavior, not self-perception, that objectively defines one's sexual orientation?

> Homosexuals, like vegetarians, are defined by what they do, not by what they believe themselves to be.

What follows next is critical. "More than three-quarters of the acts of sexual abuse of youths by Catholic priests, as shown in the *Nature and Scope* study, were same-sex acts (priests abusing male victims). It is therefore possible that, although the victims of priests were most often male, thus defining the *acts* as homosexual, the priest did not at any time recognize his *identity* as homosexual." It is a false segue to say, "It is therefore possible..." Such twisted logic suggests a failure to confront the obvious.

Let us grant that it is possible for gay priests to think they are not homosexuals. It cannot be said more emphatically that this changes nothing. If someone eats nothing but vegetables and does not consider himself to be a vegetarian, this is surely an interesting psychological issue, but it does not change reality. Subjectively, the vegetarian may think of himself as carnivorous, but his behavior belies his self-perception. Homosexuals, like vegetarians, are defined by what they do, not by what they believe themselves to be.

In the endnotes section the study says that "it is possible for a man to identify himself as 'heterosexual' because he is sexually attracted to adult women; however, he may commit an act of sexual abuse against a male youth." Let us concede the point. Yes, this may happen. But social science analysis, the authors well know, is informed by what is generally true, and is not driven by anomalies. In this vein, it would hardly change the status of a vegetarian if he were to experiment with hot dogs at a ballpark: he would not always be a practicing vegetarian, but it would not affect his master status.

The sexual identity dodge, and that is what it is, was previously noticed by Hoover Institution researcher Mary Eberstadt. After the abuse crisis hit the news in 2002, she astutely observed that "the only way to argue that gay priests are not largely responsible for the Church's man-boy sex crisis is to choke the life out of ordinary language itself."

Indeed, at that time, Eberstadt offered by way of example the kind of rationale that is strikingly similar to the line of defense employed by the John Jay professors today. "The involvement with boys is homosexual activity, but that doesn't mean the person who's doing it is homosexually oriented." She labels this defense, which was offered by a Jesuit psychologist, as "a typically contorted example" of denying the obvious.

This game is not new. In 1974, Father Donald Goergen, O.P., a member of the Catholic Coalition for Gay Civil Rights, authored a book, *The Sexual Celibate*, wherein he spoke of the "healthy homosexual in heterosexual persons" and "healthy homosexuality in homosexual persons." Sexual identity, he said, is what one *feels*, and sexual maturity, he informed, was bisexuality.

Flawed though this fixation on what sexual identity is, it would have made sense for the authors to probe the sexual orientation of priests. Remarkably, we learn that "data on the sexual identity of priests and how it changed over the years were not collected for this study." If sexual identity looms large in the authors' findings, and if it partly drives their reluctance not to see this as a homosexual crisis, then this kind of data should have been collected.

Another way of dodging the real issue is to discuss priestly sexual abuse in terms of ephebophilia, not homosexuality. An ephebophile is someone who is sexually attracted to adolescents, or to postpubescent persons. It is of such dubious merit that it is not recognized by psychiatrists as having clinical significance, something which the report notes. However, this does not stop the authors from treating it as if it bore useful fruit.

As we have seen, the report details that most of the abuse involved adolescent males, but it is reluctant to identify homosexuality as a problem. How convenient, then, to speak of abuse in terms of ephebophilia instead of homosexuality. The fact is that adult males who have sex with adolescent males are homosexuals. Dubbing them ephebophiles doesn't change reality.

One of the nation's leading students of priestly sexual abuse is Penn State professor Philip Jenkins. He once used the term ephebophilia in his writings, but by 2002 had come to the conclusion that "we should move away from the overly technical term 'ephebophilia.'" He explained his pivot this way: "I now believe that the word frankly communicates nothing to most well-informed readers. These days I tend rather to speak of these acts as 'homosexuality.'"

Jenkins attributed his conversion to Eberstadt. What she has to say about the issue rings true. "When was the last time you heard the phrase 'ephebophile' applied to a heterosexual man? The answer is almost certainly that you haven't. That is because 'ephebophile,' in the technical-sounding nomenclature of the scandal commentary, is a term whose chief attraction is that it spares one from having to employ the words 'homosexual' or 'gay' in attempting to describe exactly which sexual crimes the offending priests have committed." Nothing has changed since: the John Jay authors sport a preference for using this term because it allows them to address the problem without making mention of homosexuality.

Not only is ephebophilia shorthand for homosexuals who prey on adolescents, pedophilia is shorthand for homosexual priests who prey on children. St. Luke's Institute is the most premier treatment center in the nation for troubled priests, and according to its co-founder, Rev. Michael Peterson, "We don't see heterosexual pedophiles at all." If this is true, how can it be that the John Jay study failed to pick this up? To be exact, if Peterson is correct, wouldn't that mean that virtually all the priests who abused prepubescent children had a homosexual orientation?

It was disturbing to read that more than a third of priest abusers were themselves abused during childhood. This is not inconsistent with the general population: those who were abused as children are more likely to become adult abusers than those who were never abused. It is also disturbing for another reason. The clinical data shows that young boys of a homosexual orientation are far more likely to have been abused than their heterosexual cohorts. This alone suggests that homosexual adults are much more likely to abuse minors than heterosexuals.

The Elephant in the Sacristy

One of the most important chapters in the report focuses upon "Behavioral Explanations: Causal Factors Based on Individual Experience." Though the authors are unwavering in their determination to see this as anything but a homosexual issue, some of the data they provide actually undermine their thesis. Eberstadt nicely identifies this dodge as "The Elephant in the Sacristy."

> Clinical data shows that young boys of a homosexual orientation are far more likely to have been abused than their heterosexual cohorts.

The authors gathered clinical data from treatment centers, places where troubled priests were assigned. What they found was that "three quarters of the priests whom we have data had sexual relations with an adult and/or minor after ordination." Given that the minors were mostly male, and beyond puberty, is this not clearly an issue of homosexuality?

Sometimes the goal of trying hard not to recognize the elephant in the sacristy becomes downright ludicrous. "Priests with pre-ordination same-sex sexual behavior who did sexually abuse a minor after ordination were more likely to have a male child victim than a female child victim." But of course. Should we not expect that homosexuals who were active prior to entering the seminary would choose boys to abuse if they were to 15 engage in molestation? And should not data like this tell the authors something about the nature of the problem?

There's more. The paragraph that immediately follows is also noteworthy. "However, after considering pre-seminary and in-seminary sexual behavior separately, only in-seminary (not pre-seminary) same-sex sexual behavior was significantly related to the increased likelihood of a male child victim." In other words, those studying for the priesthood who had sex with other seminarians—that would make them homosexuals—were more likely to abuse a child (male, of course) than gays who were active before they entered the seminary and then stayed celibate. This means that all eyes should turn to the seminaries, a subject slighted by the authors, but about which we will examine shortly.

The problem of focusing on the sexual identity of the priest, as opposed to his behavior, is evident in the finding that "Those who identified themselves as bisexual or confused were significantly more likely to have minor victims than priests who identified as either homosexual or heterosexual." But if these "bisexual and confused" priests chose to abuse mostly males—and they must have since 81 percent of the victims were male (and nearly 80 percent were post-pubescent)—wouldn't that mean that these abusive priests were practicing homosexuality? Again, the emphasis on self-identity gets in the way of reality. Indeed, the attempt to skirt the obvious is not only disingenuous, it is bad social science.

The authors try to say that much of the abuse was situational, a function of opportunity. For example, they note that after girl altar servers were approved by the Catholic Church, there was a "substantial increase in the percentage of female victims in the late 1990s and 2000s, when priests had more access to them in the church." There is more to this than meets the eye.

The authors provide a chart that shows that between 1995 and 2002 there was an increase in the percentage of female victims. What they fail to mention is that the number of allegations made since the 1990s is so small that it distorts a fair comparison to use percentages. For example, between 2005 and 2010, the average number of new credible allegations made against priests was 8.3. So to employ a percentage-based comparison to judge how things have changed between the years when abuse peaked, and more recent times, is to distort reality (if three of the eight victims were female, that would greatly inflate their percentage as opposed to twenty out of one hundred). Moreover, the sharp increase in the number of unsubstantiated or false allegations—it jumped by 42 percent between 2009 and 2010—should give anyone pause when drawing realistic comparisons (this was not noted by the authors).

If we look at the overall allegations being brought since the initial John Jay study in 2004, independent of when the abuse occurred, here is what we find (the following data are taken from the annual reports published by the USCCB): the percentage of male victims in 2005 was 81 percent; in 2006, it was 80 percent; in 2007, it climbed to 82 percent; in 2008, in jumped to 84 percent; in 2009, it held at 84 percent; and in 2010 it was 83 percent.

Importantly, we find that the most recent study, the 2010 Annual Report, shows that 66 percent of new allegations (independent of when they happened) are alleged to have taken place between 1960 and 1984. It also says, "The most common time period for allegations reported in 2010 was 1970-1974." This is approximately the same time pattern that is reported year after year, and these are precisely the years when the abuse crisis took hold. What matters greatly is that these are the same years when the percentage of homosexuals in the priesthood soared, and when sanctions for sexual expression were weak.

If having access only to boys accounts for the high number of male victims at the peak of the crisis, then this should have been a problem before things got out of control. But the report emphatically shows this was not the case. "A review of the narratives of men who were seminarians in the 1950s, and of published histories of the seminaries themselves does not reveal any record of noticeable or widespread sexual activity by seminarians." The reason it wasn't a problem is because most priests put a lid on their libido in the 1940s and 1950s. When the lid came off in the 1960s, the crisis began.

There is also something unseemly about the opportunity-based argument. It suggests that if men don't have access to females, they will start hitting on men. This is patently sexist and flatly absurd. Men don't have much access to females in boarding schools and in the armed services, but virtually no one, save for homosexuals, finds himself tempted to choose other men to satisfy his sexual urges. Comparisons with the prison population are also flawed: the men housed there typically suffer from a host of deviant qualities.

There is too much evidence to plausibly conclude that there is no relationship between the overrepresentation of active homosexuals in the priesthood and their overrepresentation in the sexual abuse scandal.

The report cites the work of Kinsey, but does not say that he was the first to identify a correlation between homosexuality and the sexual abuse of minors. In 1948, he found that 37 percent of all male homosexuals admitted to having sex with children under the age of seventeen. More recently, in organs such as the *Archives of Sexual Behavior*, *The Journal of Sex Research*, and the *Journal of Sex and Marital Therapy and Pediatrics*, it has been established that homosexuals are disproportionately represented among child molesters. Even gay activists Karla Jay and Allen Young have admitted (see their book, *The Gay Report*) that 73 percent of homosexuals have preyed on adolescent or younger boys.

> The opportunity-based argument suggests that if men don't have access to females, they will start hitting on men. This is patently sexist and flatly absurd.

When the National Review Board released its findings in 2004, Robert S. Bennett, the head of the group, said that "any evaluation of the causes and context of the current crisis must be cognizant of the fact that more than 80 percent of the abuse issue was of a homosexual nature." Furthermore, the National Review Board explicitly said that "we must call attention to the homosexual behavior that characterized the vast majority of the cases of abuse observed in recent decades."

One of those who served on the National Review Board was Dr. Paul McHugh, former psychiatrist-in-chief at Johns Hopkins University. He has said that "this behavior was homosexual predation on American Catholic youth; yet it's not being discussed."

The account by Bennett and McHugh is similar to that of Roderick MacLeish Jr., the lawyer who pressed the case against the Archdiocese of Boston. He concluded that 90 percent of the nearly 400 sexual abuse victims he represented were boys, and that three-quarters were postpubescent.

Dr. Richard Fitzgibbons, a psychiatrist, has spent years treating sexually abusive priests. He says that "*every* priest whom I treated who was involved with children sexually had previously been involved in adult homosexual relationships." (My emphasis.) His experience is striking, but not unusual. Psychologist Leslie Lothstein, who also treats abusive priests, reports that "only a small minority were true pedophiles."

The Seminaries

When the report was released, the *New York Times* focused on the part which said that "homosexual men entering the seminaries in noticeable numbers from the late 1970s through the 1980s" did so at a time when the abuse problem was leveling off; this calls into question those who claim that the crisis was driven by homosexuality.

First of all, the surge of homosexuals in the seminaries was evident in the 1960s. Furthermore, those who entered at this time, and became abusers, were quicker to do so than their predecessors. The book notes that "men ordained in the 1930s, 1940s, and 1950s did not generally abuse before the 1960s or 1970s." Yes, and that is because sexual behavior was not acceptable. Psychologist and ex-priest Eugene Kennedy says that when he was ordained in 1955, the Church did not lack for homosexual priests, but, importantly, "the culture was intact." The big difference, he says, is that "there was not the acting out" that was later tolerated.

One of the reasons why the abuse peaked between the mid-1960s and the mid-1980s has something to do with what the authors mention early on in the report. "Men ordained in the 1960s and the early 1970s engaged in abusive behavior much more quickly after their entrance into ministry." This was also the time when gays made their way into the seminaries in large numbers and the Church dropped its guard.

Michael Rose, a critic from the right, wrote a book on the subject of priestly sexual abuse, and he maintains that "the big revolution in the seminaries happened in the late 1960s, when a lot of the disciplinary codes were thrown out the window in favor of a new, very much more liberalized, more university-like atmosphere with a lot of freedom and so forth."

Jason Berry, a critic from the left, also wrote a book on this subject, and he found much the same. "In the 1970s, as roughly one hundred Americans left the priesthood every month, most of them to marry, the proportions of homosexuals among men remaining in the ministry escalated." If this wasn't bad enough, consider what Richard Wagner found in his early study of sexually-active seminarians: he reported that 34 percent of his subjects called their sexual partners "distinctly younger."

Father Andrew Greeley uses the term "lavender Mafia" to describe what was going on at this time. He writes that seminary professors not only encouraged their students to attend gay bars, they said it was okay for them to sleep with each other. Things got so bad that Greeley later said the bishops must "clean out the pedophiles, break up the gay cliques, tighten up the seminary, and restore the good name of the priesthood."

Another liberal priest, Rev. Donald Cozzens, has spoken of the "gay subculture" that took hold, especially in the seminaries. The effect of this 20 condition, he said, was to deter "significant numbers of Catholic men from seriously considering the priesthood." This was certainly the case in seminaries like St. John's in Boston, a haven for practicing homosexuals and abusers in the 1960s. The gay presence was so strong that, according to the *Boston Herald*, they "established networks" that lasted for years.

The Resolution of Cognitive Dissonance

How could all of this happen? How could priests molest minors during the day and look at themselves in the mirror at night? What enabled them to disconnect their beliefs from their behavior? The report comes close to saying how this came about, but stops short of providing an adequate answer.

The best explanations about this phenomenon were made during the 1950s. With good reason, the authors cite the work of sociologists David Matza and Gerald Sykes, and the contribution of psychologist Leon Festinger.

Matza and Sykes contended that most sexual abusers adopted "techniques of neutralization," methods that allowed them, among other things, to deny self-responsibility and to condemn the condemners. The report, to its credit, mentions how abusive priests "blamed church leaders for the abuse and/or the responses to the accusations." Indeed, they "not only condemned the hierarchical leaders of the church for their response to the scandal of abuse, they also held leaders responsible for 'poor socialization' to the life of the priesthood, and in particular for poor seminary preparation." In other words, the molesters blamed the bishops for their behavior.

Festinger offered a more sophisticated account. He said that when an individual holds contrary ideas, he suffers cognitive dissonance, a condition that is ultimately reconciled when one of the thoughts triumphs. More recently, sociologist David Finkelhor has picked up on Festinger's work by applying it to sexual abusers. "According to Finkelhor," the report says, "abusers are able to excuse and justify their actions to themselves, thereby reducing the barriers of guilt and shame."

Unfortunately, the report doesn't develop this line of thinking further, though it could have. For example, in an earlier section, it notes that "priests with positive views toward homosexuality were most likely to have post-ordination sexual behavior." It is implausible to think that these priests were unaware that what they were doing was sinful. Their cognitive dissonance found relief, it seems plain to conclude, not by changing their behavior, but by holding to the conviction that homosexuality was not sinful.

A priest from the Archdiocese of Boston explained one of the ways in which homosexuals resolved their cognitive dissonance. They would say things like, "Well, celibacy only applies to not getting married, so since we're not getting married, we can do whatever we want." Jason Berry reports that in a study of 50 gay priests, only two said they were not sexually active. More important, for this discussion, "sixty percent said they felt no guilt about breaking their vows" and "ninety percent strongly rejected mandatory celibacy." This was more than "defining deviance down," as Daniel Patrick Moynihan put it in 1992: this was a collective psychological somersault.

Another reason why sexually active homosexual priests did not experience guilt was their conviction that the Church's teachings on sexuality would eventually change. The Church has changed on many issues, the popular refrain goes, and eventually the *institu-*

tional Church will come to see that many of its ideas about sexuality are anachronistic. They also comforted themselves with the belief that the laity were not abiding by many of the teachings on sexuality, suggesting that the Holy Spirit had not blessed them.

The report does not attempt to explain the etiological basis of these self-justifying notions. The evidence shows, however, that it began in the seminaries, beginning in the late 1960s. Quite simply, the resolution of cognitive dissonance finds its roots in the dramatic increase in dissent that marked this period.

George Weigel put his finger on two major events that contributed to the toleration of dissent: the "Truce of 1968" and the publication of *Human Sexuality* by Anthony Kosnick. While no doubt other factors could be cited, no discussion of this issue can ignore these two factors.

After the publication of the encyclical *Humanae Vitae*, which reaffirmed the Church's teachings on sexuality, most especially its proscriptions against artificial contraception, dissent from the ranks of the priesthood exploded. Cardinal Patrick O'Boyle of the Archdiocese of Washington sought to discipline nineteen priests who were publicly dissenting against the encyclical. But he was rebuffed by the Vatican and had to remove the sanctions. Pope Paul VI feared a schism which, ironically, happened anyway, if only in a *de facto* manner, and that is why the dissidents won.

The bishops were essentially put on warning: deal with dissident priests in a way that eschews a public controversy. This "Truce" was not lost on the dissidents, many of whom saw an opening to push the envelope. One of those who pushed the hardest was Father Anthony Kosnick.

Under the tutelage of the Catholic Theological Society of America, which commissioned Father Kosnick's work, *Human Sexuality: New Directions in American Catholic Thought*, seminarians were now introduced to a radical interpretation of sexual ethics. Virtually all sexual expression was seen in non-judgmental terms: contraception, cohabitation, homosexuality, swinging, adultery—even bestiality—were treated as morally neutral acts. Gone was the Church's teaching that there are objective moral standards governing sexuality. The Vatican eventually censured the book, but the damage had already been done.

No one seriously maintains that a seminarian who later became an abuser did so because he read Kosnick's volume. It doesn't work that way. But to those seminarians who were dysfunctional and who rejected the Church's teachings on sexuality, digesting Kosnick's moral relativism surely helped to resolve whatever degree of cognitive dissonance they were experiencing. And we know how the psychological tension was reconciled—by throwing the Church's teachings overboard.

Catholic dissidents have been at war with the Catholic Church on sexual matters for over a half century, and many continue to push their agenda. Two pro-homosexual groups, DignityUSA and New Ways Ministry, not only condemn the Church's teachings, they have a history of welcoming known child molesters and promiscuous homosexuals like Paul Shanley into their ranks.

> Catholic dissidents have been at war with the Catholic Church on sexual matters for over a half century, and many continue to push their agenda.

DignityUSA is utterly shameless. In the mid-1970s, the New York chapter proclaimed, "The evidence seems to indicate that Dignity is the work of the Holy Spirit, the vehicle through which the Spirit is welding Gay Catholics into an identifiable community within the Church." Father Enrique Rueda, who wrote a prescient book on this subject, *The Homosexual Network*, properly said that this reveals "the subversive nature" of the Jesuit-founded group.

New Ways Ministry, run by a rogue priest and nun, announced in 1980 that the Catholic Church's teaching on homosexuality was "all too reminiscent of the Inquisition, the Reformation, witch burnings and Nazi Germany." So the proscription against homosexuality, first broached by Judaism, was now seen as something that only a Hitlerian would counsel. It is tempting, but way too simple, to say that these are the words of fanatics: this is the voice that gave ideological cover to abusers. The priest who was the co-director of the group, Father Robert Nugent, was at one time a consultant on sexual minorities for the United States Catholic Conference; it was the lay arm of the bishops' conference at that time.

The really sad thing about this chapter in the Church's history is the enormous support these dissident groups got from those who worked in the Catholic Church. Rueda names the bishops, priests, dioceses, religious orders, nuns, lay groups, seminaries, retreat centers, colleges, high schools and theological institutes that lent a helping hand. That many dissidents remain working for the Church is known to every honest Catholic who knows anything about the subject.

The late Father Richard John Neuhaus attributed the sexual abuse scandal to a lack of fidelity. He was right. There is no way that priests who are faithful to the precepts of the Church's teachings on sexual ethics could possibly live a life of sexual recklessness. Only by jettisoning the teachings—casting celibacy and chastity as anachronistic—could they do so. Regrettably, such priests were not the only losers in this game of self-justification.

William A. Donohue is president of the Catholic League for Religious and Civil Rights in New York City. He is taught at both St. Lucy's School in Spanish Harlem and La Roche College. He is the author of numerous works, including *The Politics of the American Civil Liberties Union, The New Freedom,* and *Secular Sabotage.*

3

Economic Structure and the Life of the Jews

Simon Kuznets

ONE BROAD REFLECTION is that in the economics of Jews the non-economic elements are important, to the point of dominance. The very existence and continuance of Jews as a distinctive and cohesive minority is in essence non-economic—which is true also of many other minorities and even of many communities organized into independent sovereign states. Economic calculations guided by some rational principles, e.g. maximization of long term economic returns, would argue *against* rather than for the perpetuation of such a cohesive and distinct minority, and would affect the attitudes of both the minority and the majority which in one way or another *impose* unity and cohesion on the minority.

Such economic calculations on principles of maximization of long term net yields cannot be made with precision and reliability. But it can be argued that a group of X individuals, who are comprised in the Jewish minority, would, given their personal and material economic assets, most likely attain (for themselves and their descendants) a higher level of returns were they to act freely in response to perceived economic opportunities. "Freely" means without regard for other motives and considerations which intervene when they act as members of a Jewish minority, in fulfillment of a desire for cohesiveness and retention of identity as members of that minority.

Much of the analysis in the body of the paper lends emphasis to the point that no such "pure" response to economic opportunities is in fact exercised by the Jewish minority. In reality a high economic price, in the way of opportunity cost, has been paid for the sake of preserving the cohesion and identity of the minority. This was certainly true of the Jewish immigrants who went to Palestine when greater economic opportunities were available elsewhere; as well as of the sizable Jewish minorities anywhere in the Diaspora, where proximity to other members of the group and other conditions of social life affected economic decisions.

This is obvious enough. What is perhaps less obvious is that the hostile or discriminatory policies of the majorities, whenever manifest, are even more irrational economically. Given the kind of human capital that the Jews represent, the majority in any country, if it wished to maximize long-term economic returns, the majorities should have not only permitted the Jewish minority the utmost freedom—but in fact subsidized heavily any movement of the promising individual Jews to the upper levels of economic and social performance. Such help in developing more contributors to the stock of human knowledge and hence to the economic capacity of the country (which rests after all on tested scientific knowledge) would have been one of the highest yield investments. If only for this obvious reason, the discriminatory policies of many majorities—often directed specifically at retarding the usual dynamics of a Jewish minority, from trade into intellectual and professional pursuits—constitute extreme economic irrationality. The same can be said of limitations on movement within business corporations and the like.

> The discriminatory policies of many majorities constitute extreme economic irrationality. The same can be said of limitations on movement within business corporations.

Of course, people do not act on purely rational economic calculations and the preceding paragraphs are belaboring the obvious. Yet an implication for the analysis of the economics of the Jews follows from this platitude that has not been clearly recognized. The implication is double-edged. First, in explaining why and how the economics of the Jews came to be what it is, these non-economic elements must be explicitly formulated and considered. And this has to be done in greater detail and specificity than was, or could be done, in the preceding pages. Only in this fashion will the connection between motivation as members of the minority and economic choices and results become clear—a comment which also applies to the connection between the motivation of the majority and *its* actions on economic and social opportunities made accessible to the Jews. The second, and more elusive connotation, is that in any *appraisal* of the economic structure of the Jews, in any references to it as "normal" or more frequently "abnormal," desirable or undesirable, the utmost clarity must be sought in formulating the bases for such appraisal. Since these bases often include, explicitly and implicitly, a mixture of economic and non-economic elements, a combination of criteria of minimum economic attainment in the way of level, stability, and "respectability" of income and of continued life of the Jewish minority, a clear differentiation of these elements will prevent misleading shallow judgments. For what is "abnormal" or "undesirable" from the standpoint of one criterion may turn out to be desirable or indispensable from the standpoint of another. All this, applied to the economics of the Jewish minority, could also apply to the policy of the majority. This means that firm and defensible appraisals and judgment can be reached only if the bases on which they are made are clearly stated and accepted.

Historical Continuity

Since my own interest is in explanation rather than appraisal, my second reflection mirrors the impression of the pervasiveness of historical continuity in any analysis of economic changes among Jews in the recent century.

In a sense this is both obvious and inevitable—since we deal with a minority whose historical heritage stretches over centuries and the changes in whose conditions can hardly be understood except as links in a chain that extends far back into the past. But it is the major scenes in this historical drama, and the close connection between them, which strike the eye of an observer who attempts to stand, as it were, on the outside.

The dominance of Eastern European Jewry as the major reservoir of growth during the recent century, and the source from which the two largest communities in the world today—the United States and Israel—have been recruited, is clearly a link in a long chain of historical continuity. The reasons for the concentration of world Jewry at the beginning of the nineteenth century in Eastern Europe certainly lie in centuries of earlier history, when the Jews were expelled successively from the several countries of Western Europe, and were attracted to Poland and neighboring areas by the favorable conditions offered them.

But there is even more to this historical interconnection. The favorable position of Jews in Poland and Lithuania during several centuries meant their occupation of certain economic links in the structure of the countries impeded the formation of a native middle class. In turn, the weakness of the naive urban middle classes may have been an important factor in the weakness of the Polish-Lithuanian states and may have delayed their evolution to the stronger and more effective

> Changing economics of the Jews is part of world history and of the responses of the Jewish groups themselves, acting as distinctive and cohesive minorities.

national state—which in other countries was attained originally by a combination of leading units in the feudal nobility with the economically strong middle classes in the cities. It seems ironic that, having flourished and grown within the framework of these weaker, nobility dominated states, the Jewish communities in Poland and Lithuania have paid the price of partition and ended up under the domination of one of the most centralized and authoritarian powers in the world.

The observations above may be superficial reflections of the surface of history writ large—and misleading at that, but even if inaccurate, they illustrate the kinds of historical continuity that may be perceived in the changing economics of the Jews.

The changing economics of the Jews is at the same time part of world history and of the responses of the Jewish groups themselves, acting as distinctive and cohesive minorities. And each of these—the history of the countries whose actions affect the fate of Jews (whether the latter are or are not resident in them), and the responses of the

Jews themselves—has long roots in the historical past of both the world at large and the Jewish world community. The interplay of the variety of historical forces affecting the economic and other conditions of Jews in the immediate past, and likely to affect them in the foreseeable future, is almost overwhelming. Certainly, only the very broad lines can be marked out; and one must always be aware the depth of the antecedents and the shallowness of the explanations that can be offered and tested.

This applies to the position today. Of some 11 million Jews in the world, about 6 million are in the countries of the Western Hemisphere, and another million are in the relatively free countries of Eastern Europe. The economic and social fate of news in North America and Western Europe is a function of the economic and social fate of their countries and will be governed largely by the possibilities of preserving peace and avoiding a major world war. Another sizable group of Jews, about 2.5 million, remains in Eastern Europe, and its future is partly a function of the internal changes within these authoritarian states, any relaxation in the dictatorship meaning a relief of hostile pressure on the Jewish minorities; and partly a function again of the major course of international relations. The third sizable group of Jews, 1.5 million, is in Israel, an embattled bastion facing Arab hostility and still a potential refuge for the half million Jews in the disturbed areas of North Africa. Here the lines of historical continuity from the not so distant past of nineteenth century relations between the Western powers and the underdeveloped countries of the Arab belt are being played out to ends that can only be dimly perceived. Against this background, the characteristics of and changes in economic structure dwindle to mere details on a canvas in which other, non-economic factors, are clearly more important.

Simon Kuznets (1901-1985) won the Nobel Memorial Prize in Economic Sciences in 1971. His contributions to the field include the "Kuznets curve," which revolutionized the field of developmental economics. His writings include *Economic Growth of Nations: Total Output and Production Structure, Modern Economic Growth: Rate, Structure, and Spread*, and *Economic Growth and Structure: Selected Essays*.

4

Why is Africa Poor?

Greg Mills

WITH A PER CAPITA income 50 percent less than that of the next poorest region (South Asia), sub-Saharan Africa's growth has lagged since independence some 50 years ago. Many reasons have been put forward for the region's slow development—a lack of human and government capacity, poor infrastructure and trade access, the effects of too little (or too much) foreign aid, the legacy of arbitrary colonial boundaries, low productivity, the Cold War, climate, and geography. Many African leaders blame the rest of the world for African poverty, implying that solutions to underdevelopment are out of their hands.

But the world has not denied Africa the markets and financial means to compete. Far from it. The contemporary era of globalization has afforded unprecedented opportunities to billions of people in emerging markets. Globalization may have suffered a setback recently, but the current recession does not alter the fact that global wealth has tripled since 1990.[1] It is the varying abilities of governments to translate such opportunities into development and prosperity that has accounted, in large measure, for the widening inequalities within and between countries.

Africa is poor not because of aid per se, although large inflows of foreign aid have almost certainly been a disincentive to reform for many African governments. Nor is African poverty solely a consequence of poor African infrastructure or trade access. Africa has enjoyed preferential access to international markets, yet the continent has slipped behind other, less favored, competitors. True, much of Africa's infrastructure has deteriorated and fallen behind other infrastructures found elsewhere in the world. But there have often been vested interests—like local monopolies—that had no interest in making infrastructure more efficient. Similarly, many African countries have avoided putting in place policies and procedures that would facilitate more exports. Those policies and procedures could have been put in place quickly and for far less money than improvements to infrastructure.

Africa's poverty has not been caused by the lack of necessary technical and development expertise. Those can be bought on the international market—as many Asian countries have chosen to do. Such expertise could even have been accessed for free via donors. Africa has, however, been highly possessive about the direction and control of its development. That is partly due to an innately skeptical view of outsiders, but also because Africa has been able to get away with pursuing bad economic policies through subsidies from rich countries.

> Africa is not poor because its people do not work hard but because their productivity is too low.

Africa is not poor because its people do not work hard but because their productivity is too low. For example, subsistence agriculture, from which many Africans derive their livelihoods, creates very little value added. Unfortunately, without institutional and policy changes, there can be only a limited expansion of large-scale farming and of the industrial and service sectors of the economy.

Nor is Africa poor because it lacks natural resources. Compared with Asia, it is a treasure-trove of natural resources from agricultural land and precious metals to wildlife and hydropower. Yet, with few exceptions (Botswana is one), those resources have been used only to enrich elites, spread corrupt practices, and divert development energy and focus. And Africa's people are poverty stricken not because the private sector does not exist or has been unable to cope with difficult conditions. The problem is that the private sector is often not "private" at all. Rather, it is an elite-linked system of rent-seeking. Even where there is a degree of private-sector independence, government attitudes toward truly private businesses range from suspicion to outright hostility—not least since politicians in some African countries fear that economic autonomy will be followed by political autonomy.

African Rulers Deserve Most of the Blame

The main reason for African poverty is the bad choices made by African rulers. The record shows that countries can grow their economies and develop faster if leaders take sound decisions in the national interest. That is as true of the Vietnamese leaders before and after the failure and reform of Vietnam's command economy as it is of African reformers from Ghana to Botswana.

Africa's positive economic growth record in the 2000s illustrates that better choices can be made. True, African growth has traditionally mirrored the ups and downs of natural resource prices, but Africa's growth in the 2000s has also reflected better governance and more widespread democracy on the continent.[2]

The economic success of countries in other regions offers many good examples that Africans can learn from. In assigning blame for not seizing the opportunities of globalization to African leaders, it is important to recognize that those leaders have often taken decisions under difficult circumstances. No one disputes that African politicians face big challenges. Yet in other parts of the world, those challenges are usually regarded as obstacles to be overcome, not as permanent excuses for failure.

For in a half century of independence, Africa has not realized its potential. Instead, its greatest natural assets have undermined its prosperity. Africa's youth, for example, is not being regarded as a huge source of talent and energy to be harnessed. Rather, this group is regarded as a destabilizing force because it is largely unemployed and uneducated. This is not only a threat to Africa's security. By 2025, one in four young people worldwide will be from sub-Saharan Africa.[3] Most of those young people will be living in Africa's cities where, by then, the majority of the continent's citizens will be located. And if they do not find employment on the continent, they will seek it elsewhere.

Far from being the front for development, Africa's oil wealth has served instead to enrich elites. For example, Nigeria has received an estimated $400 billion in oil revenues over the last 40 years. Oil revenues per capita rose from $33 to $325 between 1965 and 2000. Yet the number of Nigerians living on less than one dollar per day rose from 19 million in 1970 (of a population of 70 million) to 90 million (of a population of some 120 million).[4] Instead of fueling development, oil has tainted governance and accountability across Africa.

Africa's agriculture potential has similarly been squandered. Many African states possess agricultural land in abundance. Yet, 35 out of 48 sub-Saharan African economies were net food importers at the end of the 2000s.[5] Africa's share of world agricultural exports halved since 1970, to under 4 percent.[6] Though agriculture was responsible for only one-fifth of the continent's economic output in the late 2000s, two-thirds of Africans (the majority of them women) lived in rural areas and were dependent on farming for their survival.[7] It doesn't take much to work out why productivity in that sector is so low. The agricultural sector was ruined through taxation that was meant to fuel Africa's centrally planned industrialization drive. Today, Africa is neither industrialized nor self-sufficient in food production. Instead, the continent relies mainly on export of natural products.

> Africa is neither industrialized nor self-sufficient in food production. Instead, the continent relies mainly on export of natural products.

Enabling Bad Leadership

If Africa's dismal economic performance can be put down to bad choices by African leaders, then we have to ask: Why have those leaders made those choices? The key reason is that Africans and the international community have enabled them to do so. The former have typically believed that they lacked the means to change the status quo, whereas the latter have been too ready to "help" Africa for reasons ranging from self-interest to altruism and pity.

African leaders have successfully managed, with the help of donors, to externalize their problems, making them the responsibility and fault of others.

Donors have typically lacked the tools or political will to manage their relationship with African leaders and the flow of money to Africa according to the democratic, economic-reform, and public-goods-delivery record of the recipients. Nowhere has this been more the case than with the many so-called "fragile" or "failed" states. Governments in those countries have frequently abrogated the responsibility, but not the authority, for rebuilding their countries to others. Too often, donors have taken up the challenge of rebuilding failing states, thus weakening the already tenuous link of accountability between the government and its people.

The fact that African leaders were permitted to get away with ruinous, self-interested decisions must be attributed, in large part, to a relative lack of democracy (or to single-party dominance) in Africa. There has been little bottom-up pressure on leadership to make better choices, although there has been encouraging growth of civil society in parts of the continent over the last decade. This apparent passivity of the populace in the face of bad leadership must, at least in part, be attributed to a neo-patrimonial culture. In that culture, the "big man" rules and dispenses favors. He uses all manner of tools to bolster his rule—from traditional governance structures and kinship ties to witchcraft and the church.

The system that many African leaders have preferred thrives on corruption and nepotism. Corruption is not particular to Africa, of course. But leaders from other societies where corruption is also a problem—Asia in particular—have displayed a commitment to popular welfare that is lacking in African leadership.

African societies, in contrast, have overwhelmingly been run along the lines of the "politics of the belly"—a primordial lust for wealth and power along crude racial, tribal, party, and familial lines. In this system, government officials and politically connected business elite use their positions and influence to enrich themselves and their families or kinsmen. Personal wealth, Jean-François Bayart of the Centre for International Studies and Research in Paris writes, "is one of the chief political virtues rather than being an object of disapproval."[8] Similarly, Patrick Chabal of King's College London and Jean-Pascal Daloz of the University of Oslo argue that "in most

African countries, the state is no more than a decor, a pseudo-Western facade masking the realities of deeply personalized political relations [where] legitimacy is firmly embedded in the patrimonial practices of patrons and their networks."[9]

Africa's traditional land holding structures have also been an impediment to entrepreneurship. Communal land holding has impeded the collateralization of land value through individual ownership and mortgage schemes. There has been little interest among the leadership of many African countries to reform the system. At the same time, a disastrous "reform" took place in Zimbabwe, where land was seized and redistributed on the basis of political allegiances.

> Top-down imposition of states and borders on Africa's rich ethnic and sectarian tapestry by colonial powers has institutionalized weak governance structures.

The top-down imposition of states and borders on Africa's rich ethnic and sectarian tapestry by colonial powers has institutionalized weak governance structures. African states were both formed and maintained not by raising taxes and ensuring public goods, as was the case in Europe, but by colonial fiat. Over the past 50 years, however, the Organization of African Unity and the African Union have been adamantly opposed to changing Africa's colonial boundaries.

Finally, and perhaps most importantly, bad choices have been made because better choices in the broad public interest were in very many cases not in the leaders' personal and often financial self-interest.[10]

The Sad Case of Zambia

Zambia is an example of a country that has suffered from this sort of policy malaise. There is probably no country as studied by development consultants as Zambia. Beneficiaries of large donor amounts since independence in 1964, and countless World Bank and other reports have been written on every conceivable topic—from transport and tourism, to regulatory reform and mining.

Thus, it's not as if Zambians shouldn't know what to do when thinking about how to deal with economic and other development problems. For nearly half a century they have debated how to diversify their economy away from mining into agriculture, tourism, and manufacturing—so far with marginal effect. In fact, most of the reports have been languishing on dusty shelves in government offices—their often replicated proposals are seldom read and virtually never acted on.

In some ways, Zambia's economy has done well during the 2000s. Privatization of its principal export asset, the copper mines, has resulted in more than $4 billion in inward investment.[11] Annual national copper production has climbed threefold in 15 years. It is now nearly back to its peak of 720,000 tons in the mid-1970s.[12] The economy has grown at an average rate of more than 5 percent per year during the 2000s.[13] Lusaka's traffic is one illustration of the rise in living standards and the emergence of a middle class in Zambia.

But Zambia needs to do even better. High unemployment, especially among young people, is no recipe for long-term stability. "Their army of numbers will, one day, make Zambia unviable," Hakainde Hichilema, a leading opposition figure, told me.[14] Zambian infrastructure is rickety and costly to business. It takes a week to get exports out via road to South Africa and at least four times longer by rail. A power shortage looms even though the country has abundant hydroelectric potential. Despite the quality and quantity of its natural endowments, the mining sector is undeveloped compared with other copper producers, such as Chile. Tourism facilities remain clustered around Victoria Falls, in spite of extraordinary offerings elsewhere from the Lower Zambezi to Lake Tanganyika.

Overall, the country has not performed to its considerable potential. There is little urgency in government to execute sound plans. And, at times, the government has made this more difficult for itself through ill-considered actions, such as the hurried adoption of farmland rent and windfall taxes on mining companies. Those measures threatened to bankrupt producers in both agriculture and mining before they were repealed.

The government says that it is constrained by politics and needs to move slowly on reforms out of a risk of appearing too "reactionary." Government officials claim that democracy has made economic choices politically risky. Others point to the deleterious effect of aid, which comprises one-third of government expenditures. Aid blunts the risks associated with policy inertia. Zambian politicians know that the donors will be around to pick up the pieces. Aid also provides a source of rent-seeking income and removes the incentive to expand the domestic productive sector and tax base.

But some observers highlight deeper underlying causes, though similarly political and cultural. Hichilema says that lack of reform should be attributed to the country's having been ruled for 27 years between 1964 and 1991 by a socialist-inclined leader, Kenneth Kaunda. During that time, the state became the largest employer, the regulator of first and last resort, and, as a result, it became corrupt.

Kaunda's socialism has *created* a civil service geared to protectionism and regulation at all costs, and a private sector attuned to working within a system that rewards insiders and discourages independent entrepreneurship. (We should not underestimate the fact that this system, a feature of most African countries, works just fine for the elite).

Africans Must Liberalize

Yet this is a very good moment for African leadership to push ahead with reforms. Commodity prices are high, allowing a fresh range of policy choices. Investors have an appetite for high-growth emerging markets. And many tough macroeconomic reforms have been carried out across the continent.

But to take matters to the next level, Africa will have to carry out sweeping regulatory reforms. For example, Zambian tourism investors should not require 33 different licenses to operate.[15] Such reforms will have to be matched by attractive tax regimes across the continent. To achieve those goals, the elites must be willing to prioritize economic growth over political power. They have to stop seeing foreign investors as predators snatching away their birthright. To do better, Africa has to signal that "business as usual," in which politics presides over economics, is truly over.

I spent much of 2008 in Rwanda as President Paul Kagame's strategy adviser. Frank, our driver there, had a great idea for a taxi business, but he was not able to get financing for it. He lacked not only a financial system that could cater to his needs, but also demand for his business. Rwanda's tourism industry has been stunted by the cost and difficulty in accessing that beautiful country, and also by the lack of tourist attractions—apart from Rwanda's world-famous gorillas. While the government has rhetorically been open to increasing the number of visitors, it has been less open to investors, including those in the tourism business. There is a clear tension between African governments' desire to control their societies and the understanding that stability and growth ultimately depend on liberalization.

> We spent one third of the duration of our journeys in Africa at borders and police checkpoints. The other two thirds we spent traveling, resting, and eating.

Tourism is one of the underutilized advantages that Africa possesses. Global tourism is a business that caters to nearly one billion people. Yet Africa has just a 4 percent share of that market. To increase its share of the tourism business, Africa will have to liberalize air flight and visa regimes. In the formerly communist country of Georgia, for example, it is not necessary to acquire a visa for visitors who come from countries with a GDP per capita of $10,000 or more. Compare the Georgian system to the difficulty of entering many African countries or, for that matter, the difficulty of leaving African countries like the Democratic Republic of Congo, where one has to run a gauntlet of security and other checks—informal and formal.

I wonder how many visitors from rich countries to Africa have been put off by the challenge of just getting to the continent or getting a visa. Yet I suspect that few, if any, overstay their welcome. The number of tourists to Georgia has nearly quintupled from 2003 to 2009—a war with Russia notwithstanding.[16] (I should add that Georgia had also adopted a policy that did away with work permits for foreigners.)

Getting to Africa is difficult. Moving around in Africa is similarly onerous. My team and I have conducted a number of route diagnostics—essentially sitting on a truck and doing time and motion studies. We spent one third of the duration of our journeys at borders and police checkpoints. The other two thirds we spent traveling, resting, and eating. Africans often bemoan the state of the infrastructure on the continent. Yet it would take no donor money to keep borders open around the clock, thus making the best use of existing resources—if the idea is to improve openness and trade, of course.

Or, take another example. It takes an average of eight minutes to clear each of the 30 million containers that move through the city-state of Singapore annually. The minimum average time in Mombasa is 72 hours per container. Yet, this main East African port handles only 600,000 containers annually.[17]

The answer to the question of African poverty lies in the difference between success and failure in worldwide trade. This difference can be found in policy choices—the distinction, to take another example, between Vietnam before and after its own reforms. And the explanation behind the choices that African governments make lies in politics. Indeed, the principal challenge to African economies is political. To succeed, African governments must, like the governments of Southeast Asia, put people and ideas rather than narrow-minded political interests at the heart of development.

Notes

1. Fareed Zakaria, *The Post-American World* (New York: W.W. Norton, 2008).
2. For an assessment of the spread of democracy in Africa, see Tony Leon, "The State of Liberal Democracy in Africa: Resurgence or Retreat?" Cato Institute Development Policy Analysis no. 12, April 26, 2010, http://www.cato.org/pubs/dpa/dpa12.pdf.
3. Based on analysis conducted by Genesis Analytics on behalf of the Brenthurst Foundation, 2008.
4. Nicholas Shaxson, *Poisoned Wells: The Dirty Politics of African Oil* (London: Palgrave, 2008), p. 4.
5. "Africa; The Commodity Warrant," Credit Suisse New Perspectives Series, April 14, 2008.
6. Ibid.
7. Brenthurst Foundation.
8. Jean-Francois Bayart, *The State in Africa: The Politics of the Belly* (London: Longman, 1993), p. 238.
9. Patrick Chabal and Jean-Pascal Daloz, *Africa Works: Disorder as a Political Instrument* (London: James Currey, 1999), p. 16.
10. For a discussion of how predatory political elites keep Africans poor, see Moeletsi Mbeki, "Underdevelopment in Sub-Saharan Africa: The Role of the Private Sector and Political Elites," Cato Institute Foreign Policy Briefing Paper no. 85, April 15, 2005.

11. Interview with First Quantum Minerals officials, conducted in Ndola, Zambia, in December 2009.
12. Ibid.
13. World Bank, "Data: GDP Growth," October 26, 2010, http://data.worldbank.org/indicator/NY.GDP.MKTP.KD.ZG/countries/ZM?display=graph.
14. Interview with the Zambian opposition leader Hakainde Hichilema, Lusaka, Zambia, March 2010.
15. Ibid.
16. Department of Tourism and Resorts, Republic of Georgia, "Arrivals of Non-resident Visitors at National Borders of Georgia by Country of Residence," November 18, 2010, http://www.dotr.gov.ge/files/files/Statistics/2000_2009vizitorebi ing.pdf.
17. Kenya Ports Authority, "Port Performance for Year 2008," October 26, 2010, http://www.kpa.co.ke/InfoCenter/Performance/Pages/default.aspx; and Maritime News, "Shanghai Can Be Seen Falling 14%, in TEUs, January 2, 2010," http:// bestshippingnews.com/transport-news/shang hai-can-be-seen-falling-14-in-teus/.

Greg Mills is the director of the Johannesburg-based Brenthurst Foundation. He previously (1996-2005) directed the South African Institute of International Affairs. In addition to being the author of more than thirty books, including *Security Intersection* and the award-winning *Wired Model*, his writings have been widely published in journals, newspapers and magazines including *The New York Times, Time, Washington Quarterly, Foreign Policy*, and *Politiken*.

5

Freedom and Exchange in Communist Cuba

Yoani Sánchez

Know this well: our ignorance, our underdevelopment, is paid for with freedom.
—Fidel Castro, speaking with students at the University of Havana,
September 1970

THE THEORETICAL ACROBATICS of Marxist dialectics sought to persuade us that only through the construction of a communist society would it be possible to make what Engels called "the leap from the kingdom of necessity to the kingdom of freedom."[1] The history of the end of the twentieth century shows us, however, that the only consequence of the suspension of fundamental freedoms, imposed on a nation with the declared purpose of satisfying its needs, is the persistence of misery and the vilification of the individual.

The proposal to use freedom as a form of payment in exchange for material advantages transcends social structures and is part of a psychological process to dominate the will of others. The loss of freedom is expressed in different degrees and at different levels. At one extreme is the example of an individual bound and gagged by kidnappers, or a nation occupied by a foreign invader. In such cases the resistance can be equally extreme. At a lesser extreme, we see those freedoms that we cede voluntarily in the name of social convention, such as the freedom to walk around naked or to smoke in a public place.

Acceptance of the lack of freedom also occurs to varying degrees and on various planes. The first moment happens in the physical plane when the individual suppresses his resistance to oppression;

it is the moment when the body stops fighting against the bonds, when one stops shaking the bars of the prison and tires of shouting, "Get me out of here!" Then, the person begins to adjust to his condition, and in extreme cases, ends up feeling comfortable in prison, or establishing complicity with his jailers.

Although freedom is usually discussed in philosophical terms, it is from the political perspective that it reverberates most strongly. A slight tilt toward one or another tendency can change the destiny of a country and affect several generations. The right of free expression and free association, firmly based on a solid legal foundation, bolsters the probability that remaining rights will be respected. There is no value in having laws that guarantee the freedom to work, education, health care, and equality, if it is not possible to protest the failure to uphold these laws and if people are not allowed to organize in a civilized way to demand that they be respected.

> The ability to complain, to point a finger at what we do not like, is inseparable from an environment in which the individual does not have to barter his freedom.

The ability to complain, to point a finger at what we do not like, is inseparable from an environment in which the individual does not have to barter his freedom in exchange for benefits and privileges.

Dictatorships cannot survive where these rights are fully observed. Indeed, by definition, where these rights hold it is not appropriate to speak of dictatorship. To eliminate or diminish these fundamental freedoms, dictatorial governments resort to the force of arms or police persecution; they invoke national security, establish permanent states of emergency, and through control of the mass media, they discredit these freedoms as if they were diseases or perversions. Perhaps the most sophisticated method an oppressor uses to mask the effects of repression is to paint the relationship with the oppressed as a kind of love pact, so that submission—achieved through pain or fear—wears the respectable face of a generous offer made to the other person through affection, faith in religion, or conviction in a political cause.

Freedom and Socialism in Cuba

The real socialism that disappeared in Eastern Europe has been maintained in Cuba, though with severe spending cuts and some variation. Although, in the opinion of some, fresh air was introduced to the suffocating Stalinist model, what is certain is that the same totalitarian way of thinking that existed in faraway allied countries has been replicated on the Caribbean island. The most obvious difference with Poland, Czechoslovakia, and Bulgaria, for example, is that socialism was not imposed on Cuba by an imperialist power; in fact, just the opposite happened. Cuban socialism has always tried to present itself in the garb of sovereignty, and as the only way to achieve independence from the United States.

Despite this veneer of liberation, Cuba is a case study of how the abolition of the aforementioned freedoms is put into practice. In January 1959, a troop of young men—armed and bearded—came down from the mountains. There they had organized the guerilla war, brought about the defeat of the Batista dictatorship (1952-1958), and proclaimed that 1959 would be called, "The Year of the Liberation." In their first speeches they hoisted the banner of "Bread and Freedom," and everything indicated that, finally, Cuba would become a democratic nation where the progressive constitution approved in 1940 would be respected. How this group of irreverent revolutionaries ended up founding a gerontocracy, under the last-ditch slogan "Socialism or Death," would become the subject of detailed historical studies. But it is worthwhile to respond to at least one question: What happened to freedom?

At what point did the liberation process mutate into a process that oppresses? At what point were the civil liberties that had allowed the emergence of the revolutionary groups dynamited? How and when did freedom begin to be an obscene word, mentioned in whispers and longed for in the privacy of one's home? In exchange for what did Cuban citizens surrender their individual sovereignty and allow themselves to be locked up in the cage of paternalism, control, and authoritarianism? Answering these questions leads to the dismantling of the cage, and prompts further questioning about whether the crumbs offered in exchange for that freedom have been sufficient and extended to all.

Citizenship Sold Off

At the beginning of the revolution, the abolition of freedoms found a favorable climate in the unthinking enthusiasm that engulfed almost the whole nation and led it to sign a blank check payable to one person only: Fidel Castro. In the name of that vote of confidence, used ad nauseum by the "Maximum Leader," within a short time political parties and all the institutions of civil society were swept away. Newspapers, radio, and television ended up under the control of the state. The same fate befell the theaters, art galleries, movie houses, libraries, bookstores, and any entity that might have an opportunity to generate information or opinion. The people offered up—on the altar of a process still not declared to be communist—their civic institutions and the level of freedom they had reached after throwing off the Spanish colonial government.

> Two years after it triumphed, the Cuban Revolution had completed the confiscation of the most important factories, businesses, and banks.

Along with the disappearance of civil and political rights, economic rights vanished. Two years after it triumphed, the Revolution had completed the confiscation of the most important factories, businesses, and banks. In March of 1968, what sadly became known as the Revolutionary Offensive left not even the smallest kiosk, workshop, or store in private hands. Even the boxes of the shoeshine boys were seized, in what seemed like a desire to remake the nation without any commercial or economic ties inherited from the capitalist past.

It might be said, although it would seem paradoxical, that the Cuban people agreed to repay the debt of gratitude they owed to their liberators with their rights. In exchange for the possessions and rights confiscated by the new government, they received promises of a bright future; payment in advance, however, was required.

As it is much easier to redistribute wealth than to create it, the government in the early years of the Revolution aimed to improve the living standards of the poor, not by an increase in production, but by doling out what it expropriated from wealthy property owners. These were the years in which it was calculated that the benefits obtained would be spectacular and immediate. The citizens' naïveté was the fruit, in part, of an ignorance exceeded only by the enormous irresponsibility with which laws and decrees were dictated to "put the patrimony of the nation into the hands of the people." The potential beneficiaries did not experience the results with the immediacy or the magnificence they expected, but those whose property had been expropriated or nationalized felt the effects immediately.

The frequent and numerous executions, the failure of several guerilla actions and invasions, and the long prison sentences for those detained without trial, resulted in a loss of opposition. Many such individuals were forced into a bitter exile. Many Cubans opted to remain silent, including some intellectuals who realized, without being negatively affected in the process, that mistakes were being made. To criticize had become inopportune and it was made clear that any gap in the ranks could be used by the enemy. It became common to cite the metaphor of little David against the great Goliath of the North, but the slings of the people were not permitted to launch a single stone at the cyclopean state.

The opponent was real and gigantic, nothing less than the all-powerful North American imperialism, some of whose citizens were among the hardest hit by the nationalizations. The existence of this enemy—some would say the creation of this enemy—fostered a sense of siege where, in the words of St. Ignatius of Loyola, dissent is treason. The history of the dispute is well known and excessively complicated. The Cuban government blamed the Americans for diplomatic pressures, military actions, espionage, a trade embargo, economic warfare, and sabotage. The Cuban government received blame for destabilizing the region through the creation and support of insurgent groups in almost all Latin American countries. The confrontation with the Cuban government also provided the U.S. government with an excuse to strengthen its Cold War policies and to intervene in Latin American societies.

What was least expected to come to fruition could, in the end, be considered the fundamental achievement of the Cuban Revolution: achieving national sovereignty in the face of a neighbor's voracious appetite. But national security was imposed at the price of renouncing the sovereignty of the people, wherein reside precisely those rights that citizens exercise whenever the state displays authoritarian leanings. To explore whether there was a real or fictitious dilemma between the two versions of sovereignty, it would have been necessary to establish a broad, pluralistic and public debate, but that was not possible.

As was widely said then by party and government officials: "In this historic moment that our country is living through" people need to close ranks and swallow their differences. Officials established priorities that stressed the longed-for national liberation while condemning individual freedoms to last place. To demand such freedoms was to loudly declare one's selfishness, like a spoilsport who is bothered by loud music while others, to all appearances, are having fun.

> Paternalism stripped citizens of their civic, family, and work responsibilities, as well as the responsibilities each person has to himself.

The Establishment of State Paternalism

Over the course of time, and thanks to a substantial subsidy from the Soviet Union, state paternalism was established. The government provided the population with necessities through a system of rationing for food and industrial products. In a short time this, along with the extension of free education and health care, plus subsidized transportation and communications, turned Cuba into a country where it was not necessary to work to support a family at a minimum level of survival. The crumbs were assured, and with every passing day the bars of the cage were harder to break.

Paternalism stripped citizens of their civic, family, and work responsibilities, as well as the responsibilities each person has to himself. From that point on, the barter trade between freedoms and privileges was institutionalized. Everything you received above and beyond the norm was not due to your own efforts or talent; rather it was a perk, a reward for obedience. A telling example was the emergence of regulations for the distribution of household appliances.

These could only be bought through certificates or vouchers given out at mass rallies, after commissions analyzed the work and social merits of each applicant. Workers would earn points depending on their unconditional ideological support, the number of "voluntary" hours they worked, and attendance at political events. The purchasing permits needed to obtain a fan or a refrigerator even took into account participation in the wars in Angola and Ethiopia. Outside this system it was impossible to buy anything. The same method was used to assign housing and the chance to enjoy tourist facilities. Everything had to be paid for twice; once in real money at a subsidized price, and again with freedom, whether offered sincerely or not.

Those who did not jump through the hoops had to continue living with their in-laws and were forbidden to own a refrigerator, television, or washing machine. Even prostitution was practiced by young women willing to give their bodies to ministers and senior military officers in exchange for privileges—never cash. These were the courtesans of socialism who, years later with the arrival of the convertible currency, were transformed into prostitutes in the traditional sense.

The Impact on Personal Freedoms

But the infringement of rights did not stop there. *Real socialism* had an ardor for atheism, and among the questions you had to answer to get a job, enroll in the university, or receive new housing, would be whether you had religious beliefs, which creed you preferred, and how you practiced it. The questions were not a formality, nor a statistical curiosity, because the answers concealed an easy-to-guess password to admission.

While homophobia is not the exclusive patrimony of communists, it is worth remembering that homosexuals could be expelled from any school or workplace. In addition, in the 1970s, many homosexuals were interned in reeducation centers under a regimen of forced labor.

Renouncing the practice of the religion you believed in, or of acting on your sexual preference, was equivalent to giving up gems of freedom. They were the currency of exchange required, and those who agreed to the exchange had the impression that it was a small sacrifice for the sake of the future they were promised. They paid with images of the Virgin, rosaries, and scapulars for a hypothetical future that seemed, incredibly, just like the celestial kingdom the sacred books spoke of.

Lowering self-esteem seems to be an essential condition to produce at least a minimum level of acceptance of the loss of freedom. In the peculiar case of Cuba, since the 1970s there has been an attempt to shape a kind of person whose aspirations would not exceed the ceiling that the state had set for him: individuals who would have a self-perception that they could not compete, men and women who should feel satisfied, and even grateful, with what little could be given to everyone equally. Mediocrity began to be called modesty, while self-confidence was branded as arrogance. Amid a widespread lack of material things, the true revolutionary embraced the austerity that labeled the slightest weakness for fashionable clothing as extravagance, while consumerism and any desire for the new was considered unpardonable. Listening to foreign music, reading literature by authors not in the socialist *Parnassus*, wearing your hair in a certain way—these manifestations were condemned as ideological deviations which sooner or later would have to be analyzed, and for which one would have to repent through public self-criticism.

> Earning the revolutionary "diploma" became an obsession for writers and artists caught between fear and complacency.

In the midst of this forced austerity and a growing effort to standardize Cuban society, art was given the task of shaping "new ideological values," thus discrediting its function as a vehicle of expression for the artist. Ernesto Guevara had already had the arrogance to enunciate the original sin of the intellectuals; referring to their poor participation in the fight against Batista, he said that they had not been revolutionaries. Earning the revolutionary "diploma" became an obsession for writers and artists who, caught between fear and complacency, accepted the maxim that governed, and still governs, the political culture of the country: "Within the Revolution, everything; against the Revolution, nothing."

Freedom of expression came to be considered "freedom of the bourgeois press," and freedom of association became an illegal act to overthrow the Revolution. Civil society found itself restricted to revolutionary organizations which were mere transmitters of official views. The unions did not represent the interests of the workers against management, but functioned as extensions of state power to instruct the workers in socialist planning directives to meet production goals. Student associations ceased to be a tool for the young to stand up to school authorities, and evolved into an instrument of the Ministry of Education to enforce disciplinary rules. Nor were women's organizations a platform to demand women's rights, but rather a bureaucratic structure to incorporate women into production. The same occurred with the other institutions, including the peasants' association, the journalists' union, the writers' and artists' union, the college of architects, and even stamp collecting clubs.

Belonging to these organizations, which function in effect as neo-governmental organizations rather than non-governmental organizations, became obligatory. Still today, on any form, whether to register for a language class, ask permission to leave the country, or apply for a new job, the same question always appears: Are you an active member of any of these organizations? On occasion, the organizations are listed and you need only to check the boxes, as if it is illogical that there might be other organizations, or because there are no others. For anything involving the slightest privilege, you must bring a letter, on letterhead with a signature and a stamp, that guarantees, "the bearer is a comrade in the Revolution who participates in all its activities." But for a higher-level request these trifles are not enough. For something truly important, one must be a member of the Party or its youth organization, and for this, surrendering a small amount of freedom is not sufficient.

The Candid Surrender of the Idealist

In all these years, now totaling half a century, many dreamers have believed that the best way to solve the country's problems, the right path, the appropriate place to correct flaws, was found only within the Communist Party. Of course, becoming a party militant is a voluntary act, but the law establishes that other political organizations cannot be founded, and as a result, it is illegal to belong to any party other than the Cuban Communist Party. All those with political concerns—or simply a sense of civic responsibility—who are interested in promoting initiatives to improve life in their country, will only find a legal space to do so within the party.

To be admitted into the ranks of this select fraternity is accepted as proof by any examiner that an applicant is genuine and his intention is not to criticize, but to help. If you express yourself you cannot enter, and if you do not enter you cannot express yourself. This is the conflict that snares those who wish to improve the system through their observations and opinions. Once in the party, they learn that at the entry level they will not be heard, and that in order to climb the ladder, where they supposedly might be able to exercise influence, they have to swallow their criticisms. In the long run they are either domesticated by the machinery or expelled from it as an undesirable excrescence.

The approach of temporarily surrendering freedoms to gain access to a place from where you might reclaim them ends—for those who believe in this dangerous equation—in a well-calculated swindle. During the long silence that supposedly guarantees a platform to eventually speak from, idealists end up confusing faces with masks, the feigned for the felt. No one is going to return the freedoms pawned in this chameleonic act, which leaves idealists trapped between frustration and opportunism.

The Hoarding of the Opportunists

Others have understood that the party card is a key that opens doors, giving access not only to the higher echelons of command, from where they can influence decision making, but also to something much more attractive: the tempting accouterments of power. In any other social system these people would have been successful entrepreneurs, but in socialism they have to settle for being leaders of the process. To pass through the filters, they adapt the text of their biography, including living the biography asked of them, as a prerequisite.

Wearing the correct mask, they put a high price on the freedom they scorn, unable to find any sense in it because they don't know what to do with it. So, they barter it in exchange for a position, a house, a car, or a trip abroad that lets them bring home material goods—technological trinkets or brand-name clothes—unavailable in the domestic market. A trip that, ultimately, allows them to succumb to the temptation to desert.

At the end of the day, their final objective is not to change things in their country but rather to improve their own life, and for this they must ascend. To get there, to climb to the positions from where the helm is controlled, they must show irreproachable discipline and loyalty. Invariably they vote in favor of the proposals that come down from above, never admitting even the slightest deviation from what is directed, making life impossible for the idealists. They accuse the rare honest party members of being pessimistic and hypercritical and sneer at their lack of faith and arrogance; they dismiss them as irrelevant.

> The ultimate objective of party cadre is not to change things in their country but rather to improve their own life.

Each in their own way—the idealist who waits for the opportune moment to influence the course of events, and the opportunist who lies in wait only for possible benefits—ends up forfeiting their freedom. They give it away, receiving almost nothing in return; only the long wait for the one and the tiny material sinecures for the other.

Small Crumbs

Even to its supporters, the revolutionary program is hopeful, but slow. Every step involves an enormous sacrifice for everyone, with minimal gain for each person. From the point of view of the leaders of the process, the mass is a conglomeration of individuals who have neither elevated ideals nor pretentious ambitions. If they do not plan to propose a political program or open a business, why do these people want freedom? They must be given their bread, instructions to make them productive, and medical services to keep them healthy.

The most commonly repeated argument in socialist-authoritarian regimes is that freedom puts all the social advances enjoyed by the masses at risk. In one sense, this is entirely true. If everyone could say what they like, the first thing they would talk about is the need to introduce market mechanisms and the associated right to ownership. If, in addition to this, they are given the opportunity to organize themselves, they would have money to pay for a promotional campaign and would convince the majority that socialism is a brake on prosperity.

It is very curious that the sellers of the socialist Utopia only accept payment in freedom, and even more curious that they are the ones with the least faith in the human condition. It goes without saying that a society without social classes, where people work driven neither by need nor by the obscene lust for profit, would have to be populated by an angelic species, noble and altruistic by nature; were it otherwise the theory would be full of holes. In Cuba, this rare specimen of human being was given the name, "The New Man" ("El Hombre Nuevo"). He was going to be a species fundamentally incapable of demanding freedom, but satisfied with the paternalistic crumbs that fell his way from above.

To construct this man—a being alien to unfair economic exchange and the temptations of the market—education, the arts, and propaganda all contributed steady doses of ideology and indoctrination. But the final result was indifference or discontent. People raised outside a framework of social, economic, and political freedoms did not become "New Men." They yearned for the freedoms they didn't have.

In the market of Utopias there are no exchanges or returns, and the freedom that pays your way into paradise is never refunded. Rarely do citizens have the option to choose; freedom is suppressed, a system is imposed on them, and then, when citizens get frustrated and begin to think about introducing changes, they feel as if they must perform a Herculean task.

Buying Time

When the socialist bloc collapsed, the Cuban government found itself trapped in a real conflict between trying to maintain socialism without the Soviet subsidy or beginning to take into account the economic laws of the market. The first would have led the country to a fate similar to that of Cambodia in the appalling times of Pol Pot. The authorities even flirted with the possibility of a project called "Option Zero," which included a massive shift of people from the cities to the countryside.

But relative sanity prevailed, along with the desire to stay in power, and the so-called "Special Period" was decreed, in which some concessions would be made to "save the gains of the Revolution." They accepted that there would be small private restaurants, authorized the holding of dollars—which, until that time, had been penalized with years in prison—and welcomed remittances from Cubans living abroad. They permitted self-employment, and as a consequence of the increasing importance of tourism, prostitution reappeared with a vengeance, with the obvious tolerance of the authorities. The Fourth Communist Party Congress, held a couple of years earlier, had made the unexpected concession of allowing people with religious beliefs to become Party members, and everything pointed the way to an opening for the proposals of the reformist sectors.

Another currency appeared on the scene (initially it was the U.S. dollar; later it was the Cuban Convertible Peso), one that allowed citizens to obtain material goods without continuing to pay in freedom and support for the government. The dual monetary system changed the face of a country that, for decades, had established rationing or favoritism as the path to goods and services. The overprotective and authoritarian father that the Cuban state had become did not look kindly on its children's ability to thrive outside its protection, but it could do little to stop them. Legal and law enforcement mechanisms were created to ensure that the misguided entrepreneurs did not accumulate too many material goods, which might lead to independence.

As an indirect result of this "slacking off" in vigilance, anti-government activity increased significantly. Some 120 opposition organizations across the country decided to coordinate and celebrate an event called the "Cuban Council" or "Cuban Assembly" (Concilio Cubano). Hours before February 24, 1996, the event's promoters were imprisoned, an unequivocal signal that tolerance had its limits. To make matters worse, on the same day the Cuban military shot down two small planes from Florida, crewed by exiles supposedly trying to drop leaflets over Havana, In response, U.S. president Bill Clinton, pressured by the Cuban-American lobby, felt compelled to sign the Helms-Burton Act, strengthening the trade embargo. As a result, the "court reformists" lost what little ground they had gained.

The reversal accelerated with Hugo Chavez's rise to power in Venezuela and the considerable financial and energy resources he put into the hands of the Cuban government. With no one able to prevent a reversal, the small openings began to shrink. There would be no new licenses for self-employment, and a pack of inspectors fell on the private restaurants, forcing the majority of them to close.

The news of Fidel Castro's retirement for health reasons offered a ray of hope. His brother, Raúl Castro, declared the need for structural changes and even mentioned the possibility of offering an olive branch to the United States. But by the end of his first year in office as president of the Council of State, his measures were only cosmetic, such as allowing Cubans to have cell phones, stay in tourist hotels, and purchase DVD players and computers. These openings were so ridiculous that they only served to alert the rest of the world to the absurd limitations faced by Cuban citizens in their own country.

The showcase of the "Raúl reforms" was the land grants announced for anyone who wanted to cultivate them. In practice, there were no title deeds, but rather 10-year terms of usufruct. Agricultural development remains an unfinished business, because of the ineptitude of the large state companies and their lack of enthusiasm with regards to giving land to private farmers. This announced process of returning certain usurped freedoms only strengthened the evidence that the greedy state rarely gives back what it takes for itself, to the detriment of its citizens.

In the area of political freedom, the most significant step has been the signing of the International Covenant on Economic, Social, and Cultural Rights, and the Covenant on Civil and Political Rights, key instruments of the United Nations that are backed by the majority of democratic governments. These covenants, however, have not yet been ratified, nor has a single law been modified to make the Cuban legal system reflect the commitments within them. More than two hundred people now serving prison sentences were convicted for political reasons, even though officially this category does not exist and these prisoners are considered "mercenaries of imperialism."

Material poverty and the inability of citizens to finance their own political projects have launched many on a new form of dependency. Faced with the impossibility of legally justifying the allocation of resources they desire, all civil action parallel to the state is marked by the same level of informality as the black market. Those people inspired to develop programs and *create* organizations at the edges of the restrictive laws are viewed as criminals of opinion and traffickers in their own ideas.

The Sheep Who Escapes

The only threat that can be made against a sheep who wants to escape is that it will be returned to the pen. But it will no longer be part of the herd because, while the pen has fences, bolts, and physical boundaries, the herd is a mathematical abstraction, a number that falls apart once the participants who make up the sum decide to exercise their free will. As soon as a citizen stops paying with his freedom for other rights that ought to be respected, the confiscator of his sovereignty must change his tactics; now, instead of stealing his freedom from him, he must buy it. He must promise him better food, a roof that won't go flying off in a hurricane, or more lucrative subsidies. But little can be done if your coffers are empty and you have not learned how to create the wealth you must offer in exchange for freedom.

Every day there are more people in Cuba who are disenchanted with the socialist system, or the scam that goes by that name. Conversely, no conversions occur in the other direction and, now, to wear that mask is becoming a bad choice. Even the opportunists, with their sensitive noses, begin to flirt with real criticism and sing in the chorus of those demanding change. People are beginning to be conscious of having been cheated; this leads to signs of discontent and, lamentably, the country bleeds through growing migration. Just by boarding an airplane, many believe they can begin to recover all the freedoms ceded and stolen, while few dare—from inside our country—to push the limits of what is permitted.

One of the tools that has helped people recover the opportunity to air their opinions is the Internet. Although a common citizen cannot contract for Internet at home, and the price of an hour's connection in a public place exceeds two weeks' wages, a web of networks has emerged as the only means by which a person on the island can make his opinions known to the rest of the world. Today, this virtual space is like a training camp where Cubans go to relearn forgotten freedoms. The right of association can be found on Facebook, Twitter, and the other social networks, in a sort of compensation for the crime of "unlawful assembly" established by the Cuban penal code.

In a printed newspaper or magazine, on the radio or television, it is still impossible to publicize opinions that stray from the trite official script, but once connected to the Internet, many possibilities open up. Up until now, the most used are the independent blogs that have begun to appear. Most of the "direct readers" are abroad, and from there they e-mail the articles and posts they like to their friends and family in Cuba, who copy and multiply them. The bloggers, for their part, put copies of their work on CDs and even distribute them on flash drives. Television stations received by illegal satellite report on the contents of the blogs and conduct interviews, showing the faces of the bloggers. In this way, in less than a year, a community of cyber-dissidents was created—a *blogostroika,* as it is also called. Spaces such as Voces Cubanas or Desde Cuba, and the digital magazine *Convivencia,* are vivid examples of this.[2] They don't need authorized spaces to exist; rather, in lieu of recovering these parcels of freedom, they have created them.

> The right of association can be found on Facebook, Twitter, and the other social networks, in a sort of compensation for the crime of "unlawful assembly."

The Loan Shark Declares Bankruptcy

The methods used by the government to kidnap the freedom of Cuban citizens over these 50 years have had at least three elements: law enforcement, ideology, and economics. These three methods of reducing and dismantling rights have not followed each other in chronological order, but rather have coexisted and intermingled. In the case of Cuba, they began to manifest themselves during the first years of the triumph of the Revolution, though the dominance of one relative to the others has shifted back and forth.

The curbing of freedom for economic benefit had its strongest period when the support coming from the Kremlin allowed the state to offer its unconditional supporters something material in exchange for their loyalty. This buying and selling plummeted as the socialist camp fell apart, demonstrating the dependence and weakness of the Cuban economy. The trading of material benefits to those who ceded their freedom did not revive once money again had value as a medium of exchange; the convertible peso bankrupted the system of political and work-related merit as the path to material possessions. To buy the appliances that now reappeared in store windows it was no longer necessary to do volunteer work or to applaud a political speech, it was sufficient simply to have money. But this money was almost always obtained in ways contrary to those still being promulgated from the political dais.

The same thing happened with ideology. Disbelief spread among those who had once bet on the Marxist path to achieve a future of prosperity and equality. It became more difficult to find people who would yield their dwindling share of civil rights under the influence of an ideology that demanded it from them. This left, then, a single possible type of exchange: imposition. One hands over freedom without thinking, however, for material perks or for ideologies one believes in, but rights are not given as voluntarily to a repressive apparatus.

> When coercion becomes the only way to make a person yield his freedom, it is easy to recognize the uneven exchange that has been imposed.

When coercion becomes the only way to make a person yield his freedom, it is easy to recognize the uneven exchange that has been imposed. Discovering yourself to be a victim, you tend to react immediately and vehemently. Although the interior freedom of a person is inexhaustible, what you yourself paid for a privilege cannot be recovered. There is always the opportunity, however, to break the contract and choose to pay the price.

Meanwhile, the loan shark is bankrupt. The same one to whom you pawned civic action, the rights of free association, of which religion in which to raise your children, of freely leaving and entering the country, of freedom to buy a house or rent a room. The same one who held captive, through prohibitions, the creative and economic potential of an entire nation. This is what has happened in today's Cuba; where there are no longer rights to surrender as a currency of exchange, nor benefits to obtain through that purchase and sale. This is the time to fall into the hands of another moneylender, or to stop, once and for all, handling freedom as if it were money.

Notes

This text was translated from the Spanish by M. J. Porter. The original can be found at the Cato Institute's Spanish language website at http://www.elcato.org/pdf_files/ens-2009-ll-ll.pdf. The essay won a prize in the 2009 essay contest "Caminos de la libertad," organized by TV Azteca.

1. Friedrich Engels, "Anti-Duhring," in Karl Marx and Friedrich Engels, *Collected Works 25* (Moscow: Progress Publishers, 1987), p. 270.
2. Voces Cubanas, http://vocescubanas.com/; Desde Cuba, http://www.desdecuba.com/; and Conviven-cia, http://www.convivenciacuba.es/.

Yoani Sánchez, a University of Havana graduate in philology, emigrated to Switzerland in 2002. Two years later, she returned to Cuba, and started her blog, *Generation Y.* In 2008, *Time Magazine* named her one of the 100 Most Influential People in the World; it named *Generation Y* one of the "Best Blogs" of 2009. Spain honored her with its highest award for digital journalism, the Ortega y Gasset Prize. In 2009 she became the first blogger to interview President Barack Obama, who commented that her blog "provides the world a unique window into the realities of daily life in Cuba," and applauded her efforts to "empower fellow Cubans to express themselves through the use of technology."

6

Regime Change and Democracy in China

Liu Xiaobo

ON 19 OCTOBER 2005, the Information Office of the State Council of the People's Republic of China released the white paper, "Building of Democratic Politics in China." Although this was the first white paper on democracy-building issued by the Communist government since it came to power, except for the fact that it was published, it broke no new ground in terms of content.

At the core of the white paper were arguments regarding the "theory of national conditions," "theory of [Chinese Communist] Party [(CCP)] authority," and "theory of the wisdom of the [CCP]."

The "theory of national conditions" in the white paper no longer stresses China's economic backwardness and the substandard quality of the population, but rather emphasizes that the central leadership position of the CCP was both a historical choice and the voluntary choice of the Chinese people—that is, it was created by history rather than the will imposed by the CCP on the people. Clearly, the purpose of the "theory of national conditions" is to refute the universal nature of democracy and to conceal the problems of legitimacy of the current CCP regime by invoking special national conditions.

The "theory of Party authority" publicly affirms China's current system of the supreme authority of the Party. Whether it is the abstract idea of democratic construction of popular sovereignty or the protection of human rights and specific human rights written into the Constitution, whether it is the institution of the National

People's Congress (NPC) and the political consultative system or the so-called democratic centralism with Chinese Communist characteristics, whether the grassroots democracy process or rule by law—all of these must follow the guidance of the CCP authority and have nothing to do with popular sovereignty.

The purpose of the "theory of the wisdom of the CCP" is to declare that the credit for all of China's current achievements is due to the CCP, going as far as to defend a string of failures as great accomplishments. Similarly, whatever little democratic achievement there has been in China since the reforms is also all attributable to the wise leadership of the CCP and is most certainly not the result of spontaneous efforts of the people.

> The purpose of the "theory of the wisdom of the CCP" is to declare that the credit for all of China's current achievements is due to the Communist Party.

As a result, the white paper is tantamount to a declaration to the entire world: Above the democracy of people's sovereignty, the CCP authority is an even higher authority, and this Party authority is supreme, which is to say that "the Party is in charge of the people" and "the Party is in charge of democracy," and that the NPC is the puppet of the Party authority, the Chinese People's Political Consultative Conference (CP-PCC) is its ornament, the judiciary is its tool, and the vocabulary of human rights, democracy, and so on is just its window dressing. Like the white paper on human rights released by the CCP authorities, this white paper on democracy is full of lies. For example, the white paper states: "All power in the People's Republic of China belongs to the people." But China's 1.3 billion people are a flock of sheep herded by the Party authority and have no opportunity to participate in the election of the country's president. Another example is that the white paper proclaims "development of democracy within the Party." Yet the great majority of the 68 million Party members are no more than Party slaves and, likewise, have no opportunity to elect the Party boss.

This is the "Building of Democratic Politics in China" flaunted by the white paper!

So this white paper is not so much an announcement of the "Building of Democratic Politics in China" as it is a public defense of "protecting the dictatorial system of the supremacy of Party authority."

On 1 October 1949, after Mao Zedong ascended Tiananmen Gate, the chorus of "he is the great savior of the people" swept through the country—an enduring song that has to this day remained a nostalgic tool used by the people to vent their dissatisfaction. On 1 October 1984, after Deng Xiaoping descended from Tiananmen to review the troops and accepted the heartfelt support [expressed in the simple greeting of] "Hello Xiaoping," with one wave of his hand, the "chief architect" bestowed upon the little people the opportunity to make a dash for the small comforts of everyday life, to "let some people get rich first," and achieved limited economic emancipation. On 1 October 1999, after Jiang Zemin reviewed the troops, despite widespread attacks from all quarters, he was still secure in the key position as the "leading figure in inheriting the revolutionary cause and carrying it into the future." He embarked on yet another theoretical innovation of vast and mighty imperial largesse and let the capitalists who had amassed great fortunes join the CCP and be politically emancipated by royal decree, so that they were no longer just the United Front partners and political ornaments of the NPC and CPPCC but had become members of the ruling party. I do not know when the new Party boss Hu Jintao plans to ascend Tiananmen to review the troops and mold an image for his own "dear people."

I do not deny that within the CCP clique currently in power there could be high-ranking officials, such as Hu Yaobang and Zhao Ziyang, who treat the people well and possess an awareness of modern politics. When they were in office, they did make quite a few good policy decisions and took risks to advance political reform. But even when this was the case, people had to wait for their rights and benefits as if they were charities bestowed from above, not to mention that such good officials could not survive for long under the CCP system.

Let us take ten-thousand steps back: If our countrymen could come across an enlightened ruler often, or if the imperial bestowing of favors was not incidental behavior but, rather, occurred every now and then, then the national inertia of waiting for these favors, although an insult to human dignity, could be excused because of the tangible benefits received. Sadly, however, our countrymen endured great suffering and endless waiting only to encounter a wise sovereign by chance or an exceedingly miserly show of mercy. What they receive are always meager compensations and pathetic consolations that arrive too late, so why is it that they are still only capable of looking up to the crown? Moreover, throughout China's cyclical dynastic history, every act of the vast and mighty imperial benevolence has occurred either at the beginning of a new dynasty, when everything left undone by the previous regime is taken up, or during the crisis-ridden final years of a reign, and never for the well-being of the people but out of political necessity, to consolidate or maintain political power or save the regime. Our countrymen are still like infants who depend entirely on adult care and who know only how to wait for a wise ruler to appear. Can it be that Chinese people will never really grow up, that their character is forever deformed and weak, and that they are only fit, as if predestined by the stars, to pray for and accept imperial mercy on their knees?!

> Throughout China's cyclical dynastic history, every act of the vast and mighty imperial benevolence has occurred either at the beginning of a new dynasty, or during the crisis-ridden final years of a reign.

There is absolutely no doubt that on the post-Mao mainland, compared with the Mao era, our countrymen have gained tangible benefits in terms of food and shelter and an extremely limited space for personal choices. The pragmatic "cat theory" initiated by Deng Xiaoping,[1] compared with Mao's ideology, which stressed class struggle, had a nimble and soft flexibility. However, none of these changes have fundamentally altered the basic mode of existence of our countrymen; the relationship between the ruler and the ruled in this land has been the same throughout the ages, and has been handed down unchanged to this day. Namely, the power to initiate and make decisions about the rights and interests of the people, the fate of the country, any progress in society, and any improvements to the lives of the common people is firmly held in the hands of the dictators. [All improvements] are charity granted from above, requiring the subjects to shout the triple "Long live!" salute to show their loyalty and gratitude to the rulers, requiring famous public figures to play the part of critics who share their goals, and requiring hack writers with skillful pens to defend and praise them, in order to demonstrate the wisdom and virtues of the sovereign.

Even though there have been improvements in civil-rights defense movements in recent years, we must also look at the grim reality facing the cause of civil-rights defense. If not used by the treacherous dictators as a tool to seize power and establish a new dynasty, the bottom-up movement to win human dignity, personal rights and interests gets completely wiped out by the brutal autocratic machine, and there is no way that a succession of large-scale movements of popular disobedience, be they the traditional violent rebellions for dynastic change or the modern political opposition movements of peaceful resistance, can arise to shake the foundations of the authoritarian system and the slavish culture.

What is the reason for this?

Repression by the dictatorial authorities is, admittedly, one of the reasons, but the indifference of the populace is an even greater cause. In the minds of ignorant, cowardly, and blind people, being used is no different from being liberated and given a new life. As to the cowardly but smart cynics, being repressed means being subjugated and, thus, becoming an accomplice, a lackey, or, at the very least, a silent, docile subject. When have our countrymen tasted the genuine liberation that comes with being the master of one's own affairs? When has China ever broken out of the vicious historical cycle of order and chaos under authoritarian dynastic rule?

For generations, up until this very day of CCP rule, expressions like "after liberation," "since the founding of the country," and "after the new China was established," and excuses such as "without the Communist Party there would be no new China," have become the most basic common understanding of history and a linguistic habit that has settled deeply into the nation's collective memory, universally used in people's speech and writing. Even the intellectuals and liberals within the Party who know the CCP's history like the back of their hands habitually use these terms for historical reference when exposing the countless crimes committed after the CCP took power.

Likewise, when common people today bring up the 1989 Movement and the June Fourth [Tiananmen] Massacre, the vast majority still casually toss around the words "turmoil" or "rebellion." Even the Beijing residents who personally experienced the great peaceful marches and the bloody massacre by and large use the vocabulary set by the government. And although the authorities have already quietly changed "turmoil" and "rebellion" to "political disturbances" in the public media, the people's language has not changed much accordingly. Since Jiang Zemin's regime persecuted the Falun Gong in 1999, the word "cult" has also entered the vernacular, spreading particularly fast among college, high-school, and elementary-school students. A few years ago, every time I heard acquaintances use the word "turmoil" to talk about the 1989 Movement, I wanted to refute it and correct them. These corrections were at first made angrily, then gravely, and, finally, with resignation. As time went on, I began to let them go. Forceful ideological indoctrination of minds that have been enslaved for a prolonged period inevitably hardens memory and language.

Linguistic philosophy's sacred monster Ludwig Wittgenstein maintained that language is not a tool of expression in the traditional sense but action itself, and that the way one chooses to express oneself linguistically is the way one chooses to think, [while] the way one chooses to think is the way one chooses to live. Therefore, by extension, if one habitually uses linguistic expressions of deep gratitude, one inevitably creates the savior mentality; the savior mentality inevitably leads to the slavish way of life of waiting for top-down charity and the fear that without the savior one will end up in a situation more desperate and pitiful than that of a homeless dog.

Time and time again, people have pinned their hopes for top-down political reform on those who have newly assumed office, but they end up disappointed each time. The most absurd part is that disappointment after disappointment still has not extinguished what little hope people have in the CCP-initiated reforms. Why? The usual response is that the national conditions make it so. Some people say that such a large country can only be controlled and governed by an authoritarian system. Others say that the CCP is too powerful and that it has too many monopolies on resources, so that unless it transforms itself no other force can challenge it. Some say that opposition groups in popular politics in many ways do not even measure up to the CCP, and that if they came to power they would be even worse than the CCP. Others say that economic development must maintain social stability, and only with the CCP in power can stability be maintained. Still others say that the mainland population is too large, inferior, and ignorant, only fit to receive charitable guidance from the elites, and only capable of carrying out top-down reforms, et cetera. All of these arguments just go to prove: Without the CCP, or if the CCP were to step down, who could effectively rule China in its place? Do not democracy activists and people who hold divergent political views in China and abroad constantly run up against this question? And that is why waiting for the gift of happiness to be bestowed from above is the common people's only option.

At a time when our countrymen do not fight, not even preparing to become their own masters, at a time when they have abandoned all efforts even before the struggle for their personal rights and interests has started in earnest, people can universally concoct a subconscious assumption that without the current rulers the country would slide into chaos. This type of assumption stems from the long-enforced ideological indoctrination of the CCP, as well as the slavish nature of our countrymen, which remains unchanged to this day. There is a reason why dictators disregard historical facts and raise this type of assumption. That is because every policy decision they make and everything they say have only one ultimate purpose—maintaining absolute power. But there is absolutely no reason for the people to believe in this assumption, because the system that this assumption supports is precisely a system that does not treat people as humans. Once our countrymen forget historical facts and believe in this assumption, they would have no qualms in waiting for the pie to fall from the sky and would look for a wise ruler or a virtuous master even if they have to die nine times looking for one; they would view all bottom-up popular opposition movements and those that fight for personal rights and interests as more of a hindrance than help that only "add to chaos," and would defend those in power, who have done one insignificant small good and 99 great ills, using that one percent of good policy to defend that 99 percent of bad government. Even when being massacred, starved, imprisoned, exiled, deprived, and discriminated against, the little people still feel eternally indebted and grateful and consider the dictators "great, honorable, and infallible."

A poem by Bai Juyi[2] says: "Wildfire never quite destroys them—They grow again in the spring wind." In mainland China, this eternal, celebrated verse is decidedly not an apt description of people who have the courage to stand up straight and tall, but rather an exquisite portrayal of our countrymen accustomed to kneeling ever so gracefully. Under the imperial throne, civil and military officials neatly fall to their knees as one and shout the salute, "Long live! Long, long live!" three times. Atop Tiananmen, the dictator waves his hand and the largest square in the world becomes a sea of subjects hailing their savior. Since the collapse of the Qing Dynasty [in 1911] and especially since the CCP came to power, even though our countrymen no longer kowtow physically like the people of old, they kneel in their souls even more so than the ancients.

> Universal enslavement and inequality are never caused by the ruler's excessive power or wisdom, but because those who are ruled kneel down.

An admonition on how to be an upright person says: "Man is born free and equal." Universal enslavement and inequality are never caused by the ruler's excessive power or wisdom, but because those who are ruled kneel down. Can it be that today, more than a hundred years after the era of imperial power based on triple kowtowing and nine-fold kneeling has been abolished, our countrymen are still humiliating themselves and finding all sorts of justifications to defend their kneeling position? Can it be that the mere favors of a good standard of living and allowing the wealthy to join the Party have made our countrymen capable only of falling to their knees and kowtowing in gratitude for the magnanimity and grace of the dictators?

For the emergence of a free China, placing hope in "new policies" of those in power is far worse than placing hope in the continuous expansion of the "new power" among the people. The day when the dignity of the people is conceptually and legally established is the day when the human rights of our countrymen will gain institutional protections.

We have had over twenty years of reform, but due to the selfish arrogation of political power by the Chinese Communist Party (CCP) and the scattering of civic forces, in the short term I do not see any kind of political force capable of changing the regime, or any liberal-minded force within the circle of official authorities, like a Gorbachev[3] or a Chiang Ching-kuo,[4] nor any way for civil society to build up political power sufficient to rival official authorities. And so, China's course of transformation into a modern, free society is bound to be gradual and full of twists and turns. The length of time it will take may surpass even the most conservative estimates.

At the same time, in terms of opposition to the might of the CCP regime, civil society remains weak, civic courage inadequate, and civic wisdom immature; civil society is still in the earliest stages of development, and consequently there is no way to cultivate in a short time a political force adequate to the task of replacing the Communist regime. In such a situation, change in China's political system and its current regime—any plan, program or even action seeking instant success—can be no more than castles in the air.

Yet this does not mean that there is absolutely no hope for a future free China. The sky of Chinese politics in the post-Mao era can no longer be single-handedly obscured by a totalitarian ruler; rather, it has assumed two hues: darkness and light. Likewise, the relationship between the officials and the people is no longer such that no one dares to speak out, except to shout, "Long live the emperor!" Rather, the political rigidity of the authorities and the people's awakening to their rights, and official suppression and civil resistance exist side-by-side at the same time. The system is autocratic as before, but the society is no longer ignorant; the officials are tyrannical as before, but the civil-rights defense movements continue to arise; the terror of literary inquisition is still there, but it can no longer produce the deterrent of "killing one to scare the rest;" the regime's "enemy awareness" is unchanged, but "politically sensitive individuals" are no longer a terrifying "pestilence" shunned by everyone.

In the Maoist era, for personal totalitarian control to be established, four major conditions had to be met at the same time:

Comprehensive nationalization, leading to no personal economic autonomy whatsoever, turning the regime into an all-powerful nanny of our countrymen, and making them economically dependent on the regime from cradle to grave;

All-pervasive organization, leading to the complete loss of personal freedom, turning the organization into the sole authenticator of legal status for our countrymen, who can hardly take a single step if they leave the organization, and making them personally dependent on the regime to the extent that without the shelter of the organization they have no social license;

Rigid tyranny of the machinery of violent dictatorship imposed on the entire social body; a dictatorial atmosphere created by an extreme rule of one man and by an "enemy" mentality, where every citizen is made a soldier; all-pervasive vigilance and ubiquitous monitoring, to the extent that every pair of eyes is turned into surveillance equipment and every person is under surveillance by his or her work unit, neighborhood [committee], neighbors, and even relatives and friends.

Mental tyranny imposed on the entire nation by an ideology of formidable cohesive power and power to inspire, and by large-scale mass movements, where the extreme personality cult and leadership authority create a kind of mind-control with one brain deciding what everybody thinks, and where artificially created "dissidents" are not just persecuted economically, politically, and in terms of social status, but are also made to suffer humiliation of character, dignity, and spirit—the so-called "criticism until they drop and stink," which is in fact a dual tyranny that is both physical and mental to the extent that the great majority of the victims succumbing to this mental tyranny engage in endless public self-humiliation.

Yet, in the post-Mao era, the society entirely based on official authority no longer exists. An enormous transformation toward pluralism in society has already taken place, and official authority is no longer able to fully control the whole society. The continuous growth of private capital is nibbling away at the regime's economic foundation, the increasingly disintegrated value system is challenging its ideology, persistently expanding civil-rights protections are increasing the challenges to the strength of the arbitrary authority of government officials, and steadily increasing civic courage is making the effectiveness of political terror wither by the day.

Since June Fourth [1989] especially, three of the four major pillars necessary for the establishment of personal totalitarian rule have been in various stages of decay and even collapse. Personal economic dependence [on the regime] has gradually been replaced by personal independence, and the living made through one's own efforts has given individuals the material base for autonomous choices, while bringing a plurality of interests to the society. Personal dependence on organizations has gradually been replaced by a smattering of personal freedom: The Chinese people need no longer live in organizations for lack of alternatives; the time when they could hardly take a step if they left the organization is gone, never to return. Chinese society is gradually moving toward freedom of movement, mobility, and career choice.

> An enormous transformation toward pluralism in society has already taken place, and official authority is no longer able to fully control the whole society.

In the ideological sphere, the awakening of individual consciousness and awareness of one's rights have led to the collapse of the one great unified official ideology, and the diversification in the system of values is forcing the government to look for excuses for the passive adjustments of its ideology. A civic value system independent of the bureaucratic value system is gradually taking shape, and although indoctrination with lies and speech control continues, [the government's] persuasive power has significantly declined. The information revolution ushered in by the Internet in particular has multiplied and diversified the channels of information access and civic discourse, causing the fundamental failure of the means of control used by government authorities to block information and prohibit political discussion. Of the four pillars of totalitarian rule, only political centralization and its blunt repression remain. However, because a social pattern where righteousness and justice reside with civil society while power resides with the authorities has gradually taken shape, the twofold tyranny of the Maoist era—persecution of the flesh and trampling of the spirit— is no more, and there has been a significant decline in the effectiveness of political terrorism. As for [the] government's persecution of its victims, it no longer has the twofold effect of using prison to deprive them of personal freedom and also using mass criticism to debase their integrity and dignity. Political persecution may cause its victims to suffer economic losses, may strip them of personal freedom, but it is unable to damage their social reputation, and even less able to place them under the siege of social isolation; and therefore it cannot destroy their integrity, dignity, or spirit. On the contrary, it has gradually turned into a vehicle for advancing the moral stature of its victims, garnering them honors for being the "civic conscience" or "heroes of truth," while the government's hired thugs have become instruments that "do the dirty work." Not only does the majority of those persecuted no longer beg forgiveness from the organization through endless self-criticism or undertake public self-humiliation; on the contrary, most are able to inspire reverence with their devotion to justice as they defend themselves in the dock under great organizational pressure, putting the Communist Party organization and courts into the moral position of defendants.

Meanwhile, following the collapse of the communist-totalitarian Soviet Union and Eastern bloc, the global trend toward liberalization and democratization has been gaining strength by the day. Pressure from the human-rights diplomacy of mainstream nations and from international human-rights organizations is making the cost of maintaining a system of dictatorship and terror politics increasingly high, while the effectiveness and the deterrent capacity of official persecution continue to decline, forcing the current Chinese Communist regime to put on a big "Human Rights Show" and "Democracy Show," both in its domestic governance and in its foreign response.

In other words, whether it is the everlasting practice of nonviolent resistance, or the prediction that the liberal system will be the "end of history,"[5] all these [theories] ultimately appeal to the spiritual aspect of human nature. Humans exist not only physically, but also spiritually, possessing a moral sense, the core of which is the dignity of being human. Our high regard for dignity is the natural source of our sense of justice. When a system or a country allows everyone to live with dignity, it can gain spontaneous approval from the people, which is how St. Thomas Aquinas understood political virtue: Virtuous good governance lies not only in maintaining order, but [even] more in establishing human dignity. [If it acts] otherwise, [a government] will provoke various forms of resistance, with conscientious objection among the principal forms. The reason why the liberal system can gradually replace dictatorship, and the end of the Cold War can be seen as the end of history, lies in the fact that the former [liberal system] acknowledges and respects human dignity, while the latter [dictatorship] does not recognize human dignity and discredits it by dragging it in the dust.

The greatness of nonviolent resistance is that even as man is faced with forceful tyranny and the resulting suffering, the victim responds to hate with love, to prejudice with tolerance, to arrogance with humility, to humiliation with dignity, and to violence with reason. That is, the victim, with love that is humble and dignified, takes the initiative to invite the victimizer to return to the rules of reason, peace, and compassion, thereby transcending the vicious cycle of "replacing one tyranny with another."

> Humans exist not only physically, but also spiritually, possessing a moral sense, the core of which is the dignity of being human.

Bottom-up reform requires self-consciousness among the people, and self-initiated, persistent, and continuously expanding civil-disobedience movements or rights-defense movements among the people.

In an unfree society ruled by a dictatorship, under the premise of a temporary absence of power that can change the dictatorial nature of the regime, the civic ways that I know of for promoting the transformation of Chinese society from the bottom up are as follows:

The nonviolent rights defense movement does not aim to seize political power, but is committed to building a humane society wherein one can live with dignity. That is, it strives to expand an independent civil society by changing the way people live—the lifestyle of ignorance, cowardice, and willing enslavement—by first endeavoring to expand the space and resources for civil society in areas where the control by government authorities is weak. This is followed by sustained nonviolent resistance to compress the social space controlled by government authorities, and then by increasing the price the dictatorial government has to pay in order to control the civic sphere, shaping a pattern of gradual inch-by-inch progress of civil liberties at the expense of the contracting power of government authorities.

The nonviolent rights defense movement need not pursue a grand goal of complete transformation. Instead, it is committed to putting freedom into practice in everyday life through initiation of ideas, expression of opinions, and rights defense actions; particularly through the continuous accumulation of each and every rights defense case, it accrues moral and justice resources, organizational resources, and maneuvering experience in the civic sector. When civic forces are not yet strong enough to change the macropolitical environment at large, they can at least rely on personal conscience and small-group cooperation to change the small, micropolitical environment within their reach. For instance, the fact that the rebellion of senior newsmen such as Lu Yuegang and Li Datong against the official news system achieved definite results was ultimately a function of the soundness of the small milieu within the *China Youth Daily.*

Regardless of how great the freedom-denying power of a regime and its institutions is, every individual should still fight to the best of his or her ability to live as a free person—that is, make every effort to live an honest life with dignity. In any society ruled by dictatorship, when those who pursue freedom publicly disclose it and practice what they preach, as long as they manage to be fearless in the small details of everyday life, what they say and do in everyday life will become the fundamental force that will topple the system of enslavement. If you believe that you possess a basic human conscience and if you heed its call, then display it and let it shine in the sunlight of public opinion, let the people see it and, especially, let the dictators see it.

One should unfailingly commit to liberal values, pursue the principle of tolerance, and promote multilateral dialogue, particularly when different voices and different choices arise among the people; and one should treat low-profile dealings as a supplement to high-profile resistance, rather than regarding oneself as an absolute hero and unreasonably assigning blame. Because even though enforced morality is different from enforced politics, it is still quite far from the tolerance that liberalism calls for. That a person is willing to pay a great price for the ideals he or she chooses does not constitute justification for forcing others to make comparable sacrifices for ideals.

Whether an insider or an outsider of the system, whether working from the top-down or the bottom-up, each should respect the other's right to speak. Even the statements and actions of people attached to the government, as long as they do not force constraints on independent discourse among the people and the rights defense movement, should be regarded as useful for exploration of transformational strategies. Their right of speech should be fully respected. Those who advocate transformation from the top-down should maintain adequate respect for the explorations of those working from the bottom up among the people. With the premise of mutual respect and equal treatment, the contention and dialogue between proponents of the top-down and the bottom-up positions will make a more useful contribution to shaping a popular consensus on the trajectory for transformation. This is the meaning of the saying, "All roads lead to Rome." Tolerance, however, does not mean tacit consent to tyranny, nor does it mean sinking into the quagmire of absolute relativism. The bottom line for the liberal nongovernmental position is, specifically, firm opposition by force of the words and deeds of the people to any government repression, whatever form this repression may take—intimidation, bribery, rectification, expulsion, prohibition, arrest, or legislation.

Institutional common sense on how to confront rather than evade an ever-present dictatorial power: [One must] take into one's own hands the initiative for improving the status of the population without rights, rather than pinning hope on the arrival of some enlightened master or benevolent ruler. In the strategic maneuvering between civil society and the government, regardless of how official policies may change, the most important thing is to encourage and assist the civil-rights defense movement and to hold fast to the independent position of civil society. Especially in a situation where one is alone in confronting bad governance amid a chorus of praise singers, one must be committed to the criticism of and opposition to the dictatorial regime from the position of an outsider. When the government's policy decisions are stiff, one must force them to become flexible; when the government's attitude loosens, one must take advantage of it to expand civic resources and space. While supporting enlightened policy making within the system, one must still hold fast to one's position as an outsider and persevere in one's criticism.

In sum, China's course toward [becoming] a free society will mainly rely on bottom-up gradual improvement and not on a top-down "Chiang Ching-kuo-style" revolution.[6] Bottom-up reform requires self-consciousness among the people, and self-initiated, persistent, and continuously expanding civil-disobedience movements or rights-defense movements among the people. In other words, pursue [the building of] free and democratic forces among the people; do not pursue the rebuilding of society through radical regime change, but instead use gradual social change to compel regime change. That is, rely on a continuously growing civil society to reform a regime that lacks legitimacy.

Notes

1. When Deng Xiaoping returned to power in the mid-1970s, after the Cultural Revolution, he famously declared, "I do not care whether a cat is black or white. As long as it catches mice, it is a good cat," to signal that he intended to put stress on pragmatism rather than ideology. This landed him in new trouble, and he was once again purged from all his official posts by Mao Zedong. However, after Mao's death Deng's position won the day, and set off decades of China's economic reform and opening to the outside world.
2. Bai Juyi (772-846 C.E.), one of the most celebrated Tang Dynasty poets, used elegantly simple verse to protest the social evils of his day, including corruption and militarism.
3. Mikhail Sergeyevich Gorbachev (b. 1931) was the second-to-last general secretary of the Communist Party of the Soviet Union, serving from 1985 until 1991, and the last head of state of the USSR, serving from 1988 until its collapse in 1991.
4. Chiang Ching-kuo (1910-88) was the Kuomintang (Chinese Nationalist) politician and leader. The son of Chiang Kai-shek, he was first the premier (1972-78) of the Republic of China (ROC), and then its president from 1978 until his death in 1988. Under his tenure, the ROC government, while authoritarian, became more open and tolerant of political dissent. Toward the end of his life, Chiang relaxed government controls on the media and speech.
5. See Francis Fukuyama, "The End of History?" *National Interest* 16 (Summer 1989): 3-18.
6. In 1987, President Chiang Ching-kuo ended martial law in Taiwan and began a gradual process of political liberalization, allowing opposition groups to form.

Reprinted with permission of the National Endowment for Democracy and translated from the Chinese by Human Rights in China.

Liu Xiaobo is a Chinese literary critic, writer, and professor who has called for the end of communist one-party rule in the People's Republic of China. He has taught at Beijing Normal University, University of Oslo and Columbia University. In 2010, he became the first Chinese citizen to win the Nobel Peace Prize while still residing in China. His writings include *A Single Blade and Toxic Sword: Critique on Contemporary Chinese Nationalism* and *A Nation That Lies to Conscience*.

7

Shifting Balances between Business and Government in the United States

Murray Weidenbaum

EVER SINCE Thomas Jefferson and Alexander Hamilton debated the merits of individual freedom and strong government, the nation's decision makers have faced the challenging task of reconciling fundamental, but conflicting objectives. Today's economy provides an especially dramatic example of that conflict as it reduces the large gap between the rich and the poor in the United States and simultaneously improves the dismal performance of the American economy.

Many popular policies that would aid in dealing with one of these two fundamental concerns would worsen the other. Unfortunately, there is no shortage of cogent examples. To start with the most obvious, reducing the tax burden on the top income group would expand the amount of saving available to finance investment and economic growth. However, the result would be a more unequal distribution of income and wealth than now exists in the United States.

The alternative of raising taxes on those in the top brackets would result in the mirror image of the first alternative. The disparity among income classes would be smaller, but simultaneously the amount of private saving available to finance investment in economic growth would decline. In plain English, citizens would receive more equal slices of a smaller income pie.

It is oversimplified, but basically accurate, to contend that the first decade of this new century has been characterized by a primary focus on expanding the income pie and also public policy in the United States now is shifting to the second alternative of giving citizens more equal shares of income. Each of these two alternatives comes with fundamental shortcomings.

From that perspective, the basic purpose of this study is to demonstrate the need for a new sense of balance in developing the economic policies for the United States in the second decade of the twenty-first century. In essence, I will be introducing the economist's notion of a "tradeoff" between important objectives. Rather than advocating the continuation of a public policy process that swings from one extreme to another, the need is for reconciliation among important but competing national objectives.

This approach is based on the notion introduced by the late Arthur Okun of the Brookings Institution: there is a tradeoff between equality and efficiency. The single-minded pursuit of efficiency in economic affairs can produce gross injustice, while the pursuit of too much equality can generate unacceptable efficiency losses in terms of economic output foregone. Okun's concept of a "leaky bucket" reminded us of the price of equalization. A loss in economic efficiency often accompanies programs to help low-income people.[1]

> The first decade of this new century has been characterized by a primary focus on expanding the income pie and also public policy in the United States.

The facts and arguments on the issue of inequality of the distribution of income in the United States are well known and can be quickly summarized. Harvard University economist Benjamin Friedman reminds us that the bottom fifth of the US income distribution received a 4.1 percent share in 2007, down from 5.7 percent in 1974. In contrast, families in the top fifth saw their share of national income rise from 40.5 percent in 1966 to 47.3 in 2007.[2]

As for the concern over economic growth, the United States is now in the midst of a long and deep recession, the longest and deepest since the Great Depression of the 1930s. The unemployment rate, to cite an especially influential statistical indicator, rose from 4.6 percent in 2007 to over 9 percent in mid-2009. Moreover, most forecasters expect the unemployment rate will not return to the 2007 level for many years.

In our complex modern economy a great many factors influence economic growth and the size of the nation's income pie to be distributed across the population. In recent months, attention has focused on a variety of governmental efforts to assist or to "bail out" strategic sectors of the economy which have been especially hard hit by the combination of credit crisis and macroeconomic decline.

Rather than attempting to repeat or even to improve upon the mass of writing on the subject, I am focusing on an important, but neglected aspect of economic policy: the cumulative impact of new or expanded federal expenditure, tax, credit, and regulatory policies on the ability of the private enterprise system to perform its traditional function of producing the bulk of goods and services required by the American people. To cite one example among many: businesses can be discouraged by government policies from making major new investments, especially those of a long-term nature with payoffs far in the future. A key discouraging factor is the likelihood of higher taxes and/or greater inflation resulting from the huge budget deficits that are likely to arise in the next several decades.

> The basic fact is that the United States has a progressive personal income tax. In 2006, 1 percent of federal taxpayers paid 21 percent of their income for taxation whereas the top 5 percent devoted 19 percent for tax purposes.

Surely, the fairness of the tax system could and should be enhanced. Nevertheless, we start from the basic fact is that the United States has a progressive personal income tax. In 2006, 1 percent of federal taxpayers paid 21 percent of their income for taxation whereas the top 5 percent devoted 19 percent for tax purposes.[3]

Thus, as we ascend the income pyramid we find that each successive level pays a higher average tax than the preceding level. That is true until we come to the very top of the income distribution. A statistical breakdown of the tax burdens of the people within the top 1 percent shows low effective rates. A key reason is the provision of the tax law that allows the highly paid managers of hedge funds and private capital pools to pay the lower capital gains rate on the fees that they earn for managing those portfolios. This special provision is a popular candidate for tax reform.

My primary focus, however, is on the major ways in which economic performance is depressed because of those government actions which are focused on other objectives. The importance of investment is reinforced by a recent and comprehensive analysis of the major sources of economic growth. Between 1948 and 2006, investment accounted for the largest share; 49 percent of the total. In contrast, labor income represented 31 percent of the total growth of the American economy in that time period.[4]

The sections that follow are devoted to identifying new governmental barriers to investment and economic growth.

Tax Policy

The general approach being taken by the Obama Administration on tax policy can be gleaned from the 131 pages it takes the Treasury to present the highlights of its tax proposals.[5] The effort cannot be accurately described either as an attempt at tax simplification nor to strengthen the performance of the American economy.

For the period 2009-2010, the largest Administration tax initiative affecting business is the expansion of the net operating loss carryback. This technical provision has the short-term merit of reducing the tax liability of business taxpayers by over $60 billion in 2009-2010 without the likelihood of arousing widespread opposition. Over the longer-term, however, the consequences are in the opposite direction—to increase business tax liabilities in the 2010-2019 time period by an estimated $9.3 billion.

International Trade and Investment

The Obama Administration has developed a great variety of proposals to increase the tax burdens on companies operating overseas. The underlying notion is to encourage domestic companies to do more business in the United States. Many of the provisions are detailed and some are quite obscure. A mere listing provides significant insight into the nature of the changes proposed:

1. To increase reporting penalties on foreign trusts;
2. To require more information reporting on offshore entities;
3. To require more reporting on the transfer of assets to foreign financial accounts;
4. To require disclosure on tax returns of the information contained in the Report of Foreign Bank and Financial Accounts (FBAR) filed with the Treasury Department;

5.   To establish a negative presumption regarding failure to file an FBAR for accounts with nonqualified intermediaries;

6.   To require reporting of transfers of money or property to foreign financial accounts;

7.   To establish a negative presumption for foreign accounts with respect to which an FBAR has not been filed;

8.   To extend the statute of limitations for reportable cross-border transactions;

9.   To double penalties on accuracy-related understatements involving undisclosed foreign accounts; and,

10.   To establish a negative presumption regarding withholding on determinable or fixed gains, profits, or income to nonresident aliens and foreign entities.

The Treasury estimates that enacting these and other similar changes in taxation of international business will raise almost $210 billion in federal revenues in the decade 2010-2019.

Paperwork Burdens

Among the Administration's tax proposals, a variety of specific provisions will increase the paperwork burden on businesses. For example, the penalties for failing to file information returns (such as Form 1099) promptly and accurately are raised in a very complicated fashion involving three tiers of penalties. Other technical tax changes would increase the paperwork burdens of life insurance companies, government contractors, companies retaining non-employee service providers, and taxpayers receiving rental income. In total, the various "tax informational reporting" changes are expected to increase revenues by over $10 billion in the decade 2010-2019.

Reimposing a Tax No Longer Levied

Buried in the fine print of the Treasury's tax proposals is the reinstatement of corporate environment taxes which were eliminated at the end of 1995. These include excises on domestic crude oil and hazardous chemicals. The proceeds go into the Superfund trust fund. The justification for reviving these special taxes is "the continuing need for funds to remedy damages caused by releases of hazardous substances." No connection is shown between the environmental tax liability imposed on any company and its release of hazardous substances.

Raising Taxes on Business

Numerous technical proposals share a common characteristic: they raise the amount of taxes collected from business. For example, the proposal to codify the economic substance doctrine (which, stripping away transactions having no apparent economic justification, ignore for tax purposes transactions only undertaken to reduce taxes) seems to be a move to improve the federal revenue system. This change would raise an estimated $4.7 billion in the decade 2010-2019. However, one technical change—repealing the LIFO (last in—first out) method of accounting for inventories—is estimated to increase revenues in the coming decade by over $61 billion.

Some of the administration's tax proposals have special attractions. Surely, at a time when public policy is concerned with limiting the discharge of carbon dioxide by users of fossil fuels, continuing tax subsidies to encourage the production of those fuels is hard to justify. Repealing all oil and gas company preferences would increase federal revenues in the period 2010-2019 by over $31 billion.

One proposed business-oriented tax increase is especially controversial. It is to tax as ordinary income the money received for managing hedge funds and pools of private equity. Of course, the capital that hedge fund managers invest in these funds would—and should—continue to receive the same capital gains treatment as other investors. However, the proposal relates only to the income that these executives receive for the task of managing these funds: that income is not now taxed at the same rate as other taxpayers who work for a living, but at the usually lower capital gains rate.

It turns out that the many of these investment managers whose income is taxed at the lower capital gains rate are some of the highest earning people in the nation. It is hard to defend the notion that they should be taxed on their earned income at lower rates than other income earners. The Treasury estimates that the proposed tax change would raise over $23 billion in the decade 2010-2019.

In May 2009, a new Assistant Attorney General announced "a shift in philosophy . . . to let everyone know that the Antitrust Division will be aggressively pursuing cases . . ." Assistant Attorney General Christine

Varney stated, "The Division will return to tried and true case law and Supreme Court precedent in enforcing the antitrust laws."[6]

To carry out the new policy, Varney withdrew the Justice Department report on *Competition and Monopoly* which had been issued in September 2008.[7] That report was issued after a year-long series of hearings involving more than 100 experts in antitrust law and economics. The withdrawn report contained a large number of seemingly sensible points about the enforcement of the antitrust laws. Making a special reference to Section 2 of the Sherman Act, which prohibits a business firm from conduct that undermines the competitive process, the report states that Section 2 standards should at the same time avoid overly broad prohibitions that suppress legitimate competition.

Surprisingly the Justice Department now attempts to link tougher, antitrust enforcement with the government's effort to improve the poor performance of the American economy. According to Varney, "antitrust must be among the frontline issues in the government's broader response to the distressed economy." She views antitrust enforcers as "key members of the government's economic recovery team."[8] This new approach ignores the already high level of litigation in the United States, a widely cited example of governmental barriers to improved economic performance.

Enforcement of the Antitrust Laws

Government policy toward the automobile industry has focused on the special aid given to General Motors and Chrysler as they go through the bankruptcy process. Much has been written on that general subject. Let us focus instead on other aspects of the developing relationship between government and the automobile industry. One such concern is that the financial dependence of the companies has forced them to acquiesce to costly impositions that will make it more difficult to become profitable businesses.

Those costly requirements typically result from introducing other interests, such as promoting the Administration's objectives in energy, the environment, and labor relations. Views on the desirability of these other objectives clearly vary. However, the Administration's policymakers may inadvertently be creating a new type of uncompetitive, government-dependent enterprise.

The new burdens cover a wide terrain. For example, tough restrictions are being imposed on the ability of General Motors to import small, fuel-efficient cars that it already produces overseas. On the other hand, the Troubled Asset Relief Program provides a special tax credit for people who purchase GM's new electric car, the Chevy Volt. Under the circumstances, it is not surprising that the major motor vehicle producers dropped their traditional opposition to enhanced fuel economy standards and CO_2 controls.

The most highly-publicized governmental efforts to participate in the internal management decisions of the automobile companies relate to the closing of company facilities and to the termination of dealer contracts. As a general proposition, members of Congress are never happy when facilities are closed in their states or districts and when constituents lose their jobs. It is not unusual for legislators to issue statements on these occasions. However, the advent of large bailouts to automobile companies has generated new opportunities for second-guessing what is traditionally a company business decision.[9] All this provides a strong incentive for the automobile company management to spend time in Washington, DC rather than in Detroit.[10]

In a very real sense, a hidden cost in the original bailouts is the new—or added—opportunities to summon management to congressional hearings to be second-guessed on the various actions they take. The likely result is for managements of the automobile companies to act more like the heads of government agencies than the leaders of private enterprises.

Wage Controls (21st Century Style)

In what could presage the shape of things to come, just one day after the Obama Administration unveiled its proposals for setting pay levels at companies that are receiving federal "bail-out" money, members of the House of Representatives Committee on Financial Services debated whether they should expand the plans to cover all US companies.

The breath of the Administration's "limited" executive pay proposals was described to the Committee by Gene Sperling, counselor to the Secretary of the Treasury:

> Our goal is to help ensure that there is a much closer alignment between compensation, sound risk management, and long-term value creation for firms and the economy as a whole . . . compensation practices must be better aligned with long-term value and prudent risk management at all firms . . .[11]

For companies that receive federal "bailout" money, the Treasury has provided specific government rules for the compensation committees of their boards of directors. These instructions range from how often the committee shall meet to how to respond to the risks facing the business.

In contrast, private compensation experts believe that corporate boards must guard against making business executives too conservative. In fact, the consulting firm Watson Wyatt Worldwide, in evaluating 1,000 executive pay plans, found that many of the practices now being criticized (such as stock options) are more common among companies with lower and improving credit risk.[12]

Simultaneously, however, the Obama Administration is easing up on the regulation of labor organizations. It is making a 9 percent reduction in the budget for the Labor Department division that polices fraud and other illegalities on the part of labor unions.[13]

Another controversial area of public policy relates to the union card check proposal. Liberals and labor unions strongly support the effort to make it easier to get a labor union recognized in the workplace. The proposed Employee Free Choice Act would let a union win automatic recognition by convincing a majority of workers, one at a time, to sign cards favoring union recognition. Managements and conservatives vehemently oppose the effort to eliminate the traditional secret ballot before a collective bargaining unit is unionized.

Under the Free Choice Act, if the union obtains cards from a majority of the covered workers, the company would then have to reach a deal with the union within 90 days or accept the ruling by an arbitrator appointed by the US Federal Mediation and Conciliation Service. The arbitrator would have the authority to set work rules, pay, benefits, and other contract terms for at least two years.

Another trend with substantial impact on business is the rapid expansion of social regulation now underway. A recent case is the legislation empowering the Food and Drug Administration to regulate tobacco products. The most far-reaching example would be adoption of legislation to respond to the rising concerns over global warming.

The Family Smoking Prevention and Tobacco Control Act gives the FDA power to set standards to reduce nicotine content and regulate chemicals in cigarette smoke. It also bans most tobacco flavorings (except menthol) which are considered a lure to first-time smokers. The control act also tightens restrictions on the marketing and advertising of tobacco products, notably specifying that black-and-white text must replace colorful advertisements and store displays.[14]

Meanwhile, writing a climate change statute that will gain the required congressional support is taking more time. In May 2009, the House Energy Committee presented a complex 932-page bill to establish a cap and trade system intended to reduce emissions of carbon dioxide (widely considered to be a major culprit in global warming).

This initial version of a climate change law was diluted substantially. Original proposals were based on the successful cap and trade system developed to reduce acid rain (SO_2). However, under the House Committee version, initially 84 percent of the permits issued under the law would be made available without charge.

The free permits would constitute a new array of "goodies" to be handed out arbitrarily. The original idea under cap and trade, however, was to auction off all of the permits, creating a strong incentive for emitters of CO_2 to change their production and consumption systems so as to emit less CO_2 in the first place.[15]

The Rise of the Financial Regulation

In June 2009, President Obama submitted to the Congress what was described as the most ambitious overhaul and expansion of financial regulation since the New Deal of the 1930s. Although the plan was criticized by some as inadequate, it would affect every area of the financial industry. Prepared by the Treasury Department, it would provide the Federal Reserve and the Treasury with additional administrative authority, create a new regulatory agency, and give the government power to take over large financial companies in trouble, among many other changes in the nation's regulatory structure.[16]

Some of the changes would not require congressional approval. These include raising the amount of capital that financial institutions must hold to deal with losses, setting new rules to deal with conflicts of interest for rating agencies, and requiring banks to hold on their own books a portion of the mortgages that they issue.

Most of the proposals would not require authorization by Congress, such as the creation of a Consumer Financial Protection Agency. Described as the equivalent of a Food and Drug Administration for financial products, the new agency would be empowered to tell banks what standards to follow in developing new types of consumer credit and to issue warnings to users. The new agency would be financed by fees assessed on entities and transactions across the financial sector and thus would be independent of the annual appropriation process.

The Administration's finance proposals also included the formation of a Financial Services Oversight Council, led by the Secretary of the Treasury, to advise the Federal Reserve on gaps in regulation and on issues that do not fit into the traditional framework. The new Council is expected to identify companies whose problems could produce system-wide shock and are in need of increased federal supervision.

Because of the great variety of changes envisioned in the Obama Administration's financial proposals, it seems helpful to array the changes by the federal agency that it created or expanded:

1. The *Federal Reserve System* is given new powers to oversee any large financial entity whose failure could generate systemic risk (in plain English, jeopardizing the stability of the financial system);

2. The *Treasury Department* heads a new Financial Services Oversight Council to identify firms that could pose systemic risks and to resolve jurisdictional disputes among agencies. A new Office of National Insurance also is to be established in the Treasury to monitor "all aspects" of the insurance industry, a sector of the economy traditionally under the province of state governments. The Office will develop expertise, negotiate international agreements, and coordinate policy on insurance matters. The end result desired is "a modern regulatory framework for insurance;"

3. The *Securities and Exchange Commission* (SEC) will register all advisers to hedge funds and other private pools of capital with assets over

a given threshold. The commission also will have the power to inspect the books of the advisers and to ensure compliance by their clients. In addition, the SEC will work to strengthen the regulation of credit rating agencies, including managing conflicts of interest. In addition, the work of the SEC will be expanded by legislative proposals to give it a more active role in guiding compensation committees of all companies (not just financial) and also by assigning it the responsibility for monitoring issues of asset-backed securities;

4. *The Commodity Futures Trading Commission* gets more authority to regulate complex financial instruments known as "derivatives;"

5. A new *Consumer Financial Protection Agency* will enforce rules regarding consumer loans, credit cards, and mortgages. This powerful new agency will have supervisory and enforcement authority and jurisdiction over everyone covered by the statutes that it implements. It will also take over the enforcement of fair lending laws and the Community Reinvestment Act. The agency will also seek to ensure that "underserved" consumers and communities have access to "prudent" financial services, lending, and investment. This far-ranging agency will also have a mandate to strengthen employment-based and private retirement plans and to encourage adequate savings;

6. The *Federal Deposit Insurance Corporation* will have new authority to take over and shut down financial institutions whose failure is deemed to pose systemic risk;

7. A new *National Bank Supervisor* is created by merging the Office of the Comptroller of the Currency and the Office of Thrift Supervision. It will regulate all federally-chartered depository institutions.

Viewed in their totality, the adoption of the Administration's proposals (or even a major portion of them) would result in a historic expansion in government involvement in and responsibility for the nation's financial systems. Comparisons with the New Deal of the 1930s may be too timid. The enactment of these recommendations would be the largest expansion of governmental financial powers since the days of Alexander Hamilton.

The Obama Administration is aware of the potential for overlap and conflict among the many new and expanded financial regulations to be established by its plan. Thus, it expresses its concern that the jurisdictional boundaries among the new and old regulatory agencies be "drawn carefully" to prevent mission overlap.

Treasury's report (which was issued by the White House) states specifically that "each of the federal financial regulatory agencies generally should have exclusive jurisdiction to issue and enforce rules to achieve its mission." But then the report concludes by reminding the reader of the painful reality: many of the questions that will arise in the various agencies are likely "to raise issues relating to systemic risk, prudential regulation of financial firms, and consumer or investor protection."[17]

We can only sympathize with the individual citizen or organization that will be caught in the regulatory crossfire. For example, the Treasury proposes that the Federal Trade Commission should retain authority for dealing with fraud in the financial marketplace, but, in the same sentence, it says that the commission should also provide such authority to the Consumer Financial Protection Agency (CFPA).[18] The tone of these proposals is contained in the justification for the CFPA: "To help ensure that no product goes unregulated merely because of uncertainty of jurisdiction."[19]

> The adoption of the Administration's proposals would result in a historic expansion in government involvement in and responsibility for the nation's financial systems.

Conclusion

One fundamental point emerges from this review of recent and planned increases in federal government power and resources: the balance between the private sector and the public sector is shifting once again. Many controversial decisions are likely to be faced by people in authority in both business and government. Rather than another sharp swing in the pendulum of national policy, the need now is to achieve a more balanced approach to public policy in the United States.

In responding to current and well-placed concerns over inadequacies in government regulation of business, policymakers should remember that the great bulk of the income and wealth of the nation is generated by private enterprise. They should take great pains to avoid inadvertently crossing the fine line between necessary government influence over the economy and government dominance of the vital private sector.

Nevertheless, the Treasury Department deserves the last word on these matters, at least in terms of describing the underlying policy environment. It warns us that its 88 pages of detailed proposals of financial regulation do not represent the complete set of desirable reforms: "More can and should be done in the future."[20]

Notes

1.   The description of Arthur Okun's views is taken from his long-term Brookings colleague, Joseph Pechman. See Joseph A. Pechman, ed., *Economics for Policymaking: Selected Essays of Arthur M. Okun* (Cambridge: MIT Press, 1983), viii.
2.   Benjamin M. Friedman, "Widening Inequality Combined with Modest Growth," *Challenge*, 52.3 (2009), 78. See also Benjamin M. Friedman, *The Moral Consequences of Economic Growth* (New York: Alfred A. Knopf, 2005).
3.   George K. Yin, "Bush Income Tax Cuts Should Not Be Extended," *Tax Notes*, April 6, 2009, 121.
4.   Dale W. Jorgenson and J. Steven Landefeld, "Implementation of a New Architecture for the U.S. National Accounts," *American Economic Review*, 99.2 (2009), 65.
5.   U.S. Department of the Treasury, *General Explanations of the Administration's Fiscal Year 2010 Revenue Proposals*, May, 2009, 131. All factual and statistical descriptions of the tax proposals in this section are taken from the Treasury Department report.
6.   U.S. Department of Justice press release, "Justice Department Withdraws *Report on Antitrust Monopoly Law*," May 11, 2009, 1.
7.   U.S. Department of Justice, *Competition and Monopoly: Single-Firm Conduct Under Section 2 of the Sherman Act*, September 2008, 201.
8.   Christine A. Varney, *Vigorous Antitrust Enforcement in This Challenging Era*, May 12, 2009, 10.
9.   Carl Hulse and Bernie Becker, "Auto Dealers at Risk Turn to Washington," *New York Times*, June 12, 2009; Josh Mitchell, "Congress Grills GM, Chrysler on Closings," *Wall Street Journal*, June 13, 2009.
10. David Brooks, "The Quagmire Ahead," *New York Times*, June 2, 2009.
11. Cyrus Sanati, "House Panel Clashes Over Pay Restrictions," *New York Times*, June 12, 2009.
12. Cari Tuna and Joann Lublin, "Risk vs. Executive Reward," *Wall Street Journal*, June 15, 2009.
13. *National Review*, June 8, 2009, 10.
14. Duff Wilson, "Senate Approves Tight Regulation Over Cigarettes," *New York Times*, June 12, 2009.
15. "A Green Resolution," *The Economist*, May 30, 2009, 14-15.
16. U.S. Department of the Treasury, *Financial Regulatory Reform; A New Foundation: Rebuilding Financial Supervision and Regulation*, June 17, 2009.
17. *Ibid.*, 21.
18. *Ibid.*, 63.
19. *Ibid.*, 60.
20. *Ibid.*, 4.

Murray Weidenbaum is Edward Mallinckrodt Distinguished University Professor of Economics at Washington University in St. Louis and Honorary Chairman of the Weidenbaum Center on the Economy, Government and Public Policy. He was the first chairman of the Council of Economic Advisers to Ronald Reagan and also served as a member of Reagan's Economic Policy Advisory Board. He is the author of numerous books including *Business and Government in the Global Marketplace*, *One-Armed Economist*, and *The Bamboo Network*.

8

The Democratic Warrior and his Social Identity

Andreas Herberg-Rothe

THE CHANGES SINCE the landmark years of 1989-1991 require a different model of the soldier in democratic societies. Since then, the model of the warrior has gradually been developing in contrast to the soldier. The warrior has always embodied the difference and distance between soldierly actions and the self-image of a civilian society, while at the same time developing his own warrior code of honor.[1] Some of these approaches, however—and especially in John Keegan and Martin van Creveld—put so much emphasis on the difference from civilian and democratic society that there appears to be no possibility of ever bridging the gap.[2] On the other hand, the decisive problem for the twenty-first century continues to be integrating the military into and reconnecting it with the standards, values, and interests of a democratic society, while at the same time recognizing its own identity and culture.

A pure adaptation to changes in duties, as in the concept of the "archaic combatant,"[3] would not only sever the dynamic bond between the military and society and open up an unbridgeable chasm, but it would also permanently define individual and possibly limited changes. On the other hand, concepts such as the "armed social worker" tend to undervalue the specifics of soldierly action which are the application and threat of force.[4] It's true that in modern armies only a small percentage of the soldiers actually fight. In that respect, the much-trumpeted differentiation of roles is as practical a perspective as multifunctionality,[5] but because of this very differentiation, it can never offer soldiers a relatively consistent meaning or solidify into a social role. On the contrary, in multifunctionality the essential professional and social identity of the soldier seems to vanish. By way of contrast, the concept of the "democratic warrior" is introduced here in an attempt to build a bridge that can both do justice to soldierly self-image and reconnect it to a democratic society and its political goals in world society.[6] At the same time, we must point out the basic difference between the social roles of the combatant and the warrior. Whereas a combatant embodies only one dimension of soldierly action, the social role of the warrior encompasses a variety of possible duties and differentiations.

> The concept of the "democratic warrior" is introduced here in an attempt to build a bridge that can both do justice to soldierly self-image and reconnect it to a democratic society.

In systematic terms, this perspective of reconciling opposite poles[7] is in line with Clausewitz's concept of the "wondrous trinity." Rather than reducing his far-reaching theoretical approach to the famous formula of "war as a continuation of policy by other means," in his "wondrous trinity" he created an arsenal that can basically encompass all types of war.[8] In my interpretation of his trinity, each war is a different historically-based combination of primordial violence, struggle between two or more opponents, and membership of the combatants in a comprehensive society—a situation that Clausewitz elucidated with the primacy of politics.[9] The specific form that a war takes is determined by the historical differences in the particular means of the force/violence, the fight/struggle, and the particular communities. According to this definition of war by Clausewitz, soldiers themselves must also be able to strike a balance between these three tendencies. In terms of the military's self-image, this means that its soldiers must be capable of exerting or threatening force/violence, they must be able to fight[10] and, finally, they must act as part of a larger community as well as being perceived as such a community.[11] For Clausewitz, the larger community was the Prussian state, and at times the Prussian nation. The model for us today is and remains the democratic state—and this community is of existential importance for intervention forces, which are perceived as closely connected to their particular social model.

From "Soldiers" to "Warriors"

To explain this connection between the state and soldiers in terms of Clausewitz, we need to take a look at German history. Often the term soldier is used indiscriminately to describe any bearer of arms. To distinguish them from other arms bearers, soldiers in the narrower sense have only been commonly referred to since the French Revolution. Ideally, soldiers serve the state out of conviction, they defend higher values, and identify with the state that they serve. Military service as a soldier is generally linked to state citizenship, and conscription is an outgrowth of the individual citizen's obligation to the state. "Defense of the fatherland is the foundation myth of modern armies" and of the soldier.[12] Naturally, this attribution of meaning does not directly correspond to reality, but besides playing an essential role in the self-image and political formation of soldiers, it is also central to the democratic legitimization of conscription in modern armies. Friedrich Engels already noted that conscription was Prussia's only democratic institution. In revolutionary France, citizenship and membership in the national defense force were seen as two sides of the same coin and related to the concept of the modern nation as a political variable that appointed the people as sovereign.[13]

As a reaction to the Prussian defeats, military reforms were also introduced that, on the one hand, were guided by the image of the victorious Napoleonic armies and, on the other hand, took into account the conditions peculiar to Prussia. From this developed a specific tension: the entire society was enlisted for the purpose of warfare with the goal of producing the patriotic and willingly self-sacrificing "soldat citoyen." At the same time, however, the political transformation had to remain limited in order to maintain the existing power structure. Prussia was no sovereign nation of citizens, it had no constitution that would have curtailed the monarch's authority and allowed citizens to participate in legislation. But how could it achieve a national enthusiasm and sense of self-sacrifice for the nation state as per the French model without an adequate social foundation, i.e. without equality and the possibility of political participation for all citizens?[14] The Prussian military reforms remained inconsistent and half-hearted, although they included some very positive elements, such as the abolishment of dishonorable and inhumane punishments. For the reformers, the only way to deal with the dilemma of needing to mobilize the entire society for the war while unable to change the existing social structure was an "educational dictatorship." From now on, the army and civil society would merge in that all (male) citizens would become potential soldiers.

What was the significance of the perspective unity of citizen and soldier—the militarization of society or the civilizing of the military? In Prussia, it could initially be seen as a civilizing of the military because of the abolishment of its especially degrading and savage practices. Over time, however, there was more and more of a militarization of society that Friedrich Meinecke described in hindsight as historically unprecedented. In particular after the successful wars during the founding of the German empire (1864-1871), the Prussian lieutenant "made his way through the world as a young god and the civilian reserve lieutenant as a demi-god."[15] However, the First and Second World Wars were decisive in establishing the image of the soldier as a member of a popular army. Two battles in World War I illustrate two different soldier images: Langemarck and Verdun. In a communiqué from the Supreme Command, the events at Langemarck were described thus: "Young regiments broke forward with the song 'Deutschland, Deutschland über alles' against the first line of enemy positions and took them." What was suppressed here was the mass slaughter of young soldiers and the fact that this was a defeat. Indeed, only one year later the story was: "The Day of Langemarck will forever remain a day of honor for the German youth. This day saw sheaves of the bloom of our youth slain. But our grief for the bold dead is so splendidly surpassed by the pride in how well they knew how to fight and die."[16] The myth that came out of the battle at Langemarck conjured up a military past that was shaped by the ideal of heroic sacrifice for the Fatherland. It was very different from the Verdun myth. Verdun is the symbol of industrialized and depersonalized war. The initial enthusiasm was gone and now it was only a matter of enduring the effects of mechanized warfare. Neither the Anglo-French offensive on the Somme nor the German offensive at Verdun achieved their goals, but both resulted in battles involving a previously unknown expenditure of soldiers, equipment, munitions, and guns. Within an area of a few square kilometers, hundreds of thousands of people were "processed." The aim of the battles was not primarily to gain territory, but to cause the greatest possible losses to the enemy. The Germans did not celebrate the subsequent military successes of World War I as a triumph of superior ideals, but considered them a highpoint in modern technological warfare.

The myth created on the soil of Verdun required a new image of the soldier. Under the constant threat of death on the battlefield, the soldier's only choice was to adapt to these circumstances. It seemed that there was no more room for honor, morality, or ideals on the industrialized battlefield of the twentieth century. Whereas formerly weapons were at the service of people, from now on people were at the service of weapons. Elements of the Verdun myth were used by Fascism to support the principle of selection: in a situation where fighting seems unavoidable, the ideal soldier is the one who submits to the principles of modern martial force. The laborer-soldier image of the front-line soldier in the storm of steel generated its own amorality that absolutized the fight. For good reason, many soldiers in the German Reich joined in World War II without belief in the justness of their country's cause. The combination of rigid modernity and pre-civilized amorality found its gruesome embodiment in the members of the SS.[17]

Following World War II, fundamentally different armed forces and ideas of the "soldier" developed. The soldier became the (democratic) citizen in uniform. According to Wilfried von Bredow, an adequate understanding of the history of the Bundeswehr since its creation in 1956 and of its sociopolitical integration, is not possible unless both are understood to be a consequence of a break with pre-1945 German history with all things military were overemphasized. In "leadership and civic education"—a complete system of measures intended to guarantee the concept of the citizen in uniform in terms of its legal status and soldierly self-image at all times—von Bredow sees "one of the Federal Republic of Germany's most innovative and creative political reforms, fully comparable in its significance to the conception of the social market economy."[18] The image of the soldier was now co-determined by a critical public, by the social demystification of the military, by the marginalization and reduction of the armed forces as part of comprehensive changes in the threat and values and, finally, by the democratization and civilization—institutionally fixed but whose enforcement was not without resistance—of the government's instruments of force. Ever since the national defense forces became intervention forces in the 1990s and conscription armies became professional armies, the model of the democratic "citizen in uniform" has been subject to an increased requirement to adapt—a development that had already taken place in the U.S. following the loss of the Vietnam War.[19]

This development reflects the transition from conscription to a professional army as well as a new self-image and growing self-awareness on the part of the arms bearers. If we summarize the many approaches, the warrior is characterized by a strong attachment to values, a clearly defined distance from civilian society, and a high measure of professionalism. The values represented by warriors do not reflect the values of the particular society or community. They are not politically or ideologically biased, but spring solely from their organization and affiliation, as well as their special capabilities.[20] Their closest counterparts in history are the medieval knights, and how they understood themselves to be warriors from a social elite.[21] John Keegan, one of the propagandists of a new warrior image, explains the rejection of the values of civil society. War reaches into the most secret depths of the human heart, where the ego eliminates rational goals, where pride reigns, where emotions have the upper hand, and instinct rules. One of Keegan's models of the warrior was the Roman centurion. These officers were soldiers through and through. They entertained no expectation of rising to the governing class, their ambitions were entirely limited to those of success within what could be perceived, for the first time in history, as an esteemed and self-sufficient profession. The values of the Roman professional soldiers were of an ideal and not a material nature. According to Keegan, these ideals were those by which their comrades in the modern era also live: pride in a distinctly masculine way of life, the good opinion of comrades, satisfaction in the tokens of professional success, and the expectation of an honorable discharge and retirement.[22]

Malicious, scheming, and womanish—these are the things a warrior should not be.[23] Malicious for a warrior means, for example, weapons that offer an unfair advantage. The poisonous gas first used during World War I filled the soldiers of that time with disgust, they saw it as unchivalrous. This image of the warrior best expresses the aspect of the duel, which is as symmetrical as possible in terms of weapons.[24] The weapon and honor of a warrior elite enter into a direct bond. The weapon of war is wielded only against the soldierly opponent, the honorable enemy. A warrior does not sully his weapon with the blood of a partisan, traitor, or "deceitful wench." Warriors do not use their weapons to kill criminals; they hang them. "Gun women" are slain with a rifle butt. Fighting with bows and arrows was especially repulsive because these were a poor man's weapons. Anyone could win with a bow and arrow, including the very poorest, "most dishonorable," and most cowardly scoundrel.[25] Despite its clear overvaluing of Medieval knighthood (especially considering the gender-specific valuations), the subject of the warrior's "honor" can play an important role in limiting violence in future conflicts. Regardless of the existence of conventions of war and the establishment of an international war crimes tribunal, current developments worldwide are tantamount to a revocation of limitations on the use of violence. Warriors, on the other hand, follow certain conventions for the sake of "honor." As part of the customs of war followed by warriors with mutual respect for one another, aspects of "conventional" warfare thus arose that—besides the fighting of battles—were based on a dissociation from combatants considered to be illegitimate. Sun Tzu could be a model for this understanding of the warrior, for despite the differences between him and Clausewitz regarding direct and indirect warfare, the two could be seen as complementing one another in the sense that Sun Tzu concentrates more heavily on the actual conduct of war and on those conducting the war, and Clausewitz concentrates more on the relationship between the war and the political-social conditions previous to and resulting from the war.[26]

Developments since 1989-91

To judge which kind of "weapon carrier" is needed in the twenty first century, we have to look at developments since 1989-1991. Since the end of the East-West conflict, terms like "risk society," reflexive modernization, and globalization have been used in both academic and social debates as part of an intensifying discussion of how the accelerating transformation of social and national identities is affecting societies. Social, political, and economic developments have devalued knowledge that has been handed down, and traditional models of interpretation have required new orientations. Cultural and social conceptions of order, in their historical and contemporary contexts, serve as orientation. As people's life-worlds are affected by processes of change and transformations, they reconstruct these conceptions of order and reorganize them so as to make the world comprehensible and explicable.[27] One makeshift solution is to establish the present state as a decline of the previous state, such as "post-Westphalian"[28] and "post-national."[29] However, the "post-" terms not only suffer from the fact that they require a fundamental hyphen separating the former and current development (similarly to the opposition between "new" and "old war"[30]), but also in their negation continue to view the current changes themselves through the lens of the old paradigm. The same problem applies to the various "de-" terms, including denationalization, depoliticization, demilitarization, decivilization, deterritorialization, and delimitation.[31] In a certain sense, these approaches hypostatize as ideal an earlier development that did not historically exist in this form. In particular, the "Westphalian system" that supposedly came to an end after 1989 was already fundamentally shaken by the revolutionary and Napoleonic wars of 1792-1815. The majority of wars throughout the twentieth century, and World War I and II in particular, can no longer be placed in the categories of the "Westphalian system," any more than can the Cold War.

The key problem with the variety of new terms appears to be not so much the dispute over empirical findings, but rather the ideal-typical reconstruction of an earlier state.[32] The result can be the absolutizing of a limited development into a general norm and projecting it as a dominant trend in the future. Processes described in terms of "failed states," privatization of violence, etc., may be undisputed, but it is questionable whether these terms express the present development in its entirety or remain spatially and temporally limited. On the other hand, a conceptualization related to the concept of order can better describe the current transformations: dissolution of old orders after the end of the global-scale bipolar system and the beginning of an intensified globalization, the resulting tendency toward privatization, and the dissolution of any widespread system of order, "conflict" (in the sense of Lyotard[33]) between different systems of order and the variety of attempts to make these systems compatible, all the way to violent conflicts over different conceptions of "world order."

In an attempt to capture the (for many) unexpected forms that excessive violence has taken since the epochal years of 1989-91, some authors have put forward the concept of "new wars,"[34] character-ized by the decline of statehood, the rise of privatized violence, the development of civil war economies, and the reappearance of types of combatants thought to be long gone (mercenaries, child soldiers, and warlords), together with armed conflicts over identity, mineral resources, and fundamental existential resources such as water. The outward characteristics of these wars are a greater incidence of appar-ently irrational violence (suicide bombings and large-scale terrorist attacks such as those of September 11, 2001), massacres carried out by right-wing or left-wing forces or by Islamist and other religious move-ments, and the sudden transformation of neighborly relations into a "war of all against all" in conflicts shaped by ethnic differences.

In addition to the idea of "new wars," political and academic discourses have also taken up terms such as privatized war, asym-metrical warfare, small wars, wild wars, low-intensity conflicts, postnational wars, wars in the process of globalization and the development of capitalism, and wars in the framework of "global fragmentation."[35] However, each of these terms describes only one segment of reality in an extremely dynamic and, above all, uncertain development.[36] The very diversity of the concepts proposed points to this uncertainty and to the changed perception of warfare on which they rest. To some extent, however, a new type of war is being discovered with each new war. However, a common point of reference for these different terms seems to be the assumption that the level at which wars are being fought has shifted from the level of the state to conflicts mainly involving non-state actors on at least one side. This is seen to lead to the conclusion that the motivation and goals of these non-state actors no longer follow political or ideological imperatives but have other sources which may be ethnic, economic, or the fact that violence has become an autonomous force. This point of view found its clearest expression in the assumption of an approaching anarchy[37] and leads directly to recent concepts such as the idea of a liberal American empire, because this is seen to be the only principle that can guarantee a minimum of order as a defense against the approaching anarchy.[38] Things would look different, however, if this diffusion onto the level of conflict "below" that of the state

> The level at which wars are being fought has shifted from the level of the state to conflicts mainly involving non-state actors.

were no more than a transitional phase, or if this indisputable development were restricted to certain parts of the world—such as the Sahara and sub-Saharan Africa and the traditional lines of conflict on the fringes of the former "empires." Additionally, one may take into account the possibility that some aspects of future conflicts will be politically or ideologically determined even though the parties involved are non-state actors. The paradigm of these wars would not be determined by the order/anarchy antithesis, but by the antithesis between different conceptions of order in the minds of both the actors themselves as well as the public, to which the various conflict parties refer and appeal. The latter refers to the "interested third parties," or rather the "alleged interested third parties" to which the violent actors refer and appeal.[39] The decisive problem here is not the value we attach to our own conception of order, but the fact that the conflict dynamic obeys rules that differ from those operating in a paradigm where conceptions of order and anarchy confront each other directly. Ideas of a "liberal empire," which may still be relevant to an antithesis between order and anarchy, would be especially likely to aggravate conflicts over the politics of order.

During the Cold War and the arms race between the superpowers, the world stood on the brink of a nuclear catastrophe on several occasions, but violence and conflicts seemed to fit into clear categories of interpretation: East versus West, or rather imperialist aggression and the economic interests of the military-industrial complex (as one side saw it) versus totalitarianism in the form of the "evil empire" (as the other side saw it). These interpretations conflicted with one another but, because they seemed to offer a rational explanation, were able to limit and contain violence in people's minds as well. The most notable attempt to circumscribe and limit the potentially unlimited violence of multiple *overkill* capabilities through intellectual effort can perhaps be found in Raymond Aron's highly respected book, *Penser la guerre*.[40] As Aron saw it, one could think about war between the superpowers but it was unthinkable that war could actually be waged. Although the world lived on the brink of the nuclear abyss during the East-West conflict, the conflict was very effective as a way of providing global political order, both in terms of Realpolitik and in relation to the real or apparent possibility of explaining violence and wars. The new forms of violence that have had such an impact since the end of the East-West conflict, and which have also to some extent been orchestrated by the mass media, seem to have removed war and violence from a sphere in which they could be easily comprehended before any new ordering framework had been found. If anything, violence itself now seems to be shaping order and providing the basis for community formation.[41]

The way in which the Cold War functioned as an order affected not only the direct confrontation between the superpowers and their alliance systems, but also the conflicts that were labeled "surrogate wars." This has become especially clear in the debate over how new the "new wars" actually are. Those who argue against the view that there has been a fundamental change in the form of war do so on the basis of a long time period, and include conflicts such as the Chinese civil war, the Russian civil war which continued into the 1920s, and the first genocide of the twentieth century perpetrated against the Armenians, in order to demonstrate that there is nothing genuinely new about "new wars."[42] Those who favor the concept, on the other hand, see a break in 1989-91. They compare the civil wars immediately before this break with those that came immediately after it, and see this as confirmation that a fundamental change has indeed taken place.[43] After the worldwide East-West conflict came to an end, numerous conflict parties in civil wars found that they were no longer receiving support from the superpowers in the form of weapons and economic assistance, and to an increasing degree they had to rely on their own efforts to obtain the necessary resources. This led in many cases to typical civil war economies[44] involving illegal trafficking in diamonds, drugs, and women, brutal exploitation of the population, extreme violence as a way of drawing in assistance which could then be plundered, and the violent acquisition of particularly valuable resources (robber capitalism). To this extent it was only to be expected as a necessary and commonly observed historical consequence that, after the dissolution of the Cold War order, a considerable number of "private" actors and armed groups would initially appear in weak states and in those traditional centers of conflict, the fringes of the former empires.

Re-ideologization and Re-politicization of War

The many more than two thousand wars that occurred in the world between 1945 and the turn of the century have not resulted in the total dissolution of state order in world society.[45] Strictly speaking, there are processes of state collapse and "failed states" only in "neopatrimonial wars," at least in states in sub-Saharan Africa. Even with regard to these conflicts, it has been argued that they are basically political conflicts. The point of departure for the study by Isabelle Duyvesteyn, for example, is a very broad definition of politics based on Robert Dahl: a political system in this sense is defined as "any persistent pattern of human relationship that involves, to a significant extent, power, rule or authority."[46] Duyvesteyn refers especially to the fact that in the patrimonial systems she studied, the differences between economics and politics are not as clear cut as westerners perceive them to be. Struggles that seem to be purely about the acquisition of resources can be motivated by power politics in order to obtain a separate constituency. Because the position of power in these conflicts is very often determined by the particular reputation of the leader, non-political issues can also be incorporated into a power-political context. Her hypothesis is not that economically, religiously or ethnically defined conflicts are always political, but that these conflicts remain embedded in a political framework within a patrimonial system.

One can point to developments in Afghanistan as an example of a re-ideologization and re-politicization of wars and violent conflicts: after the victory over the Soviet army, a civil war between warlords and individual tribes began at the end of the 1980s, until the conflict was re-ideologized, and the Taliban seized power. We can see here that civil wars do not always become increasingly privatized until they reach the smallest possible communities that are held together only by violence itself. There have also been a number of cases in history in which civil wars have been ended by re-ideologization and re-politicization or have been taken to a new level. Afghanistan is a good example because one can use it to illustrate the new quality of privatization of war and violence,[47] while at the same time it reveals very clearly the re-ideologization and re-politicization of the conflict with the rise and eventual victory of the Taliban. Claiming that the privatization of the war in Afghanistan proves the new quality of the "new wars" in general leads to a paradox if the claim is restricted to the period up until the Taliban victory in 1996. This case therefore cannot be used to demonstrate a general shift towards the privatization of war,[48] but only to demonstrate that this development was in this case only for a limited period, for the turning point of the Taliban victory introduced a new phase, the phase of world order wars.

One can supplement the temporal differentiation I am proposing by adding a geographical classification of the two phases. The privatization of violence can be observed in many parts of sub-Saharan Africa and in traditional conflict regions such as the Balkans and the Caucasus. The development of world order conflicts can be seen in the conflict between the West and militant Islam, and in the future it can be anticipated above all in relations with China[49] and, perhaps, with Russia. It follows that events are moving away from the level of interstate war and conflicts in two directions simultaneously—downwards towards "privatized" war, and upwards towards supra state war. This distinction is more fundamental than the attempts to distinguish between "privatized" or "new" wars and those fragmented wars arising in the course of globalization, and the attempts to use this as a way of challenging the legitimacy of the first set of concepts.[50] Waging war to promote values[51] and as a way of ordering the "world" (whether this order is conceived of as universal or particular) is something quite different from privatized and fragmented wars. Although, in practice, these two levels are interlinked, analytically they are distinct. States still wage wars, but for the most part they are now doing so not in pursuit of their own particular interests but for reasons related to world order, as can be seen in the use of concepts like the US "empire"[52] and the American hegemony.[53] Processes like the technological, economic-capitalistic, and communicational saturation of the world intensify this dual movement of privatized wars and global or regional world order wars dramatically, because they often link spaces of action directly with one another. During the civil war in Somalia, for example, bands of fighters could be seen using computers to buy and sell their Wall Street shares. Although it may not at first glance appear to do so, globalization does in fact re-politicize the world order.[54]

> States still wage wars, but they are now doing so not in pursuit of their own particular interests but for reasons related to world order.

This transformation is especially visible in the development of Russia and India. Although it was feared that the collapse of the Soviet Union would be followed by a general civil war, Russia has since returned to the world stage. India also appeared to be on the brink of becoming a failed state and was expected to break apart, but this is no longer probable. Rather, India has since become a great power. A total of five large or world powers are currently (as of 2009-10) fighting over "world order" and power-political influence, and are pursuing their own interests worldwide: the US, Russia, China, India, and Europe (whose fragmentation merely covers over its economic, regulatory and power-political influence).[55] Add to this the efforts of Iran, Saudi Arabia, and Egypt to organize the Middle East according to their own conceptions. The conflicts between these world and large powers as well as their common actions to achieve "world order" will dominate over the coming decades, but will be accompanied by a continuation of "privatized violence." Although Samuel Huntington's thesis of a clash of civilizations was hugely disproportionate, at least the large empires that were suppressed by European colonization such as China and India are returning as world and large powers, as is Russia. Even in the case of Iran, there is an obvious linking to an earlier Islamic and the ancient Persian Empire. If examples from history can help us to achieve a better understanding of current developments, then we are more likely to be facing a new and long nineteenth century (in which revolutions and "privatized violence" continue to be incorporated and which ends in World War I) than a return to a "Medieval security policy."

Clausewitz's "Wondrous Trinity" as a Differentiated Coordinate System

Many found the changes in warfare since the epochal years of 1989-91 to be so great that it appeared that an entirely new era in warfare had dawned and made the previous paradigms for understanding the complexity of the war experience seem outdated. In particular, Clausewitz's conception of the primacy of policy was called into question with the development of "new wars," the "Revolution in Military Affairs" and especially the development of network-centric warfare.[56] It is nevertheless noteworthy that this apparently latest development is comparable to very traditional approaches of the partisan fight, especially that of Mao Tse-Tung. Thus, General John Abizaid, Commander of the US Central Command in the Middle East from 2003 to 2007, emphasized with regard to the Taliban: "In fact, this enemy is better networked than we are."[57]

If we look more closely, however, we see that these latest developments can be easily integrated into a differentiated understanding of Clausewitz's "wondrous trinity." The interpretation of his trinity as a combination of and conflict among the three tendencies of primordial *violence*, of *fight* between two or more opponents, and of membership of combatants in a *comprehensive community* is at the same time a basis for the soldiers' identity: they must use violence and be able to fight *for* and as representatives of a broader community. The concept of the democratic warrior introduced here is based on this definition of war by Clausewitz and requires explanation: the polarities presented below identify each war as an ideal type from which these are composed depending on historical and social circumstances, without it being possible to eliminate one of these aspects. For a "theory that ignores any one of them . . . would conflict with reality to such an extent that for this reason alone it would be totally useless."[58] Following that, and sometimes going beyond Clausewitz, we will turn our attention to four polarities of the three areas of violence, fight and community (to which the combatants belong). The basic thesis is that in every real war it is possible to detect some similar but also different combinations of these polarities.

First Concept: Violence

a) Clausewitz saw the crucial polarity within the concept of force to be between instrumentality and autonomy. The instrumental pole of this pair of opposites is found in the definition, in the world-famous formula, and in the third tendency of the "wondrous trinity." Clausewitz discussed the problem of violence becoming absolute and therefore an end in itself in the three interactions to the extreme, directly before the formula, as well as in the primordial violence of war in the first of the three tendencies of the "wondrous trinity of war."

b) A significant contrast that Clausewitz implicitly and repeatedly brings up for discussion is whether the combatants are amateurs or specialists in violence. He did not formulate this opposition explicitly but made it the object of his explanation of the success of the French Revolution's troops over those of the Ancien Régime. From this, the opposite of the politically, ideologically and/or religiously-defined motivation of combatants takes the lead against that of a knightly code of honor.[59]

c) Clausewitz also brings up for discussion the fundamental opposition between distance and proximity in the use of force. Distance in time and space makes a relative rationality possible, on the one hand, while at the same time raising the problem of impersonal killings in which the humanity of the opponent is no longer perceived over greater distances. Fighting "face-to-face" with an opponent demands totally different characteristics; for example, aggressiveness and hate, which can lead to an increasingly independent use of force, but at the same time, still make it possible to perceive the opponent as human.

d)   A further criterion is the violent means used to fight, although this is not discussed separately by Clausewitz and must therefore be expanded on here. A good example relates to the financing of combatants' weapons. Very expensive weapons systems and combatants can lead to a certain limitation of war, as these cannot be so easily risked (as was the case, for example, in the eighteenth century). In contrast, wars waged with very cheap means and combatants are more likely to have a tendency to escalate.

Second Concept: Fight

a)   The necessity of escalation in war in order not to be destroyed is found in Clausewitz's three interactions to the extreme, whereas the game of chance and probability are discussed in the second of the three tendencies of the "wondrous trinity," as well as in the respective sections of the first chapter.

b)   The opposition, so often discussed today, of symmetry or asymmetry between combatants, their strategy, and their social composition is discussed by Clausewitz in the first chapter with reference to the opposition of attack and defense, and in detail throughout his book on defense, and generalized at the start of the second chapter.

c)   A crucial distinction within the first chapter is whether combat in war is directed against the opposing will (as it is in Clausewitz's definition of war) or if it relates to the "destruction" of the opposing armed forces. Clausewitz specifies that by destruction of the opposing armed forces, he simply means reducing them to such a condition that they can no longer continue the fight. But the original and lasting opposition of combat against opposing wills, or aimed at the destruction of the opponent, is merely repeated in Clausewitz's differentiation of the principle of destruction.

d)   For a long time, Clausewitz favored Napoleon's warfare—a direct strategy in which the armed forces of the opponent are attacked directly. In the literature on Clausewitz, however, a "strategy of fatigue" or "indirect strategy" was spied and criticized. For a general theory, Clausewitz thus needs to be supplemented, such that we consider not only a direct strategy against the opposing armed forces but start from the assumption that every war is a combination of direct and indirect strategies which are in each case composed differently.

Third Concept: Warring Communities

a)   When referring to warring communities, we must first differentiate between relatively new communities and long-standing communities. This is because in newly constructed communities, fight and violence play a greater role while, in the case of long-standing communities, there are more factors contributing to the war. Thus Clausewitz argues that the length of time a group has existed reduces the tendency to escalation in the interactions to the extreme, as other factors must be included: the facts that states can be involved, and that peace after war influences warfare through "an estimate of the political situation."

b)   A further opposition concerns whether the war serves the self-preservation of a community or, especially in revolutionary crisis situations, whether it leads to the formation of a new community; and,

c)   Whether war is subordinated to the pursuit of "interests," or is waged to maintain and spread the values, norms and ideals of the particular community. Herfried Münkler juxtaposed both contrasts, noting the opposition between the instrumental warfare of the later Clausewitz and the existentialism of the early Clausewitz.[60]

d)   Closely related to this, although not exactly congruent, is the question of whether the purpose of war lies outside itself or, especially in warring cultures, in the violent fight itself. The social composition of each society, like that of the combatants (regular armies, conscription armies, pistoleros, etc.), plays an important role here.

Summarizing these fundamental differences yields the coordinate system of war and violence shown in the diagram. Every war is accordingly defined in terms of the three tendencies of force, fight, and the affiliation of the combatants with a community, since in war there are always communities that fight against one another, even if the weapon carriers act on behalf of the community. Moreover, these three tendencies within the "wondrous trinity" are further differentiated into additional opposites that every war is composed of in different ways. Thus every war has symmetrical and asymmetrical tendencies, even when it may appear in certain situations as if only one of these tendencies comes to the fore. Moreover, a further distinction of this coordinate system would be the difference from a fourth emphasis, linear or nonlinear warfare, a hierarchical or a network-centric organizational structure, without one of these opposite poles defining the whole of war. Nevertheless, network structures require a different relationship between those conducting wars and civil society. Such conduct of war is characterized by "loose and diffuse organizational structures" in which the underlying political will and mandate can no longer be imposed down to the lowest level of a hierarchical system, but as in the warfare of partisans, necessarily assumes a high value placed on political content. It is because of the relative independence of soldiers in network-centric warfare that this type of warfare does not require an "archaic combatant," but rather a democratic warrior. In the event of war, the actions of these soldiers are in any case attributed to the political-cultural community for which they are acting. In the case of an "archaic combatant," his actions would be attributed to a body politic that has no stake as a democratic society. Hence, especially network-centric warfare requires the social role of a democratic warrior.

The Democratic Warrior in the Twenty-First Century

The classic image of war has largely been replaced by a comprehensive image of security in which the military plays a quantitatively smaller but at the same time qualitatively expanded role within the context of the security policy players.[61] Combining the different perspectives in the areas of foreign, economic, development, judicial, domestic, and defense policy permits a global approach to the planning and implementation of conflict resolution, for the purpose of meeting the requirements of complex conflict and crisis scenarios and thus fighting both the causes of a crisis or conflict and its consequences. For this purpose, security-related governmental and non-governmental actors must consciously coordinate, connect, and systematically integrate their goals, processes, structures, and capabilities into their long-term actions. Based on this expansion of the concept of security, a democratic army needs a specific task and function, as explained below, based on the concept of a new containment policy.

When the East-West conflict ended, Francis Fukuyama also announced the "end of history," meaning an end to the practice of war and violence.[62] The triumphant advance of democracy and free markets seemed to be unstoppable, to the point where it appeared as if the twenty-first century would be an age defined by economics and thus, to a large extent, peace. However, these expectations were quickly disappointed, not only because of the ongoing massacres and genocide in Africa, but also by the return of war to Europe (primarily in the former Yugoslavia), together with the attacks of September 11, 2001 in the US, the subsequent war in Afghanistan, the Iraq War of 2003, and the uprisings in Iraq since 2003-2004,

> The classic image of war has largely been replaced by a comprehensive image of security in which the military plays a quantitatively smaller role.

as well as the war between Georgia and Russia over South Ossetia in 2008 and, most recently, escalation of the war in Afghanistan and the threat of war due to the Iranian nuclear program. In a complete reversal of Fukuyama's thesis, a struggle against a new brand of Islamic totalitarianism appears to have begun, in which war and violence are commonly perceived as having an unavoidable role. Both are also perceived as having become "unbounded"—both in a spatial sense, because terrorist attacks are potentially ever-present, and temporally, since no end to these attacks is in sight. One can also speak of a new dimension to violence with respect to its extent and brutality—as exemplified by the extreme violence of the ongoing civil wars in Africa, and by completely new types of threats, such as those from weapons of mass destruction held by terrorist organizations.

These processes of growing disinhibition must be countered by a new containment policy that limits the expansion of war and violence in world society just as George Kennan—who formulated the original approach to the expansion of the USSR in 1946—already emphasized in 1987: "We are going to have to develop a wider concept of what containment means . . . —a concept, in other words, more responsive to the problems of our own time." Although his original concept was reduced to its military aspect by various administrations of the US government, incorporating the concept of common security during the Cold War made it possible to harmonize the actual dual strategy of curbing military expansion on the one hand and establishing mutual cooperation on the other. Contrary to the common view, it was not just the military-technological superiority of the US that led to Gorbachev's reforms. Rather, it was first and foremost the dual strategy of military deterrence plus far-reaching offers of cooperation which led to Glasnost and Perestroika in the East.

Two basic assumptions underlie this conception. The first assumption is that the escalating tendency of war and violence in world society is so multifaceted and differentiated that a single counter-strategy will not suffice. Rather, an overarching perspective is required for deciding which measures are suitable in individual cases—without being able to exclude the possibility of terrible errors and miscalculations. The second assumption is that in today's world society—as has been the case throughout history—many contrary processes are at work. Thus, a regard for only one counter-strategy can have paradoxical, unanticipated consequences.

This can be clarified using the example of democratization. If a general, worldwide democratization—which, because of the highly symbolic value of democracy, would also have to be implemented through violence—were the only counter-strategy against the processes of disinhibition of both violence and war, the results would almost certainly be counterproductive. This is particularly clear in those cases where fully developed constitutional democracies are not yet present, but societies are undergoing the initial process of transformation. It is much more justified to speak of the antinomies of democratic peace in the latter cases than when referring to developed democracies. Thus it is possible that a one-sided demand for democratic processes without regard for local conditions might, in individual cases, even contribute to the creation of antidemocratic movements. The historical experience that corresponds to this change is found in the developments after World War I. Here, too, in nearly all of the defeated states, there was initially a process of democratization, and even democratic revolutions. Yet almost all ended in authoritarian or even totalitarian regimes. In Eastern Europe and the Balkans, the "right of national self-determination" proclaimed by US President Wilson was interpreted in a nationalist rather than a democratic way, and as an exclusion of entire populations. Thus, the concept of the democratic warrior is not based on imposing democracy by force but on limiting war and violence in world society in order to enable and maintain democratic self-determination.

> The concept of the democratic warrior is not based on imposing democracy by force but on limiting war and violence in world society.

Conflicting developments are evident, above all in the following dimensions: globalization versus struggles over identities, locational advantages and interests; high-tech wars versus "combat with knives and machetes" or asymmetrical warfare; the privatization of war and violence versus their re-politicization and re-ideologization as well as "world order wars;" the formation of new regional power centers and superpowers versus the increasing juridification of international relations and the institutionalization of regional and global communities.

Dealing with these opposing developments requires a differentiated counter-strategy of curbing war and violence in world society, of a new containment policy combined with a fostering of good governance. This is the common element shared by humanitarian intervention and the development of a culture of civil conflict management. Add to this measures to limit the causes of war and violence—such as poverty, oppression, ignorance, and regional conflicts—in order to construct a "task of the century" facing both the community of states and civil society. Last but not least, restricting the proliferation of weapons of mass destruction, but also of small arms, is of primary importance. The concept of limitation implies that there will be no entirely non-violent societies or even a non-violent world society in the foreseeable future. Furthermore, the goal of completely eliminating conflicts as such would ignore the fact that, historically speaking, conflicts and their resolution have often furthered human development toward free and democratic ideals—as per the American struggle for independence and the French Revolution. The primary task of politics and social forces in the twenty-first century is therefore to radically limit violence and war so that non-violent structures can also be preserved and the mechanisms of the "social world"[63] can have an impact.

As an overarching political perspective, the concept of limiting war and violence in world society is based on the following elements: first, the option of using military force as a last political resort to limit and contain particularly excessive and large-scale violence as well as violence that has the potential to destroy societies; second, the diminishing of conditions that help cause violence, such as poverty and oppression, especially in the economic sphere, and also the recognition of a pluralism of cultures and life styles in world society; third, the development of a "culture" of civil conflict management (concepts that can be summed up with the "civilizational hexagon," global governance and democratic peace); and, fourth, restrictions on the possession and proliferation of weapons of mass destruction, their delivery systems, and small arms. In this context, soldiers have a unique significance and identity as democratic warriors. Not as those who impose democracy or peace by force—this would not only overstretch their capabilities, but would even be counterproductive—but as those who make different forms of democratic self-determination in world society possible by curbing and containing war and violence.

In Place of a Summary: the Identity of the Democratic Warrior

At first glance, the concept of the democratic warrior appears to be self-contradictory. Indeed, it combines seemingly contradictory value systems in a single conception. Based on the example of a magnet, or on the model favored by Clausewitz of the unity of polar opposition between attack and defense, a methodology can already be formulated[64] to explain how this type of conflicted unity is not necessarily a logical opposition, but can also be a dynamic interrelationship on a continuum. At one end of the continuum is democratic equality and non-violent conflict resolution; at the other end is the threat and sometimes violently enforced limitation of war and violence. At one end is a civilized society and at the other is a subsystem of society whose identity is defined by martial honor.[65]

The decisive bond that can link the two poles of this dynamic relationship without eliminating their opposition is the classical republican virtues, which can lay claim to relative validity in both spheres. Since Plato, the classical virtues have been prudence (wisdom), justice, fortitude and temperance.[66] Without a specific ethos aimed at the political functioning of the polity, a state can sustain itself only under the conditions of a dictatorship.[67] If republican virtue, which is oriented toward the polity, cannot be directly reconciled with the liberal democracy and its focus on the individual, it can take on a completely new significance as a bond linking a democratic society to democratic warriors.[68] Thus, for Machiavelli, republican virtue already guaranteed both external and internal freedom.[69] In this respect, the necessary though not yet adequate condition of the democratic warrior is to be likewise a republican soldier. Add to this the limitation of war and violence in world society in order to make democratic societies possible. A renewal of republican virtue is the link between liberal-democratic society and a warrior ethos. This conception is the direct result of an application of Clausewitz's wondrous trinity of war of the application of force, the ability to fight, and the affiliation of the combatants to a cohesive community to the definition of the warrior identity.

Notes

1. Michael Ignatieff, *The Warrior's Honor: Ethnic War and the Modern Conscience* (Holt Paperbacks: New York, 1998); Robert Kaplan, *Warrior Politics: Why Leadership Demands a Pagan Ethos* (Vintage: Washington, 2001); and especially Christopher Coker, *The Warrior Ethos* (Routledge: London, 2007).
2. Martin van Creveld, *The Transformation of War* (The Free Press: New York, 1991); John Keegan, *A History of Warfare* (Hutchinson: London, 1993).
3. Wolfgang Royl, "Soldat sein mit Leib und Seele: Der Kämpfer als existenzielles Leitbild einer Berufsarmee," in *Ein Job wie jeder andere Zum Selbst-und Berufsverständnis von Soldaten*, ed. Sabine Collmer and Gerhard Kümmel (Nomos: Baden-Baden 2005), 9-21.
4. Suggested by Wilfried von Bredow.
5. Karl Haltiner and Gerhard Kümmel, "Die Hybridisierung der Soldaten: Soldatisches Subjekt und Identitätswandel," in *Streitkräfte im Einsatz: Zur Soziologie militärischer Interventionen*, ed. Gerhard Kümmel (Nomos: Baden-Baden, 2005), 47-54.

6. Haltiner/Kümmel develop a similar methodological position with the concept of the "hybrid soldier" who must balance different and conflicting areas within himself; Haltiner/Kümmel.

7. Edward Luttwak also concentrates his reflections on strategy on reconciling opposite poles. Edward Luttwak, *Strategy: The Logic of War and Peace* (Belknap Press of Harvard University Press: Cambridge), 2002.

8. Here we should also mention that Clausewitz's concept of the wondrous trinity fundamentally differs from that of "trinitarian war." The latter concept is the construction of Harry G. Summers and Martin van Creveld only and is based on a completely misguided interpretation of Clausewitz's trinity; for a detailed treatment, see Andreas Herberg-Rothe, *Clausewitz's Puzzle: The Political Theory of War* (Oxford University Press: Oxford, 2007).

9. Clausewitz's concept of politics is not limited to the political leadership but, depending on the context, can also express the political conditions, and sometimes even the political constitution, the polity of a community. For a detailed treatment, see Herberg-Rothe, *Clausewitz's Puzzle.*

10. Nevertheless, this does not mean that the model of the soldier is the combatant or even an archaic combatant. This view not only overlooks the difference between combatants and warriors as developed below, but it also reduces the variety of soldierly action to a single aspect. Compare as an opposing view to Royl.

11. Herberg-Rothe, *Clausewitz's Puzzle.*

12. Michael Sikora, "Der Söldner," in *Grenzverletzer: Figuren politischer Subversion*, ed. Eva/Kaufmann, Stefan/Bröckling, Ulrich, (Kulturverlag Kadmos: Berlin, 2002); Michael Sikora, "Söldner – historische Annäherung an einen Kriegertypus," *Geschichte und Gesellschaft* 2 (2003).

13. Ute Frevert, *Die kasernierte Nation* (Beckk: Munich, 2001); Ute Frevert, ed., *Militär und Gesellschaft im 19 und 20 Jahrhundert* (Klett-Cotta: Stuttgart, 1997), 21.

14. See Frevert, *Militär und Gesellschaft.*

15. Friedrich Meinecke, quoted in Frevert, *Militär und Gesellschaft*, 17.

16. Bernd Hüppauf, "Schlachtenmythen und die Konstruktion des Neuen Menschen, in *Keiner fühlt sich hier mehr als Mensch . . . : Erlebnis und Wirkung des ersten Weltkrieges*, ed. Gerhard Hirschfeld (Klartext Verlagsgesellschaft: Essen, 1993), 56.

17. Hüppauf, "Schlachtenmythen;" Bernd Wegner, *Hitlers politische Soldaten: Die Waffen-SS. Leitbild, Struktur und Funktion einer nationalsozialistischen Elite* (Schöningh: Paderborn, 1997).

18. Wilfried von Bredow, *Demokratie und Streitkräfte* (VS publishers: Wiesbaden, 2000).

19. However, it is debatable whether there was a direct progression to the concept of warrior in the US. To a certain extent, even traditionalists like Westmoreland dominated; see e.g. Stefan Goertz, "Warum Streitkräfte mancher Staaten den Kleinen Krieg verlieren...," in *Armee in der Demokratie*, ed. Ulrich vom Hagen (VS-publishers: Wiesbaden, 2006), 75-100. Possibly, the full extent of the change in the US armed forces is only now being comprehended.

20. Ignatieff, *The Warrior's Honor.*

21. This is partially contradicted by the findings of historical anthropology regarding the concept of honor, of the game, and of the comprehensive agonal set of rules for social interactions, secularized in concepts like fairness, recognition, reciprocity, etc. Joh. Huizinga, *Homo ludens* (Routledge: London, 2008). According to my understanding, the warrior's concept of values is closer to that of knights than of pure fighters.

22. John Keegan, *Kultur des Krieges* (Rowohlt: Berlin, 1995), 388-391.

23. Stephan Stephan, *Das Handwerk des Krieges* (Rowohlt: Berlin, 1998), 132.

24. Huizinga, *Homo ludens.*

25. Stephan, *Handwerk*, 130-133.

26. My criticism of Sun Tzu and the American conduct of the war in Iraq was directed at their neglect of the political-social situation before and after the war, i.e. the absolutiz-

ing of Sun Tzu and, consequently, was not a dismissal of Sun Tzu totally as some have interpreted it to be. I thank Christopher Coker for the idea that the two must be seen as complementary; Herberg-Rothe, *Clausewitz's Puzzle*.

27. Silke Götsch and Christel Köhle-Hezinger, ed., *Komplexe Welt: Kulturelle Ordnungssysteme als Orientierung* (Waxmann: Münster, 2003).

28. Ulrich Schneckener, "Post-Westfalia trifft Prä-Westfalia," in *Die Zukunft des Friedens*, ed. Jahn, Egbert/Fischer, Sabine/Sahm, Astrid (VS-publishers: Wiesbaden, 2005), 189-211.

29. Bernhard Von Zangl, "der nationalen zur post-nationalen Konstellation: Die Transformation globaler Sicherheitspolitik," in *Die Zukunft des Friedens*, Jahn/Fischer/Sahm, 159-188.

30. Anna Geis, ed., *Den Krieg überdenken: Kriegsbegriffe und Kriegstheorien in der Kontroverse* (Nomos: Baden-Baden, 2006), 12.

31. Geis, *Krieg*, 19.

32. Antulio II Echevarria, *Fourth-Generation Warfare and Other Myths* (Strategic Studies Institute: Carlisle, PA, 2005).

33. François Lyotard, *Der Widerstreit* (Fink: Munich, 1988).

34. Mary Kaldor, *New and Old Wars: Organized Violence in a Global Era* (Stanford University Press: Stanford, 1999); Herfried Münkler, *The New Wars* (Polity: New York, 2004).

35. Erhard Eppler, *Vom Gewaltmonopol zum Gewaltmarkt* (Suhrkamp: Frankfurt AM, 2002); Herfried Münkler, "Asymmetrische Gewalt: Terrorismus als politisch-militärische Strategie," in *Merkur* 56.1, 1-12; Christopher Daase Kleine Kriege – Große Wirkung, *Wie unkonventionelle Kriegführung die internationale Politik verändert* (Nomos: Baden-Baden, 1999); Wolfgang Sofsky, *Traktat über die Gewalt* (Fischer: Frankfurt, AM, 1996); Bernhard Zangl and Michael Zürn, *Frieden und Krieg* (Suhrkamp: Frankfurt, 2003); Dietrich Jung et al., *Kriege in der Weltgesellschaft: Strukturgeschichtliche Erklärung kriegerischer Gewalt* (VS-publishers: Wiesbaden, 2002); Sven Chojnacki, "Wandel der Kriegsformen? – Ein kritischer Literaturbericht," *Leviathan* 32.3, 419; Senghaas, "Dieter Die Konstitution der Welt – eine Analyse in friedenspolitischer Absicht," *Leviathan* 31.1, 117-152.

36. Wilfried von Bredow, *Turbulente Weltordnung* (Kohlhammer: Stuttgart, 1994).

37. Robert Kaplan, "The Coming Anarchy" *Atlantic Monthly* (273) 1994, 44-76.

38. John L. Gaddis, *Surprise, Security, and the American Experience* (Harvard University Press: Cambridge, 2004); Herfried Münkler, *Empires* (Polity Press: Cambridge, 2007).

39. Münkler, *The New Wars*.

40. Raymond Aron, *Clausewitz: Philosopher of War* (Routledge: London, 1983).

41. Sofsky, *Traktat*.

42. Chojnacki, *Wandel der Kriegsformen*; Kahl, Martin and Teusch, Ulrich, "Sind die "neuen Kriege" wirklich neu?" *Leviathan* 32.3, 382-401.

43. Monika Heupel and Bernhard Zangl, "Von "alten" und "neuen" Kriegen – Zum Gestaltwandel kriegerischer Gewalt," *Politische Vierteljahresschrift* 45.3, 346-367.

44. François Jean and Jean-Christophe Rufin, ed., *Wandel der Bürgerkriege* (Hamburger edition: Hamburg, 1999).

45. Klaus Schlichte, "Staatsbildung oder Staatszerfall: Zum Formwandel kriegerischer Gewalt in der Weltgesellschaft," *Politische Vierteljahresschrift* 47.4, 18; while differentiating among the following real types: wars of decolonization, social revolutions, wars in developing nations, wars in neopatrimonial states, wars in peripheral socialism, *ibid.*, 7.

46. Isabelle Duyvesteyn, *Clausewitz and African War* (Routledge: London, 2005), 9.

47. Heupel/Zangl, *Neue und alte Kriege*.

48. Heupel/Zangl, *Neue und alte Kriege*.

49. Thus Australia, for example, is preparing for a possible war against China. In a report, the Australian Defense Ministry warned of a possible war in the Asia-Pacific region in the next two decades and as part of its new arms program devoted 70 billion dollars to the preparations for such a war (source: www.n-tv.de/1147623.htm).

50. Chojnacki, *Wandel der Kriegsformen*.

51. Joas, Hans, *Kriege und Werte, Studien zur Gewaltgeschichte des 20. Jahrhunderts* (Velbrück: Wellerswist, 2000).

52. Michael Walzer, "Is there an American Empire?" *Dissent Magazine* 1 (2003): http://www.dissentmagazine.org/menutest/archives/2003/fa03/walzer.htm.

53. Klaus Leggewie, "Globalisierung versus Hegemonie: Zur Zukunft der transatlantischen Beziehungen," *Internationale Politik und Gesellschaft* 1, 87-111.

54. Antulio Echevarria II, "Globalization and the Clausewitzian Nature of War," *The European Legacy* 8.3, 317-332.

55. Fareed Zakaria, *The Post-American World* (W. W. Norton & Company: New York, 2009).

56. Frans Osinga P.B, *Science, Strategy and War: The strategic theory of John Boyd* (Routledge: London, 2007); Antoine Bousquet, *The Scientific Way of Warfare: Order and Chaos on the Battlefield of Modernity* (Hurst: London, 2009). Strictly speaking, these newer approaches constitute a renaissance of Sun Tzu and Basil Liddell Hart as well as the disengagement of the military and actions in war from the primacy of policy. In contrast to the assumptions that the actions of each individual soldier on the battlefield could be controlled by computer networking through "information warfare," the latest development of networkcentric warfare is based on the relative independence of military actions.

57. Quoted in Bousquet, *Scientific Way*, 2.

58. Clausewitz, *On War.*

59. This opposition is pointed out most clearly by Keegan.

60. Herfried Münkler, *Gewalt und Ordnung* (Fischer: Frankfurt, 1992).

61. On the concept of networked security and the transformation of the armed forces, see Ralph Thiele, "Trendforschung in der Bundeswehr," *Zeitschrift für Sicherheits und Außenpolitik, ZFAS* 2, 1–11.

62. Francis Fukuyama, *The End of History and the Last Man* (New York: Free Press, 1992).

63. Ernst Otto Czempiel, *Weltpolitik im Umbruch: Die Pax Americana, der Terrorismus und die Zukunft der internationalen Beziehungen* (Beck: Munich, 2002).

64. Herberg-Rothe, *Clausewitz's Puzzle.*

65. I would like to emphasize that the basic value systems are not as irreconcilable as is suggested by the positions of Keegan and van Creveld, and are propagated by weapons fetishists who also call themselves warriors, but are simply pure fighters.

66. Josef Pieper, *Das Viergespann – Klugheit, Gerechtigkeit, Tapferkeit, Maß* (Kösel: Munich, 1998).

67. For more on this topic, see the edited volume by Herfried Münkler and Harald Bluhm, ed., Forschungsberichte der interdisziplinären Arbeitsgruppe "Gemeinwohl und Gemeinsinn" der Berlin-Brandenburgischen Akademie der . . . Arbeitsgruppe der BBAW: BD 1. Berlin 2001.

68. Article on Republicanism. *The Blackwell Encyclopaedia of Political Thought.* Edited by David Miller et. al. Oxford 2004.

69. Marcus Llanque, *Politische Ideengeschichte: Ein Gewebe politischer Diskurse* (Oldenbourg: Munich, 2008), 159.

Andreas Herberg-Rothe is currently lecturer at the University of Applied Sciences, Fulda. Previously he served as private lecturer of political science at the Institute for Social Sciences Humboldt University Berlin and visiting fellow at the Centre for International Studies, London School of Economics and Political Science. His writings include *Clausewitz's Puzzle: The Political Theory of War* and *Clausewitz: The State and War*.

9

Reconstruction of Liberal Education

Daniel Bell

"Nothing at all has remained theory, everything has become a story."
—Gershom Scholem

A story: "When the Baal Shem [The Master of the Name] had a difficult task before him, he would go to a certain place in the woods, light a fire and meditate in prayer—and what he had set out to perform was done. When, a generation later, the "Maggid" of Meseritz was faced with the same task, he would go to the same place in the woods and say: "We can no longer light the fire, but we can still speak the prayers"—and what he wanted done became reality. Again, a generation later, Rabbi Moshe Leib of Sassov had to perform the task. And he too went into the woods and said: We can no longer light a fire, nor do we know the secret meditations belonging to the prayer, but we do know the place in the woods to which it all belongs—and that must be sufficient.... But when another generation had passed and Rabbi Israel of Rishin was called upon to perform the task he sat down ... and said: We cannot light the fire, we cannot speak the prayers, we do not know the place, but we can tell the story.
—Hassidic Tale, as retold by S.Y. Agnon

ABOUT THIRTY OR SO YEARS AGO, I wrote a book, *The Reforming of General Education*. In the older reckoning, as Comte put it, thirty years was the life span of a generation. Today, as historical time has collapsed into decades, "theoretical paradigms"—structuralism, post-structuralism, deconstructionism, and post-modernism—spin dizzily through the revolving doors of intellectual fashion, my book, I suspect, if someone stumbles across it in the stacks of a college library, would have an archaic echo and a musky smell. Or, in the high-tech mode, if the book is beamed up from a microdisk or CD-ROM, the language (but one would have to say, the discourse), with its emphasis on "conceptual inquiry," or the "nature of explanation," would surely seem to be dated, if not "irrelevant."

And yet, apart from an author's pride in the products of one's youth, the book might have some standing in a contemporary discussion of the "crisis" of liberal education (crisis being the only invariant term perhaps in the history of discourse) as a benchmark from the past and as a starting point in the effort presented to offer a "reconstruction" of liberal learning.

Education is an effort to defend the value of liberal learning against the centrifugal spin of fragmentation and the whirlpools of specialization, which were turning a college curriculum into a cafeteria for many and a training diet for a few. It was an effort to defend the existence of the college as a distinctive intellectual experience or grounding in the logic of inquiry, rather than as a "corridor" of remedial learning; or as preparation for a career between the secondary school and the graduate or professional school.

> Education is an effort to defend the value of liberal learning against the centrifugal spin of fragmentation and the whirlpools of specialization.

Any venture into education (besides being an experiment in autobiography) requires an explicit relationship of philosophy, and a commitment to a particular philosophical point to justify the point of view. The traditional idea of general education was based, implicitly or otherwise, on one or another of two premises: one, that there were invariant truths about human behavior, and natural ends (*telos*) to which moral action should be shaped, as established by human reason; the other that there was a common body of knowledge (or books) that every educated person ought to know, under the pain of being judged uncultivated.

Both grounds, I would argue, remain as normative ideals. Yet neither, I argued, prepares a student to deal with structures of disciplines and the ways knowledge is revised. I was not concerned with the multiplication of knowledge, which was the belief behind the thought of the fragmentation of knowledge. Let me say here, as a necessary aside, that the argument about the exponential increase in the "amount" of knowledge (based either on the increase in the number of scientific journals or the "doubling rates" of library holdings) is completely misleading. The statements confuse data, information, and knowledge. To illustrate the distinctions, let me take the index of a book, through whose classifications we are given the necessary clues to what one finds in the book. *Data* (statistics, birth records, crop totals, minerals mined, etc.) is like a *name* index; it is easily ordered and usually alphabetized by name or ordinal amounts. *Information* (historical events, scientific results, concepts, such as democracy or equality) is grouped under the *subject index*; these are combinations of materials into some thematic form.

Knowledge is the *judgment* about the organization and groupings of information under different subject rubrics. Judgment derives from purpose, which allows the author and reader to revise and rearrange the subjects for the purposes of one's own research.

Intellectual judgment, in this vein, derives from theory, and how the information fits into or disconfirms a theory. This means that knowledge is the construct of an "analytical index," which unfortunately few students or readers use when grappling with a book. To that extent, there has been no "exponential increase in knowledge" (though in some fields, as in physics, we have the elaboration of theory, as when electricity and magnetism, though disparate in their original conceptions, are now understood as being a single unified force).

All of this points to the philosophy that underlay my book, the power of the single lexical phoneme in providing different ways of reorganizing, reordering, and rearranging aesthetic forms and knowledge. To understand the nature of "re," one must know the history of the previous forms whose spatial planes in art or sound patterns in music or topographical knots in mathematics or the logic which sets forth "transformational rules," in physics or anthropology. The theme of "re" is central of course to the thinking of John Dewey, and finds marvelous exposition in his *Art in Experience*.

I did not insist that there is one and only one orderly structure, a trivium and a quadrivium, which all must follow. But whatever curriculum one stipulates, it is incumbent that the sequences one selects and relates be articulated into a coherent intellectual structure that is rationally defensible. Without that it is not education.

My book, *The Reforming of General Education* opened with a detailed presentation and historical development of the three models of general education that had been followed by many American colleges, that of Columbia, Chicago, and Harvard. It remains, I believe, the only such comparison in the educational literature. It outlined the structural changes emerging in the society, principally that of a "post-industrial society" (a theme I elaborated ten years later in a comprehensive book on that subject) and a new intellectual technology that needs to be embodied in the curriculum. And it dealt with the break up of two intellectual hopes upon which much of the philosophy of general education had been predicated: the idea of the "unity of knowledge," and more sharply, the "unity of science."[1]

The ground of the book was the experience of Columbia College, and the major influence was my colleague, Lionel Trilling, to whom the book was dedicated, as much in intellectual temper as his reflective mode. It was the confrontation of modernity with tradition that was the issue to be mastered. As I wrote then:

> Is it the task of the university to be a clerisy, self-consciously guarding the past and seeking assertively to challenge the new? Or is it just a bazaar, offering Coleridge and Blake, Burckhardt and Nietzsche, Weber, and Marx, as anti-totalitarian prophets, each with his own call? No consensual answer is possible, perhaps "because the university is no longer the citadel of the traditional mode—only the simple-minded can believe it is—but an arena in which the critics once outside the Academy have, like Blake's the tiger (or Tyger) once outside the gates of society, found a place—deservedly—within. And the tension between past and future, mind and sensibility, tradition and experience, for all its strains and discomfitures, is the only source for maintaining the independence of inquiry itself.

And yet, there was a question. Again:

> [Art] is the freest activity of the human imagination ... the least dependent on social constraints ... and for this reason the first signs of changes in collective sensibility become noticeable in art. It is, one can say, (in the phase of De Quincy) the realm of proleptic wisdom. Just as the agonized fantasies of a Rimbaud a hundred years ago prefigured the cruder cult of adolescence today, so the writhing of a Burroughs, or the anti-art of some modernist cults, may foreshadow the vulgate language and destructive impulses of thousands more tomorrow.

The anomaly of all this is that the thrust of modernity—what Professor Trilling has called the "adversary culture"—has itself become an established force, nowhere more so than in the university, while retaining its adversary stance.[2] These were cautions.[3] The courage lay in proposing a new rationale, the stipulation of the patterns of knowledge, and a set of proposals within the three as to how these patterns would be embodied in a curriculum. Curiously, each was a set of triads.[4]

The normative commitment was comprised of three objectives: *self-consciousness*, the forces that impel an individual from within and constrict him from without, the questions derived from Rameau's Nephew of authenticity; *historical consciousness*, beyond fact and chronology, necessary as these are, to provide a "vocabulary of reference" for the historical imagination and the nature of comparison for historical explanation; logic and *methodological consciousness*, the logic of conceptual inquiry and the relation of the knower to the known.

The patterns of knowledge, I argued, are fundamentally triadic in that different principles govern the acquisition of knowledge in the sciences, the social sciences and the humanities. In the sciences, learning is *sequential* in that specified steps are necessarily defined and have to be mastered before one proceeds to the next ones. In the social sciences, the pattern is one of *linkages* in that the kinds of an economy (market or command) are dependent on different political orders, and this, in turn, on the social structures of State and civil society, and that the understanding of one, necessarily involves, the understanding of its relation to the others. And the humanities are *concentric*, in that one explores the meanings of experience as a *ricorsi*, albeit within different contexts and hermeneutic levels, such as the understanding of tragedy and comedy. (As Groucho Marx once said: It is much harder to do comedy than tragedy, for while everyone cries at the same things, they laugh at different things.)

The curriculum would be structured in three steps. The first would be a grounding in history, the second, the acquisition of a discipline, and "the third-tier" courses that would apply the history and discipline to broad, synoptic problems, moral and practical. The history I proposed was Western history for (as I shall argue again), the matrix of our intellectual schemes, particularly the very idea of *concepts*, originates and develops in the West, and the roles of science and technology derive primarily from the new thinking developed in the Renaissance, as the idea of conscience and faith are redefined in the Reformation. I do not believe in the idea of "inter-disciplinary" schemes, for a discipline is an internally coherent, integrated body of concepts (such as neo-classical economics) that are applied to subjects (such as an economy). The third-tier allows for the knowledge gained in the two previous steps to come to bear on issues such as city planning to values and rights.[5]

The final chapter of the book is a reprise of the cultural theme sounded earlier. "A great and troubling task remains—to humanize technocracy and to 'tame' the apocalypse. It will be easier to do the first than the second." The technocratic mode, to which the university is increasingly committed, stresses professionalism and technique. In reaction, the apocalyptic mode, as expressed in the humanities, becomes nihilistic or estranged from the society. "One lives," I concluded, "in that painful alienation which is the continuing knowledge of doubt, not certainty. And yet this, too, is a state of grace, for as Dante said, 'Doubting pleases me no less than knowing.'"

> *The Reforming of General Education*, though later appreciated elsewhere, had little or no impact at Columbia, the place for whom the study was undertaken.

The Reforming of General Education, though later appreciated elsewhere, had little or no impact at Columbia, the place for whom the study was undertaken. There was the resistance from an older faculty that did not wish to be disturbed, and from the career-oriented or research-involved faculty whose rewards came not from teaching, but from "the production of new knowledge," as it was called, and whose advancement comes from specialization and graduate teaching and research. Intellectual challenges fall badly on the deaf ears of the educational theorists who are concerned, usually, with classroom pedagogical problems (I mean no disparagement) or on the indifferent minds of the research-oriented professors who are committed to their own professional concerns.

Besides, this was a report of a "committee of one," which, by definition, has no constituency other than himself and some fellow teachers.[6]

But the main reason why the report sank without much of a trace at Columbia was the "storming of the citadel" by the student radicals who, in the contagion of revolution thought that by challenging the University, they were challenging (and might even overthrow) the society. In the festival of May 1968, in Columbia, as in Paris, the heady cry was that Imagination would come to Power. Imagination came to earth at the end of police clubs and many of the student leaders went underground (to surface briefly in Chicago that year at the Democratic convention, in the "day of rage,") and to live out their fantasies of revolution as Weathermen or in a spate of bomb-ings (which in one tragic instance blew up a house in Greenwich Village in New York and killed some of the Columbia students mak-ing the bombs).

Revolution, as tragedy or farce is not the setting for the "rational reconstruction" of conceptual inquiry. As some students cried, as they organized "belly-dancing" on the Columbia greensward: "Who are you to tell me what to take as courses?" To which I could only reply: "Because you don't know what you don't know. If you did, you would not need me. As it is, you do."[7]

Notes

1. The "unity of knowledge" was the theme of a symposium organized by the Smithsonian Institution on the occasion of the 200th anniversary of its founding, with essays by Jerome Bruner, Herbert Butterfield, Kenneth Clark, Claude Levi-Strauss, Stephen Toulmin, Fred Whipple, and others. The difficulty with the essays is that none of them could point to the ways the new developments in physics, art, psychology, et al. had any common founda-tions, but only, and largely through metaphor, how they had influenced one another. It was not convincing. For the collection, see *Knowledge among Men*, edited by Webster True (New York: Simon and Schuster, 1966).

    The "unity of science," was a comprehensive and heroic effort by the philosophers of the "Vienna Circle," principally Otto Neurath and Rudolf Carnap, to outline the "unifying principles of science," centered, as they thought, on the principles of logical positivism which had been developed in the 1930s. Eventually, nineteen monographs appeared, first published separately and eventually collected in two volumes, *Foundations of the Unity of Science*, edited by Otto Neurath, Rudolf Carnap, and Charles Morris (University of Chicago Press, Volume 1, 1955; Volume 2, 1970).

    One major irony is that one of the extended essays was the monograph by Thomas S. Kuhn, *The Structure of Scientific Revolutions*, a work, more singularly than any other, perhaps, which undermined the idea of the "unity of science." Kuhn's monograph, the second edition and enlarged, appears in Volume 2 of the *Foundations*, 53-272.

2. The quotations are from the Doubleday Anchor edition, 151, 149-150. The reference to Trilling is from his *Beyond Culture* (New York: Viking, 1965), ix-xviii.

3. The dedication of the book was to Lionel Trilling, who has "The Scholar's Caution and the Scholar's Courage."

4. I leave it to a new Hermes Trismegistus (Hermes thrice great) author of magical, astro-logical, and alchemical doctrines, to explain the attraction of the triad.

For Plato, the parts of the soul, and the corresponding classes of the City, were the rational, the spirited, and the appetitive. For Fichte and Hegel, knowledge proceeded through thesis, antithesis, and synthesis (though there is a question whether Hegel employed this so mechanically). And for Freud, the personality was comprised of the id, the ego, and the super-ego. And the Gnostic symbol of all this is the triskelion.

5.   The book suggests a large number of different third-tier courses in the sciences, social sciences, and humanities (see 262-279).

6.   I should point out that this inquiry was my one and only foray into the field of "education." The study was undertaken at the request of David B. Truman who was then the dean of Columbia College. David Truman, a thoughtful man, was quietly aware that Columbia University, a great institution, was in danger of faltering. In the course of events, David Truman was destined to become president of Columbia University. By 1967, he had already become the provost and, because of the confusions of Grayson Kirk, the president, was in the command post during the student disturbances of 1968. Professor Truman made a mistake, I believe, in calling in the police when negotiations with the adamant student radicals, encouraged by some middle-aged romantics, such as Dwight Macdonald and Norman Mailer, failed. This is still a disputed issue, but the outcome was that the college community was so divided that it became impossible for Mr. Truman to accede to the presidency of Columbia. Though I was one of those who strongly opposed Mr. Truman (who had been my mentor at Columbia) and who Mr. Truman may feel that he had been betrayed by, none of this diminishes the respect in which I held him and the commitment he had to the University.

7.   One admires, in these instances, the prescience of Trilling. For as he pointed out, in a wry reflection on the advance of the "adversary culture," when an intellectual institution fails to offer resistance to the new, especially that of the adversary stance which "has developed the power to overturn old canons and establish new categories of its own," they will "fall into the inertness and weariness of all conventionalities, the conventionality of an outworn radical mode" (Op. cit.).

On Columbia, see my essay, "Columbia and the New Left," for a detailed account of these events, see *Confrontation*, edited by Daniel Bell and Irving Kristol, Basic Books, 1969.

Daniel Bell (1919-2011) was professor emeritus of sociology at Harvard University and is best known for his work and contributions to post-industrialism. He had been editor of the publications *The New Leader*, *Fortune*, and *The Public Interest*. He is the author of *The End of Ideology*, *The Winding Passage: Sociological Essays and Journeys*, and *The Social Sciences Since the Second World War*.

10

The Anti-leadership Vaccine

John W. Gardner

IT IS GENERALLY BELIEVED that we need enlightened and responsible leaders—at every level and in every phase of our national life. Everyone says so. But the nature of leadership in our society is very imperfectly understood, and many of the public statements about it are utter nonsense.

This is unfortunate because there are serious issues of leadership facing this society, and we had better understand them.

The most fundamental thing to be said about leadership in the United States is also the most obvious. We have gone as far as any known society in creating a leadership system that is based neither on caste or class, nor even on wealth. There is not yet equal access to leadership but we have come a long, long way from the family- or class-based leadership group. Even with its present defects, ours is a relatively open system.

The next important thing to be said is that leadership is dispersed among a great many groups in our society. The President, of course, has a unique, and uniquely important, leadership role, but beneath him, fragmentation is the rule. This idea is directly at odds with the notion that the society is run by a coherent power group—the Power Elite, as C. Wright Mills called it, or the Establishment, as later writers have named it. It is hard not to believe that such a group exists. Foreigners find it particularly difficult to believe in the reality of the fluid, scattered, shifting leadership that is visible to the naked eye. The real leadership, they imagine, must be behind the scenes. But at a national level this simply isn't so.

In many local communities and even in some states there *is* a coherent power group, sometimes behind the scenes, sometimes out in the open. In communities where such an "establishment," that is, a coherent ruling group, exists, the leading citizen can be thought of as having power in a generalized sense: he can bring about a change in zoning ordinances, influence the location of a new factory, and determine whether the local museum will buy contemporary paintings. But in the dispersed and fragmented power system that prevails in the nation as a whole one cannot say "So-and-so is powerful," without further elaboration. Those who know how our system works always want to know, "Powerful in what way? Powerful to accomplish what?" We have leaders in business and leaders in government, military leaders and educational leaders, leaders in labor and in agriculture, leaders in science, in the world of art, and in many other special fields. As a rule, leaders in any one of these fields do not recognize the authority of leaders from a neighboring field. Often they don't even know one another, nor do they particularly want to. Mutual suspicion is just about as common as mutual respect—and a lot more common than mutual cooperation in manipulating society's levers.

> The most powerful do not always win. Sometimes a coalition of the less powerful win.

Most of the significant issues in our society are settled by a balancing of forces. A lot of people and groups are involved and the most powerful do not always win. Sometimes a coalition of the less powerful win. Sometimes an individual of very limited power gets himself into the position of casting the deciding ballot.

Not only are there apt to be many groups involved in any critical issue, but their relative strength varies with each issue that comes up. A group that is powerful today may not be powerful next year. A group that can cast a decisive vote on question A may not even be listened to when question B comes up.

People who have never exercised power have all kinds of curious ideas about it. The popular notion of top leadership is a fantasy of capricious power: the top man presses a button and something remarkable happens; he gives an order as the whim strikes him, and it is obeyed.

Actually, the capricious use of power is relatively rare except in some large dictatorships and some small family firms. Most leaders are hedged around by constraints—tradition, constitutional limitations, the realities of the external situation, rights and privileges of followers, the requirements of teamwork, and most of all the inexorable demands of large-scale organization, which does not operate on capaciousness. In short, most power is wielded circumspectly.

There are many different ways of leading and many kinds of leaders. Consider, for example, the marked contrasts between the politician and the intellectual leader, the large-scale manager and the spiritual leader. One sees solemn descriptions of the qualities needed for leadership without any reference at all to the fact that the necessary attributes depend on the kind of leadership under discussion. Even in a single field there may be different kinds of leadership with different required attributes. Think of the difference between the military hero and the military manager.

If social action is to occur, certain functions must be performed. The problems facing the group or organization must be clarified, and ideas necessary to their solution formulated. Objectives must be defined. There must be widespread awareness of those objectives, and the will to achieve them. Often those on whom action depends must develop new attitudes and habits. Social machinery must be set in motion. The consequences of social effort must be evaluated and criticized, and new goals set.

A particular leader may contribute at only one point to this process. He may be gifted in analysis of the problem, but limited in his capacity to communicate. He may be superb in communicating, but incapable of managing. He may, in short, be an outstanding leader without being good at every aspect of leadership.

If anything significant is to be accomplished, leaders must understand the social institutions and processes through which action is carried out. And in a society as complex as ours, that is no mean achievement. A leader, whether corporation president, university dean, or labor official, knows his organization, understands what makes it move, and comprehends its limitations. Every social system or institution has a logic and dynamic of its own that cannot be ignored.

We have all seen men with lots of bright ideas but no patience with the machinery by which ideas are translated into action. As a rule, the machinery defeats them. It is a pity, because the professional and academic man can play a useful role in practical affairs. But too often he is a dilettante. He dips in here or there; he gives bits of advice on a dozen fronts; he never gets his hands dirty working with one piece of the social machinery until he knows it well. He will not take the time to understand the social institutions and processes by which change is accomplished. Although our decentralized system of leadership has served us well, we must not be so complacent as to imagine that it has no weaknesses, that it faces no new challenges, or that we have nothing to learn. There are grave questions to be answered concerning the leadership of our society. Are we living up to standards of leadership that we have achieved in our own past? Do the conditions of modern life introduce new complications into the task of leadership? Are we failing to prepare leaders for tomorrow?

Nothing should be allowed to impair the effectiveness and independence of our specialized leadership groups. But such fragmented leadership does create certain problems. One of them is that it isn't anybody's business to think about the big questions that cut across specialties—the largest questions facing our society. Where are we headed? Where do we want to head? What are the major trends determining our future? Should we do anything about them? Our fragmented leadership fails to deal effectively with these transcendent questions.

Very few of our most prominent people take a really large view of the leadership assignment. Most of them are simply tending the machinery of that part of society to which they belong. The machinery may be a great corporation, a great government agency, a great law practice or a great university. These people may tend it very well indeed, but they are not pursuing a vision of what the total society needs. They have not developed a strategy as to how it can be achieved, and they are not moving to accomplish it.

One does not blame them, of course. They do not see themselves as leaders of the society at large, and they have plenty to do handling their own specialized roles.

Yet it is doubtful that we can any longer afford such widespread inattention to the largest questions facing us. We achieved greatness in an era when changes came more slowly than now. The problems facing the society took shape at a stately pace. We could afford to be slow in recognizing them, slow in coping with them. Today, problems of enormous importance hit us swiftly. Great social changes emerge with frightening speed. We can no longer afford to respond in a leisurely fashion.

Our inability to cope with the largest questions tends to weaken the private sector. Any question that cannot be dealt with by one of the special leadership groups—that is, any question that cuts across special fields—tends to end up being dealt with by government. Most Americans value the role played by nongovernmental leadership in this country and would wish it to continue. In my judgment it will not continue under the present conditions.

> Few of our most prominent people take a really large view of the leadership assignment.

The cure is not to work against the fragmentation of leadership, which is a vital element in our pluralism, but to create better channels of communication among significant leadership groups, especially in connection with the great issues that transcend any particular group.

Another of the maladies of leadership today is a failure of confidence. Anyone who accomplishes anything of significance has more confidence than the facts would justify. It is something that outstanding executives have in common with gifted military commanders, brilliant political leaders, and great artists. It is true of societies as well as of individuals. Every great civilization has been characterized by confidence in itself.

Lacking such confidence, too many leaders add ingenious new twists to the modern art which I call "How to reach a decision without really deciding." They require that the question be put through a series of clearances within the organization and let the clearance process settle it. Or take a public opinion poll and let the poll settle it. Or devise elaborate statistical systems, cost-accounting systems, or information-processing systems, hoping that out of them will come as unassailable support for one course of action rather than another.

This is not to say that leadership cannot profit enormously from good information. If the modern leader doesn't know the facts he is in grave trouble, but rarely do the facts provide unqualified guidance. After the facts are in, the leader must in some measure emulate the little girl who told the teacher she was going to draw a picture of God. The teacher said, "But, Mary, no one knows what God looks like"; and Mary said, "They will when I get through."

The confidence required of leaders poses a delicate problem for a free society. We don't want to be led by Men of Destiny who think they know all the answers. Neither do we wish to be led by Nervous Nellies. It is a matter of balance. We are no longer in much danger, in this society, from Men of Destiny. But we are in danger of falling under the leadership of men who lack the confidence to lead. And we are in danger of destroying the effectiveness of those who have a natural gift for leadership.

> We don't want to be led by Men of Destiny who think they know all the answers. Neither do we wish to be led by Nervous Nellies.

Of all our deficiencies with respect to leadership, one of the gravest is that we are not doing what we should to encourage potential leaders. In the late eighteenth century we produced out of a small population a truly extraordinary group of leaders—Washington, Adams, Jefferson, Franklin, Madison, Monroe, and others. Why is it so difficult today, out of a vastly greater population, to produce men of that caliber? It is a question that most reflective people ask themselves sooner or later. There is no reason to doubt that the human material is still there, but there is excellent reason to believe that we are failing to develop it—or that we are diverting it into non-leadership activities.

Indeed, it is my belief that we are immunizing a high proportion of our most gifted young people against any tendencies to leadership. It will be worth our time to examine how the anti-leadership vaccine is administered.

The process is initiated by the society itself. The conditions of life in a modern, complex society are not conducive to the emergence of leaders. The young person today is acutely aware of the fact that he is an anonymous member of a mass society, an individual lost among millions of others. The processes by which leadership is exercised are not visible to him, and he is bound to believe that they are exceedingly intricate. Very little in his experience encourages him to think that he might some day exercise a role of leadership.

This unfocused discouragement is of little consequence compared with the expert dissuasion the young person will encounter if he is sufficiently bright to attend a college or university. In those institutions today, the best students are carefully schooled to avoid leadership responsibilities.

Most of our intellectually gifted young people go from college directly into graduate school or into one of the older and more prestigious professional schools. There they are introduced to—or, more correctly, powerfully indoctrinated in—a set of attitudes appropriate to scholars, scientists, and professional men. This is all to the good. The students learn to identify themselves strongly with their calling and its ideals. They acquire a conception of what a good scholar, scientist, or professional man is like.

As things stand now, however, that conception leaves little room for leadership in the normal sense; the only kind of leadership encouraged is that which follows from the performing of purely professional tasks in a superior manner. Entry into what most of us would regard as the leadership roles in the society at large is discouraged. In the early stages of a career, there is a good reason for this: becoming a first-class scholar, scientist, or professional requires single-minded dedication. Unfortunately, by the time the individual is sufficiently far along in his career to afford a broadening of interests, he often finds himself irrevocably set in a narrow mold.

The anti-leadership vaccine has other more subtle and powerful ingredients. The image of the corporation president, politician, or college president that is current among most intellectuals and professionals today has some decidedly unattractive features. It is said that such men compromise their convictions almost daily, if not hourly. It is said that they have tasted the corrupting experience of power. They must be status seekers, the argument goes, or they would not be where they are.

Needless to say, the student picks up such attitudes. It is not that professors propound these views and students learn them. Rather, they are in the air and students absorb them. The resulting unfavorable image contrasts dramatically with the image these young people are given of the professional who is almost by definition dedicated to his field, pure in his motives, and unencumbered by worldly ambition.

My own extensive acquaintance with scholars and professionals on the one hand and administrators and managers on the other does not confirm this contrast in character. In my experience, each category has its share of opportunists. Nevertheless, the negative attitudes persist.

As a result the academic world appears to be approaching a point at which everyone will want to educate the technical expert who advises the leader, or the intellectual who stands off and criticizes the leader, but no one will want to educate the leader himself.

For a good many academic and other professional people, negative attitudes toward leadership go deeper than skepticism concerning the leader's integrity. Many have real doubts, not always explicitly formulated, about the necessity for leadership.

The doubts are of two kinds. First, many scientific and professional people are accustomed to the kinds of problems that can be solved by expert technical advice or action. It is easy for them to imagine that any social enterprise could be managed in the same way. They envisage a world that does not need leaders, only experts. The notion is based, of course, upon a false conception of the leader's function. The supplying of technically correct solutions is the least of his responsibilities.

There is another kind of question that some academic or professional people raise concerning leadership: Is the very notion of leadership somehow at odds with the ideals of a free society? Is it a throwback to earlier notions of social organization?

These are not foolish questions. We have in fact outgrown or rejected several varieties of leadership that have loomed large in the history of mankind. We do not want autocratic leaders who treat us like inferior beings. We do not want leaders, no matter how wise, who treat us like children.

But at the same time that we were rejecting those forms of leadership, we were evolving forms more suitable to our values. As a result our best leaders today are *not* out of place in a free society—on the contrary, they strengthen our free society.

We can have the kinds of leaders we want, but we cannot choose to do without them. It is in the nature of social organization that we must have them at all levels of our national life, in and out of government—in business, labor, politics, education, science, the arts, and every other field. Since we must have them, it helps considerably if they are gifted in the performance of their appointed task. The sad truth is that a great many of our organizations are badly managed or badly led. And because of that, people within those organizations are frustrated when they need not be frustrated. They are not helped when they could be helped. They are not given the opportunities to fulfill themselves that are clearly possible.

> So much of our energy has been devoted to tending the machinery of our complex society that we have neglected this element in leadership.

In the minds of some, leadership is associated with goals that are distasteful—power, profit, efficiency, and the like. But leadership, properly conceived, also serves the individual human goals that our society values so highly, and we shall not achieve those goals without it.

Leaders worthy of the name, whether they are university presidents or senators, corporation executives or newspaper editors, school superintendents or governors, contribute to the continuing definition and articulation of the most cherished values of our society. They offer, in short, moral leadership.

So much of our energy has been devoted to tending the machinery of our complex society that we have neglected this element in leadership. I am using the word "moral" to refer to the shared values that must undergird any functioning society. The thing that makes a number of individuals a society rather than a population or a crowd is the presence of shared attitudes, habits and values, a shared conception of the enterprise of which they are all a part, shared views of why it is worthwhile for the enterprise to continue and to flourish. Leaders can help in bringing that about. In fact, it is required that they do so when leaders lose their credibility or their moral authority, then the society begins to disintegrate.

Leaders have a significant role in creating the state of mind that is the society. They can serve as symbols of the moral unity of the society. They can express the values that hold the society together.

Most important, they can conceive and articulate goals that lift people out of their petty preoccupations, carry them above the conflicts that tear a society apart, and unite them in the pursuit of objectives worthy of their best efforts.

John W. Gardner (1912-2002) was Secretary of Health, Education, and Welfare under President Lyndon Johnson. In addition he was President of the Carnegie Corporation and the founder of two influential national U.S. organizations: Common Cause and Independent Sector. He is the recipient of both the Presidential Medal of Freedom and the Public Welfare Medal. His books include *Living, Leading, and the American Dream, Quotations of Wit and Wisdom*, and *No Easy Victories.*

11

The Social Context of Medicine

John Charles

MORE THAN a century ago, in 1873, Louis-Adolphe Bertillon rescued "mesology" from oblivion, enlarged its empire to include all animals and plants, and indicated in detail his concept of the "social mesology" of man. He suggested that as a discipline it would be concerned with the effect upon human beings as individuals and in society, of temperature, light, humidity, gravity, atmospheric pressure, meteorological and electrical influences, food and drink, urbanization, sanitary conditions, occupation, domesticity, religion, institutions, laws and psychological factors. He emphasized the importance of the economic situation of the family. Vitality and viability in children were governed to an astonishing degree by the home conditions and by the presence there of poverty or of comfortable circumstances. According to Bertillon, "there are only two possible ways of modifying man, either individually or in the mass:

1.   By modifying his ancestry, which is possible so far as future generations are concerned, but extremely difficult to apply; or,
2.   By modifying the natural or social environment."

This description of the content of "mesology" with certain additions is the epitome of "social medicine" as we know it today.

Social Medicine

The term "social medicine" was in fact first employed in 1848 by Jules Guerin, editor of the French *Gazette Médicale*. Writing at a time of intense social upheaval and distress he pleaded that the medical profession should exercise its great powers of conciliation between the classes.

"Who better than they knew the living conditions of the working classes or could assess their physical condition?" "Who was more able to help in the production of a healthier, stronger and happier society?" Social Medicine, which he defined as "all those aspects of medicine which affect society," was "the key to the burning questions of that hour of regeneration."

Throughout the quarter century which separated Guerin with his definition of social medicine and Bertillon with his catalogue of its components, much was accomplished in this country and in Europe in consonance with its principles and ideals. The British approach was perhaps more pragmatic and less academic than the continental, and the great series of John Simon's fourteen Reports to the Privy Council is replete with examples of the confluence of sociology and medicine. Perhaps the most cogent evidence of this trend is to be found in the sixth report for the year 1862 which relates to the England of almost a century ago. It is a stout volume of nearly eight hundred pages bound in the customary dark blue cover and contains eighty-four pages of Simon's perspicacious commentary and a series of eighteen appendices by various authors. These dealt with such matters as vaccination, the food of the labouring classes in England, certain dangerous industries, and a comprehensive study of the hospitals of the United Kingdom, "with the object of determining the influence of sanitary conditions upon their therapeutic efficiency."

Reports in other years discussed infant mortality, the lung-dust diseases, and the evil conditions, both physical and psychological, under which printers, tailors and the needle-women of the court dressmakers, were forced to work. Here indeed was a cumulative compendium of much that we now comprise in social medicine. But insofar as administrative practice and teaching in public health were concerned the emphasis still lay on the so-called sanitary sciences, and it was not until 1902 that the first Professorial Chair in Social Medicine was established in Berlin. There was in fact little further progress in this field, either in Europe or in America, during the next four decades.

The title of the subject may have been open to suspicion, either on political or semantic grounds, but these influences did not deter the Nuffield Provincial Hospitals Trust in 1943 from endowing an Institute of Social Medicine at Oxford, or John Ryle from assuming its Directorship and becoming the first of the British Professors of Social Medicine. Similar chairs were soon created both in Britain and abroad, but they were often disguised under other forms of description. (It is, however, a little disappointing to find that amongst this galaxy of titles there is no Chair of Human Mesology.)

Definition of Social Medicine

It will be helpful to consider very briefly how Ryle and some of his colleagues regarded their "profession," but before doing so it may be advisable to look more closely into the broader meanings of the two words "social" and "medicine." It is important to realize that "medicine" implies not only the idea of healing or making whole, but also the active prevention of disease, and the maintenance of the body in health. There is no longer the frank antithesis between medicine—"preservative" or preventive—and medicine "conservative" or therapeutic. All medicine is one. By derivation "social" refers primarily to the people with whom we are associated and allied, tied perhaps by a dependence upon one another, and so by extension it comes to include the community.

> "Medicine" implies not only the idea of healing or making whole, but also the active prevention of disease, and the maintenance of the body in health.

Ryle's definition of Social Medicine was simple and straightforward.

"Social Medicine means what it says. It embodies the idea of medicine applied to the service of man as 'socius,' as fellow or comrade, with a view to a better understanding and more durable assistance of all his main and contributory troubles which are inimical to active health, and not merely to removing or alleviating a present pathology. It embodies also the idea of medicine applied in the service of 'societas' or the community of men, with a view to lowering the incidence of all preventable disease and raising the general level of human fitness."

Other professors were neither as explicit nor as clear. For one it was a subject as the borderline between the medical and social sciences, and was concerned "with all the elements which constitute social or collective life." Others defined it as "all the aspects of medicine and hygiene which interest the sociologist, and all the aspects of economic and social science which interest the doctor and the hygienist." Again it has been described as "the hygiene of social groups whose homogeneity springs from a shared culture—a term which covers material, intellectual, psychological, and moral conditions."

Professor Francis Crew of Edinburgh at the International Conference of Forensic and Social Medicine at Brussels in 1947, after saying that "Social Medicine is coterminous with the science of Human Ecology ... It deals with the Nature-Nurture complex," went on to describe its techniques.

> Social medicine consists in effecting "class equality in relation to health."

"One of the prime objects is to demonstrate by means of field surveys and through the use of statistical techniques the exact relationship between healthiness and kinds and grades of physical and mental morbidity on the one hand, and specific ingredients of the external world on the other."

Professor Rene Sand, the giver of a classical series of clinical lectures on social medicine at the Hospital Saint Pierre in Brussels, had this simple definition of his subject: "[It] is concerned with the relations between health and the conditions of existence in society." Perhaps the most detailed exposition of this point of view was that given by Etienne Burnet in Paris in 1935:

"Social Medicine acknowledges the fact that there are rich and poor and that if diseases are to be combated, these inequalities must be made good. It has been said with some truth that social medicine consists in effecting 'class equality in relation to health.'"

Finally, in this catalogue of descriptions, there is the answer of another great Frenchman Dujarric de la Rivière to his own rhetorical question as to the aim of social medicine: "It is the science which teaches a nation to conserve and augment her human capital."

So much for definitions. There are also the twin ambivalent descriptions of the subject as "social biology," and "bio-sociology," and its anatomization into constituent parts—socio-medical demography, socio-medical anthropology, and socio-medical pathology.

From all this we may turn a little despondently, and say "Happy is the hybrid discipline which has no definition." But the despondency is unwarranted, for this vast orchestration of description is simply a series of personal variations on the same theme—the social aspects of medicine. And because, as Sir George Newman said, "Social Medicine existed even before history began, and its emergence today is simply an evolution from a negative to a positive force," we will benefit by a return to those far beginnings. Through a historical approach we can see how little by little, from one quarter or another, inspired by great men, or thrust forward by overwhelming public clamour and demand, we have proceeded beyond the incomplete mesology of Bertillon and arrived at the modern concept of the social content and context of medicine.

Its History in Ancient Times

It has been argued that Hippocrates and his school were too busy observing the progression of a disease to be interested greatly in the patient himself. They were ardent naturalists studying a series of phenomena, meditators upon death, rather than active therapists. Furthermore it has been alleged that their interest in the environmental and social situation of their patients was minimal. And yet is this strictly true? As evidence to the contrary, there are the careful meteorological observations season by season, the studies of the local water supplies, and the occasional references to the occupation of the patient, or of his or her employer. There are also the acute observations of physical, physiognomical, and psychological attributes as seen in that famous adjectival catalogue of those who died in one winter epidemic in Thasos—"striplings"—smooth-skinned—straight-haired—black-eyed—those who had lived recklessly and carelessly—the rough voiced—the lispers—the passionate. Women too died in very great numbers who were of this kind."

The Hippocratic Regimen of Health is a short pungent book of some one thousand five hundred words which gives an outline of the main rules for eating and drinking, according to the seasonal rhythm, and advice for the fat wishing to become thin, and for those whose physique and intentions were opposite. Child care is discussed; plain instruction is given for the training of the athlete; and less rigorous advice is offered regarding the walking, working, bathing, and clothing of the ordinary man. The Regimen is not by any means a comprehensive treatise, but it is at any rate a practical and coherent one.

Thus the Hippocratic physician, handicapped though he might be by the limitations of his therapy, was anxious to seek for his own proper understanding of the circumstances of his patient any information he could obtain about meteorology, hygiene, nutrition and dietetics, exercise, clothing, and those factors in the causation of the disease which were psychical rather than physical. Many of these matters were relevant to the social content of the medicine which he practised.

After the Hippocratic era of the fifth and sixth centuries BC, there is a complete dearth of Greek medical literature for over one hundred years. Greek medicine continued to flourish, particularly in Egypt, in Athens and along the Mediterranean coast of Asia Minor, but none of its learned books have come down to us. This does not mean that the modicum of social medicine we have described did not survive. It did but in its inevitable translation to Italy it underwent a characteristic Roman transmutation.

We can see that best in the *De Medicina* of Cornelius Celsus who wrote at the beginning of the Christian era. He was not a doctor but an encyclopaedically-minded writer on many subjects, keenly interested in the health and welfare of his household. Of him it could be said that he regarded the physicking of his family and his farmyard as part of the duties of the Roman country gentleman. The main interest of his book, apart from its pharmocopoeia and the precise diagnostic and therapeutic advice which it offers, lies in the regimen of life it prescribes for people like himself.

"A man in health who is both vigorous and his own master should be under no obligatory rules and have no need either for a medical attendant or for a rubber and anointer. His kind of life should afford him variety; he should be now in the country, now in the town, and more often about the farm; he should sail, hunt, rest sometimes, but more often take exercise, for while inaction weakens the body, work strengthens it; the former brings on premature old age, the latter prolongs youth."

Then follows advice on bathing, diet, drinking, and such exercise as reading aloud, handball, running, walking, but nothing in excess. "For the weak, amongst whom were many townspeople, and almost all those who were fond of letters, greater care was needed."

There remains, 150 years later in date, the great masterpiece of Claudius Galen, the *Hygieia* or *De Sanitate Tuenda*, which in its own discursive fashion is a compendium of personal hygiene, and an exposition of social medicine. It was written in Greek, not for "any savage or barbarian people, any more than for bears, boars, lions, or any of the other wild beasts, but for Greeks, or for those who, born barbarians by nature, yet emulate the culture of the Greeks." It is the source of many of those definitions of health, which are all so apt despite their variety.

"Health is a sort of harmony, but its range is wide, and does not exist to the same degree in all of us." "Health is the condition in which we do not suffer pain and are not impeded in the exercise of our bodily functions or the enjoyment of life. Medicine has two main subdivisions, Hygiene and Therapeutics—the former to maintain the body in health, the latter to cure it when diseased. But as health takes precedence over disease, it is of the first importance to study its preservation."

He divides life, as so many have done subsequently into "septads" and prescribes for each of them a regimen which is rarely concerned with the administration of medicaments, but rather with bodily care and culture, exercise and education. Much of the advice is exceedingly detailed. Gentle exercise of the limbs commences with the creeping and later with the walking child, and is followed by more advanced body movements such as those that result from being driven in a vehicle or carried in a boat. At the age of seven the boy is put astride a horse for the first time. The programme of the youth growing to manhood is based on education, the inculcation of good habits, and serious discipline. Galen debates whether exercise or physical work are of equivalent benefit, and in the end agrees that both have their virtues, and that fatigue is the evil to avoid. So far then we have had a "Regimen Sanitatis," socially rather than medically orientated, in which nutrition, exercise, regularity of habit of mind and body, and education all play their part.

In his recommendation for the members of the later "septads" Galen touches on such matters as the type of living accommodation, the heating of rooms, the enjoyment of the sun and the fresh air in summer, self-medication chiefly through the alternation of laxative foods with those of a more astringent type, the necessary modicum of work, and the pleasant exercise of the mind in conversation. These are simply obvious things, but for Galen they were important components of the art of living and of preserving health.

It would be easy to continue this pursuit of health and to quote extensively from the "Regimen Sanitatis Salerni"—a thousand years later in time than Galen. We would note how it was dedicated to the cultivation of health and the avoidance of disease amongst such members of the upper classes in the Middle Ages as might consider themselves as leisured enough to follow its rules and counsels. The popularity of these was far reaching and they were practised even in the monasteries. John Mirfield, author of the *Brevarium Bartholomei*, was, for example, a member of the Priory of St. Bartholomew, a fellow-foundation of the hospital established by Rahere in 1137. He was presumably an ecclesiastic though he had studied medicine, and knew the patients in the hospital. In addition he had views on physicians, and deplored their undue interest in money. Knowing prelates and their tendency to be corpulent, he advised them to have a rope hanging from the ceiling and knotted at the end on which they might take exercise by swinging or raising their weight. Alternatively, other forms of exercise not being available they might walk about their chambers carrying heavy weights in their hands.

His tract was written in the last quarter of the fourteenth century, at a time when the monasteries through their hospitals were providing not only geriatric care, but were also beginning to look after the acutely ill. This, curiously enough, was a consequence, at any rate in England, of the development of the inn, which by relieving the religious houses of their duties of hospitality to travellers and guests, made available accommodation for the equally charitable purposes mentioned. It is strange that a change in the social habits of the people should so influence the growth of medicine. In course of time the monastic hospitals began in their turn to specialize. Some devoted themselves to cripples, others to the mentally afflicted, and some to organize the solitary lives of the lepers.

For generations the hospital systems of Western Europe were based on these mediaeval institutions and their successors. Medicine began its slow advance in a religious, humanitarian, and social milieu, which has only begun to alter materially in the past two hundred years.

> **Medicine began its slow advance in a religious, humanitarian, and social milieu.**

Housed like Mirfield, within easy distance of St. Bartholomew's Hospital, but never a member of its staff, was John Caius. He comes into this story, firstly because of his little book, published in 1552, *A Counsel against the Sweat*, with its studies of that influenzal-like disease. His descriptions dealt not only with the march of the epidemic, but also with the physical and social characteristics of its victims—being "either men of wealth, ease, and welfare, or of the poorer sort, such as were idle persons, good ale drinkers and tavern haunters." He prescribed a preventive regimen of exercise, rest, cleanliness, the care of the skin and the use of perfumes, and advocated the appointment of "certain masters of health in every city and town as there is in Italy."

But more especially does he come into this picture because of his association with the Royal College of Physicians of London, of which he was President for nine years, spread over three terms of office during the years 1555-60, 1562-63, and 1571.

The Annals of the College have been the repository over the centuries of much information regarding epidemiological phenomena, professional attitudes and ethics, and the effects of social change. Caius's own reelection as President was postponed for a few days in the early autumn of 1558 because of the dispersal of the Fellows of the College "giving help in various parts of the City to people suffering from tertian fever." The social consequences of that epidemic were thus described: "There were hardly any healthy people to look after the sick and hardly any reapers who would bring in the harvest or store it in the granary." His next period of office was marked by an outbreak of colds and catarrhs accompanied by fever and pleurisy or quinsy. The environmental concomitant is noted in these words: "The air was smoky and dank so that for the first twelve days of December the sun hardly ever appeared or shone for one continuous hour, and the dense and foetid gloom took possession of everything." Here is history anticipating the great smog of London which took place 390 years later in December 1952.

Medicine about this time began to interest itself in the quality of drugs and also, to some extent, of foodstuffs, for the line of demarcation between grocers, pepperers, and druggists was not very clear. They were all enjoined by the College Authorities "to display their medical ingredients in their shop windows so that the physicians might judge of their goodness." This supervision, and often correction, of druggists and apothecaries continued for many years. Its primary object was to obtain for ordinary people a proper standard of medicinal substances and preparations. It ultimately led to the publication of the first London Pharmacopoeia in 1618, an event of both medical and social importance.

The Approach in the Seventeenth and Eighteenth Centuries

The College's interest in the Public Health was often made manifest in other ways; sometimes spontaneously, sometimes at the urgent request of the government.

In 1627 the College received a request to carry out within six days an investigation into the complaint which had been "brought full cry to the Privy Council against the farmers of the Alum Works near St. Katherine's." It was alleged that "the loathsome vapour from these works" was a "great annoyance to the inhabitants within a mile compass, tainting the pastures and poisoning the very fish in the Thames." The Committee of six which promptly investigated the matter included William Harvey and its plainly expressed opinion was to the effect that "works standing in that place must necessarily breed great annoyance to the inhabitants and endanger their health."

Apart from the physicians, the professors of other disciplines were beginning to take an interest in the health of man, particularly as an economic unit. In brief, they had begun to realize the cash nexus of health. Already in 1576 the Frenchman, Jean Bodin, had written *Il n'ya ni richesse ni force que dhommes*. William Petty, physician, anatomist and economist, with interests ranging from medicine to the administration of Ireland, carried these ideas further in the "Verbum Sapienti" which he wrote in 1665-67. It set out in numerical terms his estimates of the national income, national capital, and the economic value of the population. He concluded by drawing attention to the fact that the recent epidemic of Plague in London, in causing the loss of one hundred thousand lives, had deprived the state of human capital to the value of nearly £7,000,000. In his opinion an expenditure of one-tenth of that sum could have prevented the catastrophe.

> The knowledge of the relationship between economics and the public health was not commonly recognised by the medical profession.

The knowledge of the relationship between economics and the public health was not commonly recognised by the medical profession, but towards the end of the seventeenth century, its members became increasingly cognisant of the effects of the social habits of the population.

After the accession of William and Mary in 1688, such restrictions as had previously been placed on the manufacture of spirituous liquors were virtually withdrawn, and the standards of quality which had previously been supervised by the Distillers Company rapidly deteriorated. Between 1690 and 1721, the amount of spirits on which duty was paid rose from 43,000 gallons to 2,800,000. Burials had simultaneously increased and exceeded baptisms in the ratio of 3 to 2. This is the evidence of the London Bills of Mortality, and to it could be added the experience of the hospitals with their steadily increasing load of patients, to which the "dropsies" made a notable contribution.

It is not clear from the College Annals over what period of time the Fellows deliberated about this growing evil, but in the week before

Christmas 1725, they felt themselves impelled to inveigh against it in very forthright terms. The representation to the House of Commons which was then authorized, was submitted a month later, and was couched in these polite but vigorous words:

"We the President, and College or Commonalty of the Faculty of Physicians at London, who are appointed by the laws of the Kingdom to take care of His Majesty's Subjects in London and within seven miles circuit, do think it our duty to represent that we have observed with concern for some years past the fatal effect of the frequent use of several sorts of distilled spirituous liquors upon great numbers of both sexes, rendering them diseased, not fit for business, poor, a burden to themselves and neighbours, and too often the cause of weak, feeble, and distempered children, who must be, instead of an advantage and strength, a charge to the country. We crave leave further most humbly to represent that this custom doth every day increase notwithstanding our repeated advices to the contrary. We therefore submit to the consideration of parliament so great and growing an evil. In consideration thereof, we have this 19th day of January 1725, caused our common seal to be affixed to this our representation."

These strongly expressed opinions had also the support of the Magistrates who were able to demonstrate the destitution and crimes which were rightly attributable to the gin trade. This was the period when every tenth house in the majority of parishes was a dispensary of gin; and "even the workhouses were beginning to give an opening to the traffic."

More than thirty years were to pass before Parliament was ultimately driven by the scathing irony of Henry Fielding, and the grim and pungent satire of Hogarth and his cartoons to end this period of national social inadequacy by means of appropriate legislative and administrative acts. Nevertheless for the continuance of those evils the Government by reason of its pusillanimity has been largely responsible.

Here again we have history anticipating itself, for the Royal College of Physicians has drawn the attention of the Government to the situation as regards to excessive cigarette smoking, not perhaps an evil so charged with deleterious social consequences, but nevertheless a menace to the health of many of Her Majesty's subjects, and the cause of their untimely death.

These sordid aspects of the early years of the eighteenth century should not detract from our understanding and appreciation of the immense progress in knowledge of every kind which made its later years one of the outstanding periods of our social history. A coarse and robust epoch it may have been, but it was also one of intense intellectual activity.

Abroad it was the age of Rousseau and Voltaire. In England it saw the scientific discoveries of Priestley, the physiological and pathological advances of John Hunter, the introduction of inoculation against smallpox at the beginning of the century, and the triumph of vaccination at its end.

Commonly regarded as the era in which the Industrial Revolution began, it was also the period during which changes in agricultural practice, stemming from the introduction of clover and root crops, revolutionized the feeding habits of the Englishman to such an extent that one observer in 1770 was able to say "the quantity of meat, butter, and cheese consumed by all number of the people is immense."

During a lifetime which was almost coterminous with the century, for he was born in 1703 and died in 1791, John Wesley preached his gospel of man's redemption of man in almost every town and village of the land. He was amongst the first in this country who, in the words of George Trevelyan, helped "to diffuse common sense and reasonableness in life, to civilize manners and to humanize conduct." Wesley shared with many other great spirits both in this country and on the continent in the emergence of humanitarianism. That as a by-product of his activities he should find time to write a little book entitled *Primitive Physic*, which by 1747 had reached its 35th edition, is not altogether surprising. In it he set out a "regimen sanitatis" which was in keeping with his evangelism for the life of the Spirit. Its rules were simple. "Nothing more conduces to health than abstinence and plain food with due labour—eight hours sleep, fresh air and exercise, and above all contentment and serenity of mind."

Contemporary with John Wesley, and equally dedicated, was another great Englishman, John Howard. He was a puritan, a man of delicate health and constitution, and from certain points of view a "late developer." He came to be a protagonist of practical philanthropy, a reformer of prisons, and a powerful influence in the advancement of public health not only in England and Wales, but throughout Europe. In one of his notebooks there is an incomplete account of the number of miles he had travelled on the reform of the prisons. The total was over forty-two thousand miles. Later, he added to the length of his pilgrimage by an investigation on the sources of the plague, and embarked upon a tour of the lazarettos of Europe. It was while engaged on these journeys that he died from typhus fever at Cherson in the Crimea. Howard was an evangelist but he was also a scientist. His observations were accurate, his hypotheses firmly based, and his conclusions affected every aspect of prison and penal reform, including the physical well-being of prisoners and the prevention of their institutional diseases. He deplored the introduction of any kind of liquor into the prisons except milk, whey, butter-milk, or water, and advocated the addition of meat and vegetables to the diet.

There are two other names, both of foreigners, which must be brought within the conspectus of this discursive narrative, before we move on from the age of humanitarian ideals and action and return to Bentham and the nineteenth century. They are those of Bernardino Ramazzini and Johann Peter Frank. Both these men exercised their special gifts and genius in enlarging medicine in its social context, and were primarily scientists in the line of descent from René Descartes. In the latter's *Discours de la Méthode* there is a notable paragraph referring to the utilization of science in obtaining for mankind the enjoyment of:

> the fruits of the Earth and all its comforts but also for the preservation of health, which is without doubt of all the blessings of this life, the first and fundamental one. For the mind is so intimately dependent upon the condition and relation of the organs of the body, that if any means can ever be found to render men wiser and more ingenious than hitherto, I believe it is in medicine that they must be sought for. It is true that the Science of Medicine, as it now exists, contains few things whose utility is very remarkable ... but 'all that is known at present is almost nothing in comparison of what remains to be discovered, and that we could free ourselves from an infinity of maladies of body as well as of mind and perhaps also from the debility of age if we had sufficiently ample knowledge of their causes'.

It was in this spirit that Bernardino Ramazzini in 1700, having collected his material over many years, and being then in the sixty-seventh year of his own age, published his memorable *De Morbis Artificium Diatriba*. (In this context a diatribe is a discourse rather than an invective!) He sought to link many of his findings with the brief and often casual references to occupation and industry which are scattered throughout Greek and Latin literature, but this attribution of knowledge to the ancient writers is more generous than convincing. It is true that the occupational hazards of warriors are described with clarity and precision in Homer, and that there are references in Hippocrates to patients who might possibly have been suffering from pneumoconiosis. But it is not until the time of Lucretius, (circa 50 BC) that we find in *De rerum natura* that reference to the miners on certain Thracian islands which enquires "What malignant breath is exhaled by gold mines? How it acts upon men's features, and complexions. Have you not seen or heard how speedily men die, and how their vital fail when they are driven by dire necessity to endure such work?" Vitruvius, an architect and not a doctor had remarked upon the pallor of workers in lead glazes, and the risks of working in well shafts, with just the same observant eye as he had noted the goitrogenic powers of Alpine waters, and that the livid and unsound livers of animals might indicate deficiencies in local water supplies or contamination of the pastures. Most of these references in the ancient authors, however, are largely incidental—even semi-humorous, as in the frequent and detailed discussions of the hazards of the sedentary life—corpulence and varicosities. The only substantial contributors to the problems of the health of workers before Ramazzini, were Philipp Theophrast Aureolus Bombast von Hohenheim, otherwise known as Paracelsus and his contemporary Georg Agricola. Always a wanderer, though practising for a time at Einsiedeln and Basle in Switzerland, Paracelsus had arrived at certain conclusions on the basis of his studies amongst mine workers in Carinthia. He declared that all metals were harmful, and those who were employed in their production by washing or roasting were liable to suffer from asthma and consumption, and other grievous conditions, and in short to be the victims of "the metallic plague." Agricola, writing in 1550, was more specific in his description of the diseases affecting miners and metal workers and in his proposals for their prevention. Some diseases affected the eye, others the joints; others again, and these the most fatal, attacked and ulcerated the lungs. He instanced the fact that some women in the Carpathian Mountains had seven husbands, all presumably killed by these diseases.

One hundred fifty years later, Rarnazzini's great book was published in Modena. It appeared sixteen years after the death of Sydenham who, almost contemporaneously with Ramazzini, had added to the lustre of English medicine by his classical Hippocratic studies of the clinical features of disease, identifying individual infections with an unequalled precision of bedside observation against a meteorological and epidemiological background. Ramazzini, though an excellent clinician did not follow Sydenham's methods. During the twenty-two years which he spent at Modena before his translation in 1700 to the Chair of Medicine at Padua he had reviewed over fifty occupations ranging over the whole field of human activity. His points of observation were not limited to the hospital, but included the shop, the farm, the workplace, whether domestic or factory, even the study and the court. Amongst his human material are to be found the cleansers of cesspits, soldiers, scholars, midwives, opera singers, washerwomen, and many more. In the tradition of the Arabian physicians he proffered advice on the preservation of the health of princes. He did not suggest, however, like one of his predecessors that "no prince should rely on one physician, but rather on ten all speaking with the same voice."

The great value of Ramazzini's contribution lies in four things: his accuracy of observation and the application of the scientific method; his broad differentiation of occupational diseases into those which are due to contact with noxious materials, and those in which some other factor, such as ventilation, lighting, or posture, is, if not the primary, at any rate a contributory cause; his advocacy of simple, sensible methods of prevention, which took into account avoidance of poisonous materials, the other physical factors already mentioned, and the question of fatigue and monotony; and finally his proclamation that many of the diseases of workers were directly attributable to poverty. His own words are these: "It is hardly ever possible to give them any remedies which would completely restore their health. For they suffer from yet another drawback—they are very poor." Ramazzini placed his finger on two of the points which came within the social context of medicine—the effect of occupation and the impact of poverty.

When Ramazzini died at the age of eighty-one in 1714; Giovanni Battista Morgagni, then thirty-three, was with him. Morgagni became one of the greatest figures in medicine of all time. In his "magnus opus" the *De sedibus et causis morborum*, published in 1761, he continued in that rich treasury of human pathology, the tradition of Ramazzini. He identified the occupation of those upon whom he performed postmortems, noting wherever possible some vivid indication of their habits of life, so that we read of the ostler, near sixty years of age, being used to eating much and drinking very freely; the lady of leisure who nevertheless died of angina pectoris; the soldier with his aneurysm of the aorta eroding the chest wall; a certain man skilled in the art of music and his use of its instruments; a monk, who was noble both in his birth and his manners. In this approach to medicine as a science which comprehends the symptoms, signs, pathology, social conditions of the sick man or woman, and accepts the integrity of their personalities as individuals he had few who followed him until a much later date.

In this country Charles Turner Thackrah, dying prematurely in 1835 at the age of thirty-seven, was one of the pioneering spirits. A man of many gifts, a surgeon, and educationalist, he was also interested in the physical and social effects of environment, as visible in the evil conditions of the factories and the sordid housing of Leeds. The title of his book published in 1831 spells out the range of its interests as follows: *The Effects of the Arts, Trades and Professions and of Civic States and Habits of Living on Health and Longevity: With Suggestions for the Removal of Many of the Agents which Produce Diseases and Shorten the Duration of Life.* It was a serious, detailed study of some 250 branches of British industry and their respective significance for the health of those who worked in them. It went beyond the consideration of the purely occupational factors, and took into account the notoriously bad housing, the environmental squalor and the poverty which were associated "causae causantes."

Simon wrote both an epilogue to Thackrah's achievement and an epitaph on the man himself in these words:

> This special service Thackrah set himself to render, not under any official obligation or inducement, nor with any subvention from government but as his own free gift to a public cause ... Not less meritious than the assiduity and the care for truth with which he collected his facts were the unprejudiced good sense and moderation with which he weighed them ... He made it a matter of common knowledge and of State responsibility, that with certain of our chief industries, special influences, often of an evidently removable kind are apt to be associated, which, if permitted to remain, give painful disease and premature disablement or death to the employed persons.

Thackrah's own words are less circumspect than Simon's: "These evils are tolerated, even though the means of prevention is known and easily applicable."

If one were to seek to nominate candidates for the title of the "Father of Social Medicine," the claims of the great Bavarian, Johann Peter Frank would rank high. Born in 1745, he lived until 1828, and was thus almost an exact contemporary of Jeremy Bentham (1748-1832). Their minds and their ideologies had also much in common. A clinician of great skill, Frank was also an exceedingly able administrator, both of hospitals, and in the wider field of State Medicine. He was one of the most peripatetic of all European physicians moving from one professorial chair to another, and serving in turn at the Universities of Gottingen, Pavia, Vilna, St. Petersburg, and Vienna. He became the Director of the monster "Allgemeines Krankenhaus" in Vienna, in 1795, and later declined a chair in Paris which was offered to him by Napoleon himself.

Although Frank is reported as a student to have been already seized of the idea which ultimately blossomed forth as *The System of Medical Policy*, one is more tempted to believe that the actual stimulus and inspiration to embark upon his masterpiece were due to the death of his wife from puerperal fever. His first administrative reaction was to institute not only the inspection of midwives but to draw up a course for their better training. And from this he moved on to think about the whole question of the mother, the infant, and child care. This was at a time when Jean-Jacques Rousseau had already in *Émile* provoked European thought on the subject of the care of the child, much of it sentimental in substance, but much also of practical insight and importance. During Frank's wanderings

Rousseau's writings and their penumbra may have influenced him, but he was a powerful thinker in his own right. His thought moved both vertically and horizontally, and was never lost in any cloud of uncertainty. The *System einer vollstandigen medizinischen Polizey* sometimes inaccurately described as *A System of Medical Police* is a continuous study of the life of the human being. It begins before birth and extends to the very end of life. So planned it must deal with marriage, and having both the eugenic and the psychological outlook, advocates pre-marital examination and consultation, marriage guidance and sex instruction. It anticipates all our modern notions and practices by insisting on the early registration of the expectant mother, organized care at the confinement, and breast-feeding. It is enlightened about illegitimacy, and would provide adequately for foundlings and orphans, and as a preventive measure against the abandonment of the unwanted child, advocates something which very closely approaches our system of family allowances. These broadly constitute the subject-matter of the first volume published in 1779.

The second appeared a year later, and here the effect of *Émile* is obvious. It is devoted to child hygiene, and concerned with the school child, his properly heated schoolroom provided with appropriate furniture, his cleanliness, his physical training, his punishment (only rarely, if ever, corporal), and his careful avoidance of the strain of early rising, and the bolting of mid-day meals.

Volume by volume until the seventh and final one is reached, all the components of an elaborate and coherent system of health care are brought under review. The purity of food and beverages and the protection of the water supplies were amongst the subjects dealt with in his third volume. The question of clothing and the appropriate mode of dress were amongst his more minor concerns. But it was on the hygiene of the environment in all its sanitary ramifications, on good housing, on local amenities and facilities for recreation, and above all on the organisation of hospitals that he was most knowledgeable and insistent. He abhorred the social vices—alcoholism, prostitution and venereal disease—and advocated their suppression. His absolute modernity is shown in his concern about the prevention of accidents.

Only the control of communicable disease and the supervision of the workplace and the worker fail to find a place in this Utopia where even theatre-going and dancing were permitted but regulated. It was a panorama of life organized, if not disciplined on the most scientific bases and with the most beneficent but humourless intent. Garrison says of it: "Packed full of detailed regulations it might have lead to a social slavery, worse than that of feudalism, and in the hands of corrupt politicians might have become a stalking-horse for private vindictiveness in the regulation for marriages for instance."

It is a curious phenomenon that as and when humanitarianism was breaking the ice of indifference and apathy, when hospitals were being built throughout the country, when the first steps were being taken to abolish the slave-trade, when the prisons were being reformed, and the penal code was being shorn of much of its savagery, when the effects of obstinate, obstructive political restrictions had led in 1776 to the American Declaration of Independence, there were still those who yearned, like Johann Peter Frank, for the statutory limitation of personal liberty in action if not in thought. On the other hand, there were still many who regarded the elementary principles of the New Humanitarianism as being based on mutual helpfulness, and the congruence of social duties and social rights. It was to this conception, leading ultimately to the greatest happiness of the greatest number, that Bentham applied his energies and intellectual powers.

> It is a curious phenomenon that as and when humanitarianism was breaking the ice of indifference and apathy, there were still those who yearned for the statutory limitation of personal liberty.

John Charles was chief medical officer for the Ministry of Health, United Kingdom from 1950 to 1960. In addition he served as the chairman of the executive board of the World Health Organization and is a founding member of the Faculty of the History of Medicine and Pharmacy of the Society of Apothecaries of London.

12

Crane Brinton, the New History, Retrospective Sociology, and *The Jacobins*

Howard Schneiderman

THE JACOBINS was published in 1930, at the end of the first recognizably modern decade in American history, and at the beginning of the decade known for the worst economic disaster in that history. Both decades were revolutionary, each in its own manner, sparking the interest of then contemporary social scientists. Many of these intellectuals, already preoccupied by the events of the Russian Revolution and by Joseph Stalin's rise to power in the new Soviet state, were very much interested in theories of change in general and, more particularly, in revolution.

Indeed, accompanying Brinton's *Jacobins*, there were numerous books published within a few years of each other that looked deeply into violent means of change and ideological radicalism. In 1925, Brinton's colleague at Harvard, Pitirim Sorokin, published *The Sociology of Revolution*, soon followed by Lyford Edwards' 1927 study *The Natural History of Revolution*. In 1929 and 1930 a host of now classic works on revolution and ideology were published. Among these were Karl Mannheim's *Ideology and Utopia*, Harold Lasswell's *Psychopathology and Politics*, Ortega y Gasset's *Revolt of the Masses*, and Sigmund Freud's *Civilization and Its Discontents*. Another classic study of social change, albeit of a non-revolutionary sort, was Robert and Helen Lynds's *Middletown*, published in 1929. Besides these indispensable works on ideas and change, another of

Brinton's colleagues at Harvard, Talcott Parsons, brought out his English translation of Max Weber's *Protestant Ethic and the Spirit of Capitalism*, in 1930. Certainly Weber's *Protestant Ethic* must be numbered among the greatest and most important studies of how ideas interact with and impact social, political, and economic structures. All told, these were a few very fruitful years in social science history.

Brinton's book on Jacobinism was the first of three volumes that he wrote during the 1930s on revolution which, taken collectively, helped him become the most prominent theorist of revolution for decades to come. The best known of these three books, *The Anatomy of Revolution*, published in 1938 was revised twice and continues in print today as one of the most highly cited works on the subject. The third of Brinton's books on revolution, *A Decade of Revolution*—specifically about the revolutionary events in France beginning in 1789—was published in 1934 and remains a useful volume for those interested in the subject.

Pareto was the most well-known and discussed sociologist of the period beginning in the late 1920s through the decade of the 1930s.

Brinton was fascinated by two strings of thought which he weaved together in *The Jacobins*. The first was the Jacobins as a revolutionary party, and as a case study of how such parties are organized and operated. The second strand of thought was about how one can gather pertinent information to describe and analyze a political party.

As he worked his way through the material, Brinton based much of his thinking on a narrow band of the available social science theories of the day. He only mentioned three social scientists: Vilfredo Pareto, James Bryce, and Moisey Ostrogorski (these last two were mentioned in passing). These three were emblematic because they crossed disciplinary lines easily and with intellectual alacrity, and because they each wrote definitively about things essential to understanding the Jacobin movement.

Although we might not think of him as such today, Pareto was the most well-known and discussed sociologist of the period beginning in the late 1920s through the decade of the 1930s. Today, economists consider his Pareto efficiency, or Pareto optimality theory an indispensible intellectual concept. In Brinton's day, Pareto, who was ubiquitous in the sociological literature as well as in the popular press, was best known for his theories of residues and derivations which set the stage for understanding the relationship between ideas and behavior. More important to Brinton, however, was Pareto's theory of "the circulation of the elites," which helps us to make sense of much of the data about the revolutionary Jacobin party presented in the book.

Bryce, author of what may be one of the two best books ever written about American political society, *The American Commonwealth*, was the first president of the British Sociological Society, and the fourth president of the American Political Science Association. His pioneering studies of public opinion, and of political parties had an obvious influence on Brinton's thinking about the Jacobins. Ostrogorski was a lawyer, historian, political scientist, and sociologist whose *Democracy and the Organization of Political Parties* was one of the founding works in political sociology, and obviously known to Brinton. Based on his understanding of these theorists, Brinton was able to conceive of *The Jacobins* as a work of "retrospective sociology." It was also, as the subtitle indicates, *An Essay in the New History*.

Among other things, the New History was about the place of "great men" in historical context, an issue still argued about today, but wildly so a century ago. In March of 1906 William James famously addressed faculty and students on Founders' Day at Stanford University. "The wealth of a nation," he said, "consists more than anything else in the number of superior men that it harbors." During that same year one of Columbia University's well-known historians, James Harvey Robinson, was already formulating his thoughts about what would soon become known as the "New History." In his article, "Recent Tendencies in the Study of the French Revolution," published a month after James' speech at Stanford in the April issue of the *American Historical Review*, Robinson called for a more pragmatic and populist history that leaned on the social sciences, and that separated itself from the military and political modalities that most often led to mere biographies of superior men. Indeed, Robinson's New History was a leveler: down with the high and mighty, up with the average man. While both James and Robinson were a generation ahead of Brinton, their differing views about elites and elitism would have a notable affect upon him.

While James emphasized the creative and leadership roles of superior individuals, Robinson emphasized the history of common men and women. James died in 1910 after a brilliant career in philosophy and psychology at Harvard University, during which he became one of the founders of Pragmatism, America's only home-grown school of philosophy. James represented the prevailing opinion of social scientists in the late nineteenth and early twentieth centuries that great men were the engines of social change and progress. Thus, in a famous essay published in 1880, "Great Men, Great Thoughts, and the Environment," James likened genius to Darwin's notion of variation:

> The relation of the visible environment to the great man is in the main exactly what it is to the 'variation' in the Darwinian philosophy. It chiefly adopts or rejects, preserves or destroys, in short *selects* him. And whenever it adopts and preserves the great man, it becomes modified by his influence in an entirely original and peculiar way. He acts as a ferment and changes its constitution, just as the advent of a new zoological species changes the faunal and floral equilibrium of the region in which it appears.

But this elitist viewpoint was about to come under fire by the New Historians, such as James Harvey Robinson.

Two years after James' death, Robinson published *The New History*, which challenged historians to become more like quantitatively oriented social scientists and less like biographers of superior men and notable events. Indeed, Robinson laid out his populist manifesto for history in his chapter "History for the Common Man," which amounts to a call for a history *of* the common man.

In 1915, three years after Robinson's *The New History* was published, Clarence Crane Brinton entered Harvard University as an undergraduate. Brinton returned to Harvard in 1923 to teach history after having received a PhD from Oxford University that same year. In 1930 Brinton published *The Jacobins: An Essay in the New History*, and thus began a decade-long opening act in a remarkable career that made him one of the leading American public intellectuals from the 1930s until his death in 1968.

An acolyte of Robinson's New History, Brinton began his book on Jacobinism by placing history among the social sciences and by relegating "kings and courtiers, statesmen and generals to the more graceful talents of the new biographers." "History," he said, could no longer "make the study of exceptional individuals an end in itself." Thus, the home-side of James' pragmatism was echoed in Brinton's idea that the historian must "study the behavior of many men in the past because he ultimately wishes to understand the behavior of many men in the present." But, the far side of James' philosophy that considered the study of superior men essential to the workings of democracy was a challenge to Brinton's outlook as a New Historian. Mere chronology was not enough according to Brinton. The discovery of laws that predicted the uniformity of human behavior was the stuff of the New History. Brinton's own evaluation of his book as a study in "Retrospective Sociology," is a key for us to unlock the meaning of *The Jacobins*, and beyond that to think about why sociology drifted away from making better use of its own "great man" theory: Max Weber's theory of charisma.

Who were the Jacobins? Or, perhaps, a better question would be what was the Jacobin Club? The original, and eponymous, Jacobin Club was named such because the Dominican convent in which it was housed was located on Rue St. Jacques, Paris. The Club took its name from the Latinate form of Jacques: *Jacobus*. As Brinton nicely put it for his American readers, "they were unofficial political groups, similar in many ways to the Anti-Corn Law League, the Anti-Saloon League, or the Ku Klux Klan. They got things done. They were, in short, the sort of agencies of political action made familiar by the studies of Bryce and Ostrogorski." With this last reference, of course, Brinton suggests that the Jacobin Clubs were first and foremost political parties. This is a key point, because as a party the Jacobins vied for power in the government, but they were not the governing body itself.

Before Brinton's time, sociologists as varied as Herbert Spencer, Lester Ward, John Commons, Moisey Ostrogorski, James Bryce, Max Weber, and Robert Michels had published analyses of parties that are still relevant today. Brinton who modeled his work so as to be able to call it retrospective sociology, was aware of at least significant parts of this literature, and he was well aware that parties take many shapes one of which was represented by the Jacobins. Through political organization, propaganda, and violence, the Jacobins promoted paranoid visions of enemies within France, and were by and large responsible for bringing on the Reign of Terror soon after the Revolution had begun. These extremist visions led to the public executions of King Louis XVI, Queen Marie Antoinette, and many thousands more during the thirteen months of the Terror, which lasted from June 1793 through July 1794. At its end, the Terror turned upon its own leaders, including Saint Just, and Maximilien de Robespierre, who were themselves executed by their own infamous guillotine that had beheaded thousands, perhaps tens of thousands, "enemies of the Revolution."

Robespierre was surely the most famous Jacobin, but he isn't mentioned by Brinton until the middle of the second chapter of *The Jacobins*, and then only in passing. For many old school historians and biographers it would have been inconceivable to understand the political force and importance of the Jacobin Clubs to the French Revolution without placing Robespierre at the head of the line. Thus, John Morley's *Robespierre*, published in 1886, Jules Michelet's 1899 biography, *Robespierre*, and Hilaire Belloc's *Robespierre: A Study*, published in 1901, are representative pre-New History works concentrating on the Jacobins through their most famous representative. Brinton, who knew that there were hundreds of thousands of Jacobins spread throughout thousands of Clubs during the Revolution relegated Robespierre to a mere signpost pointing to a chronology of events that readers would have to turn to biographers to learn more about. It speaks volumes about the New History that it took Max Weber, a sociologist rather than an historian, to capture the irreplaceable and ironic part played by Robespierre to the Revolution, when he wrote that "the charismatic glorification of 'Reason,' which found a characteristic expression in its apotheosis by Robespierre, is the last form that charisma has adopted in its fateful historical course." Brinton and the New Historians were enamored with quantitative analysis, while charisma, a singular manifestation of the great man theory of historical change, which couldn't be easily quantified, was all but ignored.

Other than it being written by one of the foremost historians of the twentieth century, what is the specific value of *The Jacobins*? There are two answers to this question. First, Brinton does a brilliant job uncovering the demographic, ideational, and historical nature of the Jacobin's political movement. He carefully combed through the innumerable primary and secondary sources to firmly supplement the biographical material available about Robespierre and the other Jacobin leaders. Taken together, the older type of political and biographical history and the new, more sociological history gives us a remarkably in-depth view into the nature of the Jacobin movement. Second, by offering such a detailed and useful collective portrait of the Jacobins, Brinton ignites fireworks between the old and new histories. By doing this, Brinton sheds light on an essential difference between history and sociology that still needs to be resolved; namely, the relationship of theory to explanation and vice versa.

In the mid-1960s when discussions in the social sciences were often focused on "the new sociology" and the old clash between qualitative versus quantitative approaches, George Homans, a long-time friend and colleague of Brinton published a small book called *The Nature of Social Science*. As young scholars at Harvard, both Homans and Brinton had been key figures in the Pareto seminars organized and led by Lawrence Joseph Henderson, a biologist turned sociologist. Homans dedicated *The Nature of Social Science* to Henderson, his mentor as well as Brinton's. Both Homans and Brinton dealt with the question of how to reconcile the scientific aspects of social science with the humanistic elements of their books.

Homans sums up the problem of theory and explanation in history and sociology as follows: "History ... possesses an enormous range of empirical findings, findings, that is, of a rather low order of generality... The historians have looked for general propositions in their subject matter, found none that they recognized as such, and concluded that they had no theories." Homans' wasn't through yet, and he later suggests that "if history has many explanations and no theories, sociology sometimes appears to have many theories and no explanations." In many ways, Homans' critique of both history and sociology is derived from his early study and embracement of Vilfredo Pareto's theories about the place of reified ideas—or what he called sentiments—to sociological explanation. Homans learned this, as did Brinton, under Henderson's tutelage. Both incorporated these concerns over theory and explanation in their work and we see this as early as 1930 in *The Jacobins.*

Brinton's description and analysis of the organization of the Jacobin Clubs relies in part on his knowledge of the sociology of voluntary associations. It is clear that he was acquainted with the burgeoning literature in this area, including Simmel's *Soziologie*—especially the chapter on "The Secret and the Secret Society"—and Charles Horton Cooley's *Social Organization.* Indeed, Brinton's own contribution to this body of theory, namely his 1930 essay on "Clubs" in the *Encyclopedia of the Social Sciences*, demonstrates his expertise in this subject so crucial to his work on the Jacobins.

As he begins his chapter on the organization of the Jacobin Clubs, Brinton suggests that our preconceived view that these revolutionary Clubs represented something new because voluntary political associations "could hardly have a place in a polity molded by Louis XIV." True, but, as he shows, the real antecedents of the Jacobin Clubs were not political bodies, but the well-known literary societies, on the one side, and the mostly Masonic secret societies, on the other.

As Brinton describes them, the literary societies, *chambres littéraires*, started out as clubs for bourgeois scholars in the seventeenth century, but by 1760 they were ubiquitous in both urban centers and provincial towns. What had begun as associations for intellectuals to spread egalitarian and reformist propaganda, as Brinton called it, had now become social clubs, and among their members were middle class lawyers, merchants, doctors, and *rentiers.* In the three decades between 1760 and the outbreak of the Revolution "the literary societies closely organized by committees of correspondence and united by a central committee did, by propaganda, caucuses, electioneering, and public manifestations, influence political events."

If the literary societies constituted in Brinton's words a "political machine," then the secret societies, such as the freemasons, were a cultural one. Warning his readers that reliable information about secret societies is difficult to obtain, Brinton nevertheless ventures forth and shows that "many freemasons were among the founders of the first Jacobin Club."

More important than the sheer number of masons who were also Jacobins is the ritual and normative effect that the freemasons had on the clubs. Here Brinton allows the reader to flesh out some of Simmel's brilliant insights into secret societies in general and freemasonry in particular. Although Simmel is not mentioned by name in *The Jacobins,* we know that Brinton was very much acquainted with his work because he cited it prominently in his article on "Clubs" cited above, published in the same year. Simmel says that "there are perhaps no other external traits, which are so typical of the secret society ... than the high valuation of usages, formulas, and rites." Simmel uses the freemasons to show that "the vow of secrecy refers exclusively to the form of the Masonic ritual," rather than to its contents. Brinton's discussion of the Masonic origins of Jacobin practices underscores Simmel's point. Hence, among other rituals, both the masons and the Jacobins shared the "fraternal embrace" between high officials and guests, the use of "brother" as a form of address, the use of "blackballing" as part of the secret voting procedure for admission to the clubs. As with the masons, the Jacobins had elaborate secret codes for recognizing each other, detailed examples of which Brinton provides.

Having shown that the Jacobin Clubs did not arise *de novo*, but out of the wellsprings of long established middle class voluntary associations such as the Masonic and literary societies, Brinton turns his attention to the enormous pleasure that the Jacobins took in participating in politics. Brinton shows no acquaintance with Max Weber's essay "Politics as a Vocation," published a decade before in Germany, but his description of the exuberance of the Jacobins for political life with no financial rewards evokes Weber's dichotomy of "living for" as opposed to "living off" of politics, as only an upper-middle-class leadership could do. As Brinton puts it, the Jacobins "had talked about politics, and read about politics for years, but until this blessed Revolution they had never been able to give themselves the illusion that they were in politics."

To round out the organizational aspects of the Jacobin movement, Brinton gives the reader a detailed description of the estimated number of Clubs, which he thinks may be near seven thousand and the number of members which, during the Terror, may have ranged from five hundred thousand to one million. Perhaps Brinton's most sociologically advanced thinking about the Jacobins concerns the relationship of leaders to the rank and file. He shows that only a very small minority among the Jacobins actually took the lead in one Club after another. These elite groups manned the committees and formed what Brinton calls an "undisguised oligarchy." Brinton's discussion of this oligarchy echoes the ideas of Vilfredo Pareto about the "circulation of elites," which is not surprising since Pareto was the most prominent sociologist during the late 1920s through the 1930s. Besides the general fascination with Pareto among social scientists during this time, Brinton was, as mentioned above, a prominent figure in the famed Pareto Circle at Harvard University. Indeed, *The Jacobins* might be read as a case study in "the circulation of elites," as the middle class Jacobins replaced aristocrats and the monarchy in positions of authority.

According to Pareto, the circulation of the elite could induce social changes in leadership in either a gradual pattern of replacement or by violent revolution. Brinton takes up this question of how changes in the elite occured in his chapter on membership in the Jacobin Clubs. "There is a current theory," he wrote, "that all violent revolutions are the work of men who are disconnected with the society from which they rebel almost wholly because they are failures in that society." One would have thought that Tocqueville's beautifully researched and argued theory that revolutions are more likely to occur in places where the people have rising expectations rather than among the more permanently poor would have forestalled what Brinton called "the maladjustment theory" of revolution. The effect of Brinton's analysis of the membership of the Jacobin Clubs was to underscore Tocqueville's premise, namely that the most active areas of violence during the French Revolution were those where the middle classes were on the rise. According to Brinton, "the names of Jacobins are almost never found among the poor."

So "the Jacobin was neither noble nor beggar." In fact, as Brinton carefully shows, the Jacobin Clubs cut across class lines, sometimes accepting nobles as members, sometimes those who were working class, and mostly those who were middle and upper middle class. These revolutionaries were by and large successful in their occupations and communities. These observations brought Brinton closer to Tocqueville than to Marx.

The middle class orientation of the Jacobin Club was consistent with their tactics. One of the earliest and most enduring elements of political action associated with the Club was the shaping of public opinion through propaganda. Brinton uses both public opinion and propaganda in a thoroughly modern way because he thought that these methods of mass appeal and manipulation are often thought to be "primitive until quite recent times." This wrote Brinton is "quite false, like so many other assumptions based on the dogma that men were never ingenious before the industrial revolution."

Brinton's understanding that contemporary hubris about our supposed superiority is unwarranted leads the reader to rethink commonplace assumptions about progress and modernity. The many thousands of Jacobin Clubs became centers of news and views. They had reading rooms filled with newspapers from across France, as well as pamphlets and books. They all had committees of correspondence, and Brinton demonstrates that the Clubs spent a small fortune on printing and mailing packets of propaganda circulars and pamphlets. This emphasis on the power of the word harks back to the Jacobin Clubs' antecedents in the literary societies, and underscores the middle and upper middle class backgrounds of most of their members.

The revolutionary propaganda efforts of the Club extended to public education of young and old alike about the rights of man, and popular sovereignty. They sponsored prizes for reading aloud the Rights of Man, which Brinton calls the "new gospel." The Jacobins' insight about using propaganda methods for mass persuasion shows them to be more modern than we might think at first blush. This observation extends to the political acumen of these societies. Brinton carefully shows that the success of the Jacobins in pushing their agenda in elections and in policy making was "due to the simple fact that they were organized and disciplined, that they voted as a unit." Here we could easily see the relevance of the political sociology of Michels, Ostrogorski, Bryce, and Weber, all of whom saw that politics is driven by these tactics.

Up to 1793 the Jacobin Club was more or less "at peace with the government," according to Brinton, even though as a collective political party they tried to unseat incumbent officials in elections.

During the thirteen months of the Reign of Terror stretching from the summer of 1793 through the summer of 1794, the Jacobins had effectively eliminated all opposition, and its members had taken control of government. In the year-long Terror, according to Brinton, "all government officials, both elective and appointive, were for the moment of the same party; all were Jacobins." During this period we could easily make use of Pareto's work on the circulation of the elites to understand how the Jacobin Clubs "provided a reservoir from which the new officialdom could be drawn," as Brinton put it.

Even before the Terror—and certainly during it—the Jacobins use of violence, both physical and mental, was notable, especially in the form of rioting and hazing against their opponents. The numerous examples Brinton provides allow us to see just how apt is Lord Acton's famous phrase, "Power tends to corrupt, and absolute power corrupts absolutely." Without significant opposition during the period of the Terror, the Jacobins used violent means to get their way in the public life of France, as well as to insinuate their ideas into the private realm. They did this by interfering with morality and exerting pressure on individuals to conform to collectivist economic positions. A lock box hold on power always seems to open up possibilities for totalitarian temptations to come to the fore. The Jacobins were neither the first nor the last movement to monopolize power and use violent means for glorified ends. From the Inquisition centuries before to the Nazi and Communist monopolies of power centuries after, the Jacobin inspired Terror demonstrates what can happen when viable opposition parties disappear.

> Even before the Terror the Jacobins use of violence, both physical and mental, was notable.

While various forms of radicalism have been institutionalized throughout history, the Jacobins mounted one of the most successful campaigns to insinuate their ideas into the institutions of their society. In his attempt to create an "ideal typical" understanding of the Jacobins, Brinton sums up the aims of his average model:

> An independent nation-state, a republican form of government, universal manhood suffrage, separation of church and state; equal civil rights for all, and the abolition of hereditary distinctions and social privileges; a competitive industrial and agricultural

society, with private ownership of property, but without great fortunes and without dire poverty; a virtuous, hard-working society, without luxuries and without vices, where the individual freely conforms to standards of middle-class decency.

Brinton's description of the average or ideal-type Jacobin makes him seem to be much like an average contemporary European or American. Herein lays the eternal problem of reconciling ends and means, and the issue is not aims, but the means by which one pursues those ends. Radicals such as the Jacobins rarely seem to trust people to arrive at the same conclusions, or to share the same goals that they have without forcing them to move in those directions. Contrarily, liberals seem more readily to trust that individuals can and should make up their own minds about value-laden issues, and that they can be persuaded through reason to share the same goals as they have.

In America, from the Revolution on, liberalism has been prevalent, while radicals have been positioned to the left and right of the prevailing liberal center. Not so for the Jacobins. Not only were they cultural Puritans, as Brinton put it, but they were radicals who wanted to force their ideologies upon everyone else. Nothing new here under the sociological sun: think of radicals on the left and right such as Mao-ists, Soviet, and Chinese communists; Nazis, Khmer Rouge, and Mc-Carthyites. Brinton, an old-school academic liberal, understood that the Jacobins, though middle class and well-intentioned, had become dangerous radicals that fostered terrorism. *The Jacobins*, published almost on the eve of the European democratic meltdown that would lead to the unspeakable horrors perpetrated by Hitler, Stalin and their like, is a sound guidebook for understanding an earlier, different, but, kindred meltdown of democratic morality and liberalism.

Certainly one of the most notable parts of *The Jacobins* is Brinton's chapter, "Ritual." A commonplace concept today among social scientists, ritual was a relatively new addition to their theoretical toolbox when Brinton published this book. Here again we see his debt to Pareto, who discussed ritual extensively as a social need to express one's sentiments through actions, as part of his third type of "residues." Three of the most prominent participants in Lawrence J. Henderson's Pareto seminars at Harvard, later remarked about the importance of ritual to Pareto's theory of society: Brinton himself in his 1954 retrospective article "The Residue of Pareto" published in

Foreign Affairs; Talcott Parsons in *The Structure of Social Action* and in reviews of *Pareto's Mind and Society*; and George C. Homans, in his 1941 article on "Anxiety and Ritual," in *American Anthropologist.*

Others at Harvard who were heavily influenced by Pareto, especially by his thoughts on ritual, and who were well-connected to Brinton at this time were Elton Mayo, whose office was next to Henderson's in the Business School, and W. Lloyd Warner, an anthropologist whom Mayo brought to Harvard. The fifth and final volume of Warner's still important Yankee City series, *The Sacred and the Dead*, shows that he found ways to link Pareto's and Durkheim's work on ritual in one of the great ethnographic accounts of American rites. As a footnote to the rippling and enduring influence of Pareto, consider the now well-known influence of W. Lloyd Warner on Erving Goffman, his student at the University of Chicago, whose work relied on the ritual concept that Warner derived in part from Pareto and Durkheim. Brinton's chapter in ritual among the Jacobins is an earlier, but no less important manifestation of the ritual concept.

As the Revolution progressed toward its most famous phase, the Terror, Jacobin rituals progressed too, from the pedestrian to the almost fanatical. At the beginning these rituals entailed mostly communal meals, festivals, the planting of liberty trees in town squares, and other cultish imitations of religious rites. As Brinton writes, "there were civic marriages, civic baptisms, civic burials. Revolutionary songs were written, and the songs became hymns. The Declaration of the Rights of Man took on the authority of scripture." In time, these rites of revolution were underscored with statuary; for example, busts of the apostles of the Revolution were placed throughout the Jacobin meeting halls. Brinton makes the obvious connection between Jacobinism and forms of fanatical religion, and he shows that the divide between political ritual and religious rites can easily be blurred in what the anthropologist Victor Turner would later call "liminal periods."

This exercise in the New History, or what Brinton eventually called retrospective sociology, offers less of an alternative to the older narrative forms of history and more of an addition to it. Brinton's collective biography of the Jacobins is an early trend setting example of what Lawrence Stone labeled "prosopography" in his eponymous 1971 *Daedalus* article. Thus, Brinton's book is an important contribution to the social sciences as an example of a successful new methodological technique, a correction to previous historical assumptions of the lower class origin of the Jacobins, an insight into how elites circulate, and as an exploration of the use of ritual in revolutionary movements.

Based on his early work on revolution, Brinton became one of the most popular commentators on revolutionary activity during the middle of the twentieth century. His work extended beyond revolutions to the history of ideas, and among his many other books he is known for publishing *Nietzsche* in 1941, *Ideas and Men: the Story of Western Thought* in 1950, *A History of Western Morals* in 1959, *The Shaping of the Modern Mind* in 1963, and *The Americans and the French* in 1968.

Brinton was also one of the most prolific public intellectuals writing in influential journals and magazines. Thus, he published a staggering number of articles and reviews—over a hundred in all—in the *Saturday Review of Literature* during the 1930s and 1940s. Brinton also published twenty-nine essays and reviews in the *New York Times* between 1946 and 1965. He also published articles in such diverse but important venues as *Daedaus, Journal of the History of Ideas, The Sewanee Review, The Journal of Modern History, The American Historical Review, The Journal of Economic History, The Harvard Theological Review, Foreign Affairs, Political Science Quarterly,* and *The Journal of Higher Education,* among others. He served as President of the American Historical Association in 1963. In February 1968, Brinton testified at the Fulbright Senate hearings during the Vietnam War about the nature of the Viet Cong. He died in September 1968 at the age of seventy, having just retired from Harvard University.

Howard Schneiderman is professor in the department of anthropology and sociology at Lafayette College. He is the editor of *The Protestant Establishment Revisited, The Hindrances to Good Citizenship,* and has authored numerous articles. In addition, he has won numerous awards, including the Marquis Distinguished Teaching Award and the Crawford Award for classroom instruction.

13

Herbert Spencer and the Science of Ethics

Jonathan H. Turner

HERBERT SPENCER was born in Derby, England, in 1820. For a man who would become one of the most read scholars of the nineteenth century, it is interesting that he had only a few months of formal education; instead, he was tutored by his father until the age of thirteen and subsequently by his uncle in Bath. Spencer was thus trained privately, "home schooled" in today's terms, but he nonetheless received a very solid education in mathematics and science. This more technical education led Spencer to see himself as a philosopher and, as would become clearly evident, he thought "big" at a time when the sciences, and academia in general, were becoming more specialized. Perhaps, if he had had a formal education, he would have been more restrained in his thinking, and yet, despite the fact that his work swam against the intellectual tide, Spencer was to be widely respected among scientists, academics, and the lay public. His books sold more than one hundred thousand copies, even after most of them had been issued in serial form in various journal-like publications. His work was not a popularization of topics. Instead, it was a grand philosophical scheme that sought to unify the physical, biological, and social sciences under a general set of evolutionary principles. Just to be sure that the scheme of his philosophy was sufficiently grand, these evolutionary principles were the "first principles" or "cardinal principles" of what he termed his Synthetic Philosophy, which was to include ethics in addition to all of the sciences.

Spencer's intellectual star rose rapidly in the five decades following 1850, when his first major work, *Social Statics*, was published and in the subsequent decades he produced *The Principles of Psychology* (1855), *First Principles* (1862), *The Principles of Biology* (1864-67), *The Study of Sociology* (1873), *The Principles of Sociology* (1874-96), and his last work, *The Principles of Ethics* (1894-98). These books represent thousands of pages of scholarly endeavor, and the two bookends to Spencer's Synthetic Philosophy, *Social Statics* (1850) and *The Principles of Ethics* (1894-98), serve as the treatises on ethics. Even though Spencer had first began publishing what became *The Principles of Psychology* in 1854, *First Principles* lays out the basic laws governing the operation of the physical, psychological, biological, sociological, *and* ethical universes. *First Principles* is the theoretical equivalent of Emile Durkheim's *The Rules of the Sociological Method* (1895) in that they come after the first major work in his Synthetic Philosophy. Spencer seemed to feel that it was necessary to formally lay out the "laws," loosely derived from the physics of Spencer's time, that explained the operation of the psychological, biological, sociological, and ethical domains of reality. Only in sociology in his *The Study of Sociology* did Spencer make a more methodological and epistemological argument for a science of human societies; indeed, Spencer makes a much better case for social science than does Durkheim in *The Rules*.

> Spencer's work was not a popularization of topics. Instead, it was a grand philosophical scheme that sought to unify the physical, biological, and social sciences.

What were these "laws" of the universe as conceived by Spencer? He offered three general principles:

1. The indestructibility of matter;
2. The continuity of motion in a given direction; and,
3. The persistence of the force behind movement of matter.

From these three general principles, he developed several corollaries:

4.   The transferability of force from one type of matter and motion to another;

5.   The tendency of motion to pass along the line of least resistance; and,

6.   The rhythmic nature of motion.

Spencer added even more principles when he began to talk about the laws of evolution and dissolution:

7.   The instability of homogeneous;

8.   The multiplication of effects when force strikes homogeneous matter;

9.   The segregation of matter in motion to explain differentiation of matter during the course of evolution; and,

10.   The integration or dissolution of differentiated matter.

These principles are, to say the least, not very clear, but they connote an image of how evolution occurs. For Spencer, evolution revolves around forces hitting homogeneous or simple forms of matter, with the force and motion pushing on the homogeneous to create differences, which as matter is segregated in space leads to differentiation of matter as the forces pushing on it continue to do so. Differentiation produces new forms of integration of differentiated matter into a more "coherent" whole. Whether the matter be physical, biological, sociological, or ethical, this same set of principles ultimately explains the evolution of these various realms of reality.

Let me try to make more sense of this rather convoluted terminology, even for Spencer's time. Here is Spencer's "law" of evolution as it was laid out in *First Principles*: evolution is "an integration of matter and concomitant dissipation of motion; during which the matter passes from an indefinite incoherent homogeneity to a defined coherent heterogeneity; and during which the retained motion undergoes a parallel transformation."[1] Let me restate his ideas in simpler language. For Spencer, evolution is the movement of domains of reality from simple to more complex forms, driven by forces that continue to push on the elements of these forms and that cause differentiation. Differentiated forms are, however, vulnerable to dissolution as they become isolated from each other, and thus, there must be mechanisms by which these differentiated elements are integrated to produce a more coherent whole. Spencer did not argue that integration is inevitable; indeed, disintegration often occurs. What he did argue was that integration of differentiated matter or elements of each realm of reality is a condition of evolution from simple to more complex forms. Thus, whether "the matter" is the physical elements of the universe, the forms of life, the structure of mind as it affects thought and behavior, the structure of societies, or the conduct seen as ethical, these all evolved from simple, homogeneous to more differentiated and coherent whole that, by various mechanisms, became integrated.

Ethics were seen by Spencer as a kind of conduct unique to human beings, and like the evolution of the physical, biological, psychological and social universes, the evolution of ethics is governed by the first principles. Spencer thus pursued a "science of ethics," a chimera that he along with countless others have pursued but could never firmly grasp. Yet, throughout *The Data of Ethics*, Spencer invokes his "law" of evolution to explain how the biology, psychology, and sociology of human conduct moves from a simple to more complex forms. This differentiation of the body, psychology of organisms, and their organization into social structures sets the stage for the fullest and most "coherent" expression of ethics, which evolve along with bodies with larger brains, with greater capacities to think, reason, emote, sympathize, and cooperate (by building divisions of labor and social structural interdependencies). Until these conditions are in place, ethics is limited and often conflated with religious morals, law, and political authority. Ethics in its most developed and coherent form is a morality in which individuals seek to meet their own needs, while at the same time taking into consideration others' right to do the same. Morality is, in Spencer's eyes, the most evolved form of coherent heterogeneity because it increases the integration of individuals by activating a kind of "altruistic egoism" that leads people to meet their own needs, while sympathizing with others and attempting to increase these others' happiness.

Like much of Spencer's work, *The Data of Ethics* (1879) was initially published as a book and then integrated into the two-volume *The Principles of Ethics*. In his multi-volume treatises on psychology, biology, and sociology, Part I of each of these sets of volumes is devoted to "the data of" psychology, biology, and sociology; and so, in *The Principles of Ethics*, this volume on the data of ethics is Part I of the last big work by Spencer. In all of his scientific volumes, save for *First Principles* (1862), Part I is followed in Part II by a set of chapters termed "The Inductions of (biology, psychology, sociology, and ethics)." Spencer's books are filled with illustrative data and in his work on sociology, Spencer even developed a tabulation system for recording data on a wide variety of societies. These data were assembled by professional scholars and constitute the fourteen volumes of *Descriptive Sociology* (1873-1932), which continued to be published long after Spencer's death in 1903 (he left money in his will for their completion). But, Part I of each set of volumes in his Synthetic Philosophy is not like *Descriptive Sociology*; the chapters do not summarize data but, rather, lay out the terrain to be

> Woven through Spencer's analysis of ethics is a struggle for existence, with the fittest winning out in this struggle and the unfit losing.

explored with his law of evolution. In the case of The *Data of Ethics*, Spencer develops somewhat more systematically the argument first articulated some thirty-five years earlier in *Social Statics* (1850).

In *Social Statics*, Spencer made a name for himself and coined one of the most famous phrases in the English language: "survival of the fittest." Spencer was, in reality, the father of Social Darwinism, but it is Darwin's name that became attached to the unfortunate school of thought that emerged in the early decades of the twentieth century. In Spencer's philosophical works, this kind of language is very prominent and it is repeated in *The Data of Ethics* and in all of the subsequent parts of *The Principles of Ethics*. In his autobiography, Spencer complained about the grief this view of selection—that of nature picking out the fittest and vanquishing the less fit—had caused him, and his complaints might ring more true if he had not invoked these arguments again four decades later in *The Data of Ethics* and in the other Parts of *The Principles of Ethics*.

Thus, woven through Spencer's analysis of ethics is an undercurrent of social life involving a struggle for existence, with the fittest winning out in this struggle and the unfit losing—all for the betterment of persons and society. This does not seem to be a happy view of the biological and social universe, and yet, the subtitle of *Social Statics* is revealing: "*or, the Conditions Essential to Human Happiness Specified, and the First of Them Developed*." The basic argument is summarized well near the end of *Social Statics*:

> Each member of the race ... must not only be endowed with faculties enabling him [sic] to receive the highest enjoyment in the act of living, but be so constituted that he may obtain full satisfaction for every desire, without diminishing the power of others to obtain like satisfaction: nay, to fulfill the purpose perfectly, must derive pleasure from seeing pleasure in others.[2]

The chapter titles of *Social Statics* carry this theme through such topics as "The Rights of Life and Personal Liberty," "The Rights to Use of the Earth," The Right of Property," "The Rights of Exchange," "The Rights of Women," "The Right to Ignore the State," "The Limit of State-Duty," and so on. Spencer was a utilitarian when arguing about ethics, and in today's language, he would probably be characterized as "right wing," "libertarian," or even sympathetic to the Tea Party in the United States. Individuals have rights to use their abilities to achieve happiness, as long as they allow others to do so and rise to their level of competence in the struggle for existence. Yet, this would be too simplistic because Spencer was a sophisticated scholar, and these kinds of arguments are recessive in all his other works outside these first and last volumes on morality and ethics. Still, despite the several decades where these ideas in his work on psychology, biology, and even sociology were downplayed, they all come back in Spencer's last major work. This basic argument remains the same in *The Data of Ethics* and now, after four decades, Spencer developed this argument with embellishments from his general law of evolution and a legacy of work in the biological and social sciences. His goal, as noted earlier, was to develop a "science of morality and ethics." And thus, the "data" in *The Data of Ethics* are more of a conceptualization of the nature of ethics and their evolution to the point where they can provide a new level of "coherence" to the biology of humans, to their psychology and behaviors, and to their patterns of organization in highly differentiated societies.

Spencer opens his analysis of ethics with a more general statement on conduct, which he sees as the behavioral adjustment of "means to ends." Ethical conduct is a special case of conduct in general and carries a conception of right and wrong. Like all else in the universe, conduct has been evolving. As differentiation and complexity increase, so does the range of means that can be adjusted to ever-more ends or goals. When societies and organisms are simple, there are limited means and ends, but out of "the struggle for existence" of organisms, including humans, conduct evolves. Unfortunately, Spencer falls prey to ethnocentric visions of savages only living in the "here and now," but his general point that complex forms of social organization have evolved out of the "struggle for existence" generate the conditions where individuals have more options and means to realize goals is perhaps sound. Yet, "the perfect adjustment of acts to ends in maintaining the individual ... and rearing new individuals ... is only possible as war decreases and dies out." This is a constant theme in Spencer's sociology, and it carries over to his analysis of ethics. War increases the centralization of power (what Spencer termed "militant societies"), which imposes morality and limited options on persons. Only with the development of what he denoted as "industrial societies" (not to be confused with "industrialized societies"), where power is recessive and individuals have more freedom to choose options, is truly ethical conduct ever possible. Such industrial societies can evolve among relatively simple and small populations, but with population growth and social complexity of industrial societies (again, not industrial in the modern sense), the potential for ethical conduct increases. And, with the evolution of markets as dynamic forces, militant societies should finally give way to industrial societies (Spencer's "end of history" argument), thereby increasing the capacity for humans to engage in ethical conduct.

For Spencer, the definition of ethical conduct emphasizes that when actions positively affect the person, his or her offspring, and more remote others in society, it becomes ethical. Thus, as persons adjust means to ends, conduct should produce "agreeable feelings" for self, offspring, and others; indeed, there must be a "surplus" of positive to negative feelings as means are adjusted to ends. And, emphasizing the major theme in *Social Statics*, Spencer argues that ethical conduct must not only produce positive emotions in self, offspring, and others, it must always allow others the right to realize pleasure for self, offspring, and others in their conduct.

For Spencer, the essence of ethical conduct is often obscured and obfuscated by moral, theological, and political preaching. He devotes considerable energy to rejecting any view of ethical as defined by institutional systems and he does so with an interesting twist. Religion, morals, politics, social contract theories, and all similar imposed thought systems, he argues, lack an adequate conception of causation. They simply assert a causal agent that imposes its will, ignoring the real causal dynamics in human societies. Thus, there is need for a scientific basis for determining morality because the "business of science [is] to deduce, from the laws of life and the conditions of existence, what kinds of action necessarily tend to produce happiness, and what kinds to produce unhappiness."[3] Spencer then goes on to employ his vocabulary of evolution as laid out in *First Principles*, stressing that there are physical, biological, psychological, and sociological aspects to all conduct, and especially ethical conduct. Thus, a science of ethics must be based upon how evolutionary dynamics have operated to move realms of reality from simple and unstable homogenous masses to more complex and coherent structures. Thus, "[we] have to enter on the consideration of moral phenomena as phenomena of evolution; being forced to do this by finding that they form a part of the aggregate of phenomena which evolution has wrought out."[4] These considerations set up the next few chapters that examine how the process of evolution as manifested in the physical, biological, psychological, and sociological realms can add to a proper view of ethical conduct.

Physically, life never reaches an equilibrium, but only an "moving equilibrium" and displays a movement from "an indefinite incoherent homogeneity to a definite coherent heterogeneity..."[5] which is manifested in people's avoiding excess, being more precise and calculating, and thus adjusting appropriate means to measured ends.

> For Spencer, the essence of ethical conduct is often obscured and obfuscated by moral and political preaching.

Biologically, the body has more complex structures and functions, and thus moral conduct revolves around sustaining not only the vigor of the body's moving equilibrium, but also that of offspring and others.[6] He emphasizes that vigor of the body is based upon positive emotions and that "each individual and species is from day to day kept alive by pursuit of the agreeable and avoidance of the disagreeable..."[7] For "every pleasure rises the tide of life" and "every pain lowers the tide of life." Thus, evolution works to produce a "balance of functions,"[8] by adjusting the smooth functioning of bodies and the emotions aroused in performing these functions. Pleasure is, therefore, a part of the evolution of life, and so it must be for humans with their advanced psychology.

Psychologically, mental life adjusts acts to ends, and in "higher forms" becomes "the subject matter of ethical judgments," which in turn are linked to the arousal of feelings as these constitute the motives that direct thought and action.[9] Evolution has also changed the nature of self-preservation, which has moved from immediate and proximal responses to events to more instrumental, long-term calculations of potential outcomes in adjusting means to ends. Immediate impulses and feelings are subordinated to more complex and compound mental states and feelings that are essential to civilization. Immediate gains are sacrificed for the greater good of society at large; and thus, the evolution of morality and ethical conduct is for the "general good" to be increasingly considered in preference to proximate satisfactions, immediate feelings, and simple mental states. More complex feelings and thoughts that take into consideration of acts on others and society are essential to ethical conduct, but this new way of thinking and feeling has only been possible "after political, religious, and social restraints have produced a stable community [which gives people] sufficient experience of pains, positive and negative, sensational and emotional, which crimes of aggression cause, as to generate a moral aversion to them..."[10] From these experiences a more general, "abstract consciousness of duty" arises, thereby increasing the likelihood of ethical conduct.

The evolution of society, like the body and mind, produces a more complex set of structures and functions, which, over time, evolves to a recognition that individuals must learn to cooperate to achieve ends. With high rates of conflict and concentrations of power in the state, this fundamental property of "industrial" (decentralized politically) societies cannot be realized, but as war gives away to cooperation, the expansion of the voluntary division of labor leads individuals to see that the "maintenance of agreements…depend(s) on the special and general welfare."[11] Ethical conduct can evolve under these conditions because the goal of conduct is to meet one's own needs, those of offspring, and more remote others in the divisions of labor, and in so doing, promote the general welfare. And in so orienting conduct, a person experiences even more positive emotions, because with cooperation there is an extra dose of pleasure from the positive sanctioning of ego by others; and since there are many

> Altruism has been essential, but must always be secondary to egoism.

potential means and ends in complex societies, so there is more ways of generating pleasure for self and others.

After addressing various potential criticisms of this line of argument, and unfortunately, portraying "savages" as cruel compared to the "harmonious cooperation" of industrial societies, Spencer employs a clear turn of logic in *The Data of Ethics* to analyze egoism and altruisms. He begins by asserting that egoism has a primacy over altruism and, moreover, that it evolved first. Sadly, he repeats his "survival of the fittest" arguments when arguing that altruism supports the less fit and burdens the superior and keeps them from realizing their full level of fitness. For Spencer, "the undue subordination of egoism to altruism is injurious…"[12] It is these kinds of statements that ruined Spencer's reputation in the twentieth century; and they appear mostly in this crude form in *Social Statics* and *The Principles of Ethics*, and yet, they sully the much more scientific work in his biology, psychology, and sociology. And, he certainly cannot complain, as he did near the end of his life, about the consequences that these rather extreme statements have had on our retrospective view of Spencer's philosophical work.

From this rocky beginning comes the more interesting part of the argument. He duly notes that altruism has been essential, but must always be secondary to egoism. Altruism is critical to giving pleasure to offspring and others, and it has been evolving, from the biological basis of parental sacrifice for children, to a new basis built around cooperation in more complex societies revealing extended divisions of labor. Along with altruism, sympathy becomes an essential mental and emotional state because it disciplines pure egoism, pushing people to meet their own needs and, at the same time, to give pleasure to others. Altruism alone erodes the drive necessary to build societies, but egoism without sympathy erodes the capacity to cooperate in complex societies. And so, the best egoism is altruistic; and it is this growing interdependence between egoism and altruism that allows more complex societies to be built from ethical conduct.

Spencer takes a mild swipe at John Stuart Mill's greatest happiness principle, modifying this basic idea to emphasize that informal and legal contracts cause voluntary cooperation and "all [of] this growth of voluntary cooperation—this exchange of services under agreement, has been necessarily accompanied by decreases in aggressions of one upon another, and increase of sympathy; leading to exchange of services beyond agreement." There is now a substantial body of findings in the exchange literature to document that frequency of exchanges increases positive emotions above and beyond the utilities of the things exchanged; and so, Spencer was not far off the mark in this assertion. The key is *voluntary* cooperation rather than cooperation imposed by structures of power, religion, and even law. The "right mix" of egoism, efficiency of means to ends, and sympathy can only evolve when war and conflict (and hence consolidation and centralization of political power) are eliminated. It is from the evolution of complexity in divisions of labor, coupled with the decline of militancy, which sets the stage for ethical conduct in which individuals gain egoistic pleasure from giving pleasure to others. As egoism is conditioned by altruism, it gives rise to sympathy of others; and the more complex the division of labor and the means to be adjusted to ends, the more this mix of egoism, altruism, and sympathy can radiate across the conduits provided by networks of structural differentiation, and the more pleasure will be experienced by individuals at locations in these networks.

In this way, ethical conduct is simply an outcome of the more general evolutionary movement from simple, homogeneous to complex, heterogeneous formations in physical matter, bodies, psychologies, social structures, and conduct in these structures. There is a sound line of argument here, although it is tainted by some rather extreme statements about peoples in simple societies and by assumptions about "survival of the fittest." The last chapter in *The Data of Ethics* addresses the scope of ethics, revealing the same kind of complex mix of useful and highly biased thinking. Ethics are, Spencer concludes, tied up with justice, which is displayed by the most highly evolved of all animals: humans. Conduct is "just" when there is a "due proportion between returns and labor"[13] or what today we would conceptualize as distributive justice or equity: rewards should be proportionate to the costs and investments of individuals in receiving rewards—a line of argument well supported by experimental research. Spencer emphasizes that perfect equality is contradictory to happiness, which is not supported by data under all conditions, but for Spencer, happiness only comes from efficient adjustment of means to ends, disciplined by a sense of sympathy, a commitment to realize one's own needs and goals in proportion to effort while allowing others to do the same and, most importantly, trying to increase the pleasure of these others. As he always argued, coercively based inequalities cause pain and thus get in the way of happiness because such inequalities are not just. Rewards are not proportional to efforts undertaken to receive these rewards and, moreover, ends to means are neither efficient nor guided by egoism disciplined by altruism and sympathy for others but, instead, by the imposition of power and constraint.

> Ethical conduct is simply an outcome of the more general evolutionary movement from simple, homogeneous to complex.

What, then, can we say about Spencer's main line of argument in *The Data of Ethics*? Much of it does not fit with contemporary views on ethics, and yet, the underlying utilitarianism does resonate with the contemporary capitalist world. The more general theoretical argument—which seems overdrawn at first, especially because of its ethnocentric portrayal of pre-literate peoples—is perhaps salvageable. Evolution has produced more complex organisms, more complex mental and emotional capacities in higher mammals (and some birds as well), and more complex societies. Behavior and conduct have thus become more complex because in differentiated societies, there are more options, and more potential means to more ends. Individuals must form relations with many diverse others in more types of situations, and in order for them to operate, egoistic impulses must be constrained by sympathy and a sense of the need to sustain the more inclusive structures in which conduct occurs. Exchanges do evoke positive emotions when rewards are proportionate to costs and investments, and the data indicate that one consequence is that people develop commitments to each other and larger-scale social structures. Commitments are fueled by positive emotional energies that force individuals to consider the general welfare of others, along with the desire to meet the egoistic needs of self. Thus, if we backfilled much of Spencer's argument with findings from contemporary social and biological science, the argument does not seem as preposterous as it does in Spencer's rather ideologically and ethnocentrically loaded prose.

Still, is it possible to have a science of ethics, as Spencer firmly believed? I think that the answer here must be very qualified. Spencer used his laws of evolution to cast his argument that conduct evolves like all other realms of the universe; and that the most evolved conduct is ethical. Is this true? Only by assertion. Thus, Spencer's "science of morality" becomes a kind of *ad hoc* justification for his ideological biases rather than a reasoned use of science to explain the conditions under which morality evolves and ethical conduct is perceived to occur. We can use science to establish these conditions, but Spencer's search for the true form of ethical conduct reflects his own morality dressed up in the language but not substance of science. Indeed, his definition of ethical conduct might be something that you and I could agree is a good thing, but others in religion, politics, law, and other domains of society, where ideologies always generate a corresponding ethics, might disagree. Moreover, is it really possible to have big, complex societies without concentrations of power, conflict, stratification, and other forces that get in the way of ethical conflict as conceptualized by Spencer? Certainly not, and Spencer's own sociology makes this very clear. Thus, Spencer appears to ignore his treatise on sociology, written just before *The Data of Ethics*. Moreover, his accumulating volumes of *Descriptive Sociology* that laid out ethnographic and historical data on societies certainly do not support his argument for the evolution of ethnical conduct, or even a society where complex divisions of labor (inevitably) lead persons to be efficient goal seekers trying to meet their egoistic needs while giving pleasure to others. Such behaviors do occur, not just in complex societies, but also in those inhabited by what Spencer, like most Europeans at the time, portrayed as "savages."

> Spencer's works do not portray a world that has ever existed, but a world that is likely to exist only in Spencer's industrial utopia.

Thus, there is a naïve quality to all of Spencer's works on ethics. They do not portray a world that has ever existed, but a world that is likely to exist only in Spencer's industrial utopia (or in Marx's, Durkheim's or any other theorist's who begins with a theory of progressive evolution). But, Spencer does try to bring science—a rather crude version of it, in some respects—to discussion of morality. The issue of morality and ethics is as relevant today as it was in Spencer's time and there has been no lack of effort since to define what is "absolutely moral." Science can perhaps answer questions about when actions are likely to be seen as moral, perhaps even about what kind of moral world view is produced under different social and psychological conditions, but I doubt if science can establish by any set of standards that denote what the "best morality" or the "most ethical" form of conduct is. Thus, Spencer employed his science to address the wrong question; instead, he should have emphasized more than he did that complex, differentiated societies with decreased concentrations of power and less inequality than in other societal formations have a tendency to produce a particular kind of moral and ethical worldview—perhaps something along the lines of his utilitarian-inspired views. But to assert that this is the most ethical and most moral view is to jump from science to advocacy, from explaining why something occurs to what *must* occur.

The debris of intellectual history is filled with such efforts and Spencer, like all of those today who offer a moral vision, will only add to this pile of misguided moralizing. The question is not what is absolutely moral, but why people under what psychological and sociological conditions act (or fail to act) in terms of some morality of their own making. As scientists, this is a question that we can answer; and we can even pursue this question beyond the social sciences, as Spencer did, and ask: what forces of evolution have produced animals with brains that are capable of constructing morality? This too is an answerable question. And so, if ethics is to be our subject matter, science can answer some questions, but not the ultimate question of what is the best morality, or what is the most ethical ethics. There will always be no shortage of ideologues hell bent on telling us what is ethical and immoral, but science should not be one of them. And this is perhaps Spencer's biggest mistake.

I have long believed that Spencer has been mistreated and ignored and that he is just as important an intellectual figure as other canonized figures of the nineteenth century. Indeed, I have advocated that if we ignore his two bookend projects on morality, his contribution to social science is considerable. Yet, because he mixed his science with his ethics, the integrity of his science is often called in to question. This is rather unfair given the propensity for most social thinkers in the nineteenth and even twentieth centuries to do so. Thus, it is the "conservative slant" of his ideology—liberal in his time, conservative in our time—that is perhaps the real problem. Moreover, even though the argument is conservative by today's standards, Spencer did go part of the way explaining the structural conditions—high differentiation, low levels of stratification, and restrictions on use of power—under which the ethics he saw as evolving will emerge. Thus, *The Data of Ethics* is worth our reconsideration, both for the mistakes that it makes, and for its suggestions about why "industrial" societies—driven by markets in political democracies—tend to favor utilitarian-inspired ethical views.

Notes

1. Herbert Spencer, First Principles (London: Williams & Norgate, 1862), 343.
2. Herbert Spencer, *Social Statics: or, The Conditions essential to Happiness specified, and the First of them Developed* (London: John Chapman, 1851), 448.
3. Spencer, *Social Statics*, 91.
4. Spencer, *Social Statics*, 96.
5. Spencer, *Social Statics*, 101.
6. Spencer, *Social Statics*, 113.
7. Spencer, *Social Statics*, 118.
8. Spencer, *Social Statics*, 132.
9. Spencer, *Social Statics*, 139.
10. Spencer, *Social Statics*, 155.
11. Spencer, *Social Statics*, 178.
12. Herbert Spencer, *The Data of Ethics* (London: Williams & Norgate, 1884), 125.
13. Spencer, *The Data of Ethics*, 311.

Jonathan H. Turner is distinguished professor of sociology at the University of California, Riverside. He has been visiting professor at numerous universities around the world, including Cambridge University, Universitat Bremen, and Shandong University. His latest book is *The Sociology of Emotions* (with Jan E. Stets).

14

Hannah Arendt as Radical Conservative

Irving Louis Horowitz

I.

THE EMPHASIS HANNAH ARENDT placed on totalitarianism, as a social system in which legal authority is rooted in a total political institution with an organizational fabric to match, transformed her work from one of many studies of "the authoritarian mind" into the study of a totalitarian behemoth—an investigation far removed from mental acrobatics or leadership crazes. Were traces of fascism and communism to have been buried in the rubble of World War II, concern about totalitarianism might not have been possible. But it is precisely the continued force of extremism in politics after the war that made possible the reception given to Arendt's *Origins of Totalitarianism* in the early 1950s.[1] Not only did certain regimes—though defying labels, retained the strong odors of fascism and communism—remain in force, but the outcome of World War II did not so much eliminate totalitarianism as provide it with a humanist ideology. The peace that followed the war only minimized the scourge of the fascist arm of the "ism" in totalitarianism. Arendt knew this, and others did as well, but she uniquely attached the label that defined the dangerous organism as a whole.

The outcomes of the war led to a great deal of concern about state power. Even more, it created strong opposition to top-down solutions. The Depression came to an end, not with a federal program but with munitions requirements and mass mobilization. Such apparently remote areas like mental health and illness and hospitalization were subject to withering examination. Solutions based on massive institutions for everything from housing to hospitals became suspect; they did not do away with poverty nor reduce illness. The total institutions within social systems became subject to the same withering critiques as Arendt proposed in relation to the political systems. In some strange way, Erving Goffman's dissection of the hospital as a total institution became the personalized equivalent of Arendt's analysis of the nation-state as a total institution.[2] The social consequences of the defeat of National Socialism made for a new situation. There was a collective sigh of relief that the totalitarian regime could be defeated in at least one end of the European political scale, while at the psychological end collectivism could be put back in the box—at least temporarily—by David Riesman's lonely crowd operating in highly privatized persons.[3]

> The defeat of National Socialism made for a collective sigh of relief that the totalitarian regime could be defeated in at least one end of the European political scale.

It was the survival of a democratic culture that made Arendt a possibility. She was preceded by Karl Popper[4] and the sources of the open society; George Orwell and the technological wellsprings of the closed mind. Their experiences with war, along with many others, gave the culture of post-World War II a different flavor in the West than what remained ensconced by totalitarian systems in Eastern Europe and Southeast Asia. Indeed, all these tendencies reinstated the psychology of the person into a high status, even more than direct confrontations of democratic modalities with authoritarian systems, account for this turn in the popular culture. Whether conservative or radical, whether by Philip Rahv and William Phillips in the *Partisan Review* or William Buckley and Whitaker Chambers in the *National Review*, the same undercurrent of the return of the person capable and entitled to make free choices in an open society was re-established.

Some people do not fit easily into conventional categories on the political spectrum. I have discussed this myself on two other occasions: to describe George Sorel in my *Radicalism and the Revolt against Reason*,[5] and later in *C. Wright Mills: An American Utopian*.[6]

But since there are different kinds of radicalisms and no less distinct forms of conservatism, such categorizations continue to attract my attention. Variations on the theme of totalitarianism also help to remind us that absolute systems, even those self-promoted, are subject to laws of sociological change and biological evolution.

Dictionary definitions are not much help in this search for a sure footing. *The American Heritage Dictionary* for example has as its first definition of radicalism an ideology "arising from or going to a root or source." Then as its second definition it speaks of the word in terms of "carried to the utmost limit; or extreme." Turning next to conservative, this popular dictionary of knowledge speaks of the word as first signifying "tending to oppose change; favoring traditional views and values. Its second definition is rather aesthetic rather than political: "Traditional in style, not showy." It continues with a psychological twist: "moderate, cautious and restrained." For my purposes, by combining going to the root or source while favoring traditional "views and values," we have an individual who spends a lifetime on an intellectual tightrope. I believe that this correctly summarizes what Hannah Arendt sought to achieve. If she at times fell short of such an ambitious undertaking, she at least attempted to bring about some sort of synthesis of competing, indeed combative ideologies in the world of political power.

In the case of Hannah Arendt, I have proudly worn her name as an honorary attachment to my own for more than thirty three years now, although Horowitz (and its spelling variations) is not exactly a feeble name in the world of scholarly endeavor and artistic achievement. Such gratuities expressed, the broad picture of personal traits and professional achievements is extremely complex. Writing about Hannah is an exercise in how the biographical constantly intersects with the academic. The purpose in this essay is to deal with a person who has incited strong opposition, even rage, as someone who clearly tried to bridge gaps in academic training and intellectual outlook. This is a most dangerous game. It is also the most rewarding.[7]

II.

I hope here to summarize the passion of Hannah Arendt's scholarship, and the diversity of her writings on important public issues and philosophical underpinnings. To do just this is itself quite a challenge, which I have undertaken with a keen sense of its fragmentary nature. But how could it be otherwise? She was a feminist who loathed the idea of being defined in such a way; a dedicated worker for and writer about specifically Jewish causes, who invited scorn and even vilification from Jewish writers for her views; an advocate of German values of its highest aspirations who assumed their superiority to just about any other linguistic and national tradition; and also a person whose very name is identified with anti-Nazism and loathing for its murderous totalitarian traditions. For her, "Nazism owes nothing to any part of the Western tradition, be it German or not, Catholic or Protestant, Christian..." She was a passionate figure who remained intellectually wary about excesses of emotions; a severe rationalist who feared that such a frame of mind could easily lead to the engineering of the human soul.

> Arendt's is not, nor was she ever, one of Heidegger's "children."

Hannah Arendt's career is a lesson in the life of the human mind: I have argued that she is not, nor was she ever, one of Heidegger's "children" as the very fine historian of ideas, Peter Watson claims in *The German Genius*.[8] Rather, she was very much the child of Immanuel Kant, as she herself persuasively argues in her trilogy of volumes on that greatest of German philosophers. This is not a small argument about intellectual pedigree. Kant is author of a large masterpiece on perpetual peace, and Martin Heidegger, when looking to incite a "planet in flames," could draw as a solitary conclusion that "only from the Germans can come the world historical reflection, provided that they find and preserve their German element." As a rather different German, Karl Marx, once remarked, all cats may not be gray, but neither are they all black and white. Indeed, usually discussing shades of gray is what makes reflections on our universe, whatever be the areas, interesting and even compelling.

Those who identify themselves firmly within a single tradition or culture may escape the problem of relativism, but they suffer greatly from the problem of absolutism. It is that tension, that strain between traditions, cultures, and systems that I have taken from Hannah's writings. The dialectic on the ground is what makes her such a compelling figure in twentieth-century ideas and, I would argue without doubt, makes her a compelling force well into the twenty first century. The title selected for this essay, "Hannah Arendt as Radical Conservative," is not aimed at word play, but as a painful illustration of a society and a culture at odds with itself for most of the twentieth century. Unlike the French, who thought of the Enlightenment as a struggle against the shackles of religion and theology, the German Enlightenment attempted an accommodation of religion and theology as gnarled braches of the Enlightenment well worth preserving. Even such a supreme logician, rationalist, and marginal Jew as Ludwig Wittgenstein could end his philosophical investigations leaping into the arms of mysticism and subjectivism. One might well argue that Hegelianism as a system broke apart and left for the twentieth century in tatters: a German Right and a Russian Left, with little to show for synthesis as Hegel himself expected from history. Arendt was scarred by a tradition, but never beaten by it.

III.

What I take to be a supreme virtue of a scholar whose ideological tendencies were never simplistic or tendentious in its demands from others made her a target for those who think of Left and Right or Radical and Conservative as self-bestowed badges of honor. As a result political rhetoric often degenerates into what logical positivists from the Carnap School decried: Here are my preferences, do thou likewise. What follows from this position are the charge of Michael Knox Beran, who claims in the *Pathology of the Elites* that Hannah Arendt's work represents essentially "The Tyranny of the Social Imagination." He argues the case against those "arrogant classes" elites operating from ivory towers and in violation of public squares. How or why Arendt fits into such a mold remains more a puzzle than critique.[9] He states:

First: Arendt makes a "fetish out of politics." She recognized the dangers in absolute state power, but provides no options for its limitations in the town square or the public space. She failed to develop a sense of how the "social managers of capital" could be halted.

Second: Arendt asserts that politics bring forth that which is great and radiant. It is the presumed source of transcended freedom and the greatest achievements of what people are capable of. In this way, the critic of dictatorship she offers does not and cannot get beyond politics into a public arena of culture.

Third: Arendt flirted with millennial politics that incorporated the prophetic element of the French Revolution. Her regard for the Greek tradition is based on a skewed reading that even in democratic Athens, politics were essentially shabby political animals.

Fourth: The sources of her mistakes were a result of undue emphases on politics and a failure to see the problem in terms of individualism, or in some cases, the absence of a private sphere that could make room for poetry.

Fifth: Arendt failed to provide a prescriptive setting for her concerns. They were embedded in political process and political history. The cultural domain of architecture, music, and literature seemed alien to her character and professional interests.

Sixth: Some of her works were written with the support of the Walgreen, Rockefeller, and Guggenheim Foundations, and hence her positive interpretations of the civic arts and culture in general were tilted and tainted.

These sorts of commentaries reveal a conservative reflection of what the hard Left held against Arendt. Many of the charges seem limp in retrospect not to mention quixotic—a crooked public square at best. The idea that political power can be offset by poetic power is still a holdover from the romantic age of paternalistic fascism, especially the moderate sort of D'Annunzio. Indeed, the prospect of poetry even holding on to the margins it has is more of an issue. Arendt does not claim nobility for politics as such, so much as the nobility of the struggle for democratic options confronting totalitarian realities. In this, Arendt did not flirt with the French Revolution so much as confront it with the greater success of the American Revolution that preceded it. It was the compassion of the latter rather than the passion of the former that ultimately held the key to democratic rule.

The idea that Arendt did not advance a series of predictions is especially unfair, since it is precisely the nature of a democratic regime to provide descriptions that can be debated rather than prescriptions that can be enforced. The final charge that she received funds from major foundations is especially absurd, since it presumes that such foundations have ideological axes to grind that can be imposed, when in fact they are directed by boards quite independent of the name brands providing the original funding. Such a line of criticisms from the Right not only mirrors Left imaginations of a devious united elite, it reflects unease with new conspiracies that reflect a continuing concern with the very fears Arendt had of a totalitarian state.

> Arendt does not claim nobility for politics as such, so much as the nobility of the struggle for democratic options.

IV.

When the shouting of acolytes abates, and the hissing of critics turn to whispers, we are left with the last woman standing—Hannah Arendt. That is not because she was infallible or did not make terrible miscalculations in personal judgments even more than in intellectual assessments. Rather it has to do with the infusion of one enormous word, totalitarianism, as part of the rhetoric of the century—hers and now ours—of an "ism" that transcended inherited notions of nationalism, patriotism, and globalism. She went beyond the horrors of World War II, of struggles between Nazi Germany and Soviet Russia, above the war cry of democracy and dictatorship. She saw and understood in her heart and soul the unified nature of political evil as wrapped in the word totalitarianism.

Few words reach that level of consciousness to move people to understand that which unites and divides. Perhaps Alexander Solzhenitsyn's *Gulag* provided a summarized unifying element. These simple words embraced so much in a compact way. Whether the concentration camps were built by Nazis in Poland or by Communists in Siberia, the meaning of death by political will, and life spent resisting such leadership, organized the penumbra under which we all must travel. It is not that Arendt invented a word; just that she gave it a unifying dimension that made horror a quotidian event. She gave the word not only its meaning, but defined the source of its horror. Such an achievement must not be ignored or ever forgotten.

The word itself was introduced, largely by European scholars, before the outbreak of World War II. We can thank Michael Florinsky in 1938 and Carlo Sforza in 1941 among a small handful of political theorists for giving the term some shape, although hardly with a sense of a dynamic that extended beyond the nation state.[10] In the aftermath of Hannah Arndt's work, we have efforts to deepen its theoretical meaning by people such as Carl J. Friedrich in 1968,[11] Jean-François Revel in *The Totalitarian Temptation* in 1977,[12] Franz Borkenau in *The Totalitarian Enemy* in 1982,[13] and a substantial number of dissertations and histories in the later part of the twentieth century, including works by Michael Curtis, Ellen Frankel Paul, and Abbott Gleason.[14] They all share a deep concern and most often a loathing for the implications of the absolutist state. But for the most part, they had a European vision limited to the Nazi-Communist framework.

The present day literature has moved beyond a single geographical sphere, or political leadership. The cultural framework bequeathed to us by British scholars like Leonard Schapiro[15] and earlier, the expatriate novelists working in English are owed a deep and abiding gratitude for this development, especially Aldous Huxley in *Brave New World*, and in a more coherent format, George Orwell in *1984*[16] and *Animal Farm*, and Arthur Koestler in *Darkness at Noon*.[17] They provided a serious framework in a popular literary format for a rebuke of totalitarianism that found expression in all sorts of popular media. It may be a failing, but it is a sad fact that people respond with a greater sense of urgency to specific killings and compulsive assaults on human dignity than to news releases on mass slaughters or terror bombings.

It is intriguing as a matter of the history of ideas to see how, with the migration of scholars to North America as a result of the Nazi regime in particular, the center of research in the subject of totalitarianism also shifted its locus and center of gravity. After the explosive 1951 publication of Arendt's *Origins of Totalitarianism*, a new generation of post-Arendt scholars emerged who do not debate the term, or even need to promote her achievement. She neither had a "school of thought" nor sought such a dubious honor. These people first summarized the living, breathing expression of horror that is deeply embedded in the societies that persisted and still exist long after the Europeans lifted above the ashes of two World Wars. Now the term has moved on to studies of specific cases in which totalitarians fused and cemented a variety of evils that went under all sorts of more limited names with which we are all quite familiar—now more than ever cloaked in political religions of great pretence and little accomplishment for ordinary people. Unwittingly, Arendt advanced a word to the level of a paradigm, a mode of organizing thought so that the world of ideas would never quite be the same. The literature on totalitarianism, indeed on Hannah Arendt as such, has grown to such proportions that we can only provide a sample of the new literature, and its implications for understanding the importance of Arendt to the present.

If there was a distinctly American element introduced to the discussions Arendt's book stimulated, it was in the 1980s, in which people like Peter Berger[18] and Michael Novak,[19] went beyond her in linking anti-totalitarianism between nations to exploring connections between capitalist dynamics and democratic options. In this context, they asserted that the open market allowed for the free expression of ideas and human rights as a central concern. In an odd way, for them the capitalist economy displaced the Protestant Ethic as the keys to Max Weber's insight. In tandem, the two keys of economy and religion made possible a large number of channels for building a wall between freedom and tyranny. To be sure the economists of an earlier European period preceded such formulations of economic sociology, but not quite with the intellectual certainties the Americans expressed. In this, the American style differed from Arendt in emphasizing the potential for escaping totalitarianism not so much through State power as such, but on the capacity of the economy as an instrument from below. Electoral politics in Europe were never quite a populist activity such as trade union industry shut downs. The rough and tumble of American expansionism westward fueled a political system, while it calmed the thirst for urban rioting.

For the most part, it is historians, and not social scientists, who in particular have taken the lead in such efforts at synthesis. One fine such effort is by Timothy Snyder of Yale University, whose work on the Ukraine as the soil upon which Hitler and Stalin engaged in a slaughter of the innocents so transparent as to require both dictatorships to develop ad hoc theories to explain differences that might account for their slaughters.[20] Stalin had to obliterate the fact that Jewish history was uniquely singled out by the Nazis on Russian soil. He "explained" it by identifying the carnage as between German troops and Russian nationalists. Hitler had a similar problem of seeing the slaughter of the Jews as a stage in the purging of his empire of other victims—sexual deviants, communist gangsters, and medically deficient weak individuals.

> The rough and tumble of American expansionism westward fueled a political system, while it calmed the thirst for urban rioting.

This immense falsification endorsed by totalitarian instruments in the legal codes as well as the military barracks could hardly obscure the fusion of the Holocaust with the Great Terror. Snyder is wise enough and forthright enough to say that "the Nazi and Society Regimes have to be understood in light of how their leaders strove to master these lands, and saw these groups and their relationships to one another." With an understanding of the totalitarian chain of command, such apparent anomalies remained. Now they can be revealed. Snyder speaks for himself in this regard—and for the present killing fields as well.

"Today, there is widespread agreement that the mass killing of the twentieth century is of great moral significance for the twenty-first. Mass killing separated Jewish history from European history, and East European history from West European history. Murder did not make the nations, but it still conditions their intellectual separation, decades after the end of National Socialism and Stalinism." The author appreciates that the homelands of the victims lay between Berlin and Moscow, and that they became blood lands after the rise of Hitler and Stalin. What Arendt's critics did not understand is that she was not and never was "the child of Heidegger," only a teenage intellectual, star-struck lover.

In point of fact, it is the children of Hannah that have won the day. The work of Mark Mazower, program director of the Center for International History at Columbia University, covers another part of the totalitarian tapestry: the linkage of the Nazi State and how it managed to rule Europe—clumsily, filled with contradictions, but with increasing dosages of terror unknown to any earlier civilization.[21] In its efforts to conquer all of Europe and its variegated peoples, the Nazis encountered a myriad of ethnic figures, and working class laborers that it could not easily control. Indeed, the regime turned increasingly to terrorizing its own people. The rate of executions rose exponentially as the war went badly for the Wehrmacht.

Occupation of foreign territories, especially in areas of strong opposition to Nazism on both religious and political grounds required exceptional measures—first to accommodate and then to suppress all opposition. In that process, the needs of the German armed forces for allies diminished, and the capacity to move victims of the Nazi regime diminished sharply. The imperial ambitions of Germany under Hitler fueled the totalitarian system to the point of crystallizing opposition on the part of foreign nations and the passive subservience on the part of the German people. The Third Reich found that totalitarianism while a potent weapon when confined to the State apparatus, loses much of its compelling force as it moves to quiet the occupied masses. The recourse to the Holocaust in this sense was the last attempt to the consequences of anti-Semitism upon the Jewish people as a mechanism for constraining opposition. The existence of a military force placed at the disposal of a Nazi ideology that determined that *all* Jews, gypsies, homosexuals, and physically disabled were to be exterminated. Such a strategy made the Nazi war machine unable to solicit external support on a mass basis.

Mazower is clear in demarcating 1945 as a turning point. "Human rights talk in the 1940s was mostly just that, and took a long time to become politically influential." He concludes that "in the early 1950s, commentators such as Hannah Arendt saw things very differently: for her the point was to force states to grant rights and to solve the problem of statelessness that way." Thus, quite unlike Beran's critique of her position, Mazower points out that the "sheer scale of the postwar refugee problem itself not only bolstered international cooperation among agencies and relief works, it also constituted a powerful argument for rebuilding strong states with the capacity to take in and care for those people who needed help." It turns out that it was Arendt's critics who carry the burden of what Norman Podhoretz disdainfully terms Arendt's "flights of metaphysical fancy."

The critics of Arendt saw the theme of totalitarianism as a more advanced stage of authoritarian rule. It was seen as something different than Stalinism, and even a reason to support Soviet actions. This certainly was the view of Gershom Scholem, who saw World War II as an attempt to eradicate not only the entire Jewish people, but its history and culture as well.[22] This is indeed a theme articulated by the Nazi ideologists, and it is not one that Arendt openly challenged. Rather her view as expressed in *Eichmann in Jerusalem* was that forces were at work that made the destruction of the Jewish people the centerpiece of the destruction of all cultural formations alien to the Nazis. Arendt in this sense was not indifferent to cultural issues, but rather viewed them as embedded in the struggle over the Jewish Question. In that sense, her differences with many Zionist elders was not about emigration to Israel, or to Zionism as such, but rather to how the Jewish Question fits into the larger puzzle of the totalitarian machinery of death.

Another contemporary figure of note, Ben Kiernan, is important to understand the impact of Arendt's significant paradigmatic victory. Not only is the issue of totalitarianism writ large in European history, but it is central to the study of Southeast Asia in the major conflagrations of the 1970s and beyond. In the struggles between Cambodia, a genocidal State, Vietnam and, to as lesser degree, Maoist China, it became apparent that totalitarianism, whatever its claimed blessings, did not resolve issues of national, ethnic and racial differences. What came to the surface belatedly in World War II Europe became central in the study of Southeast Asia. The very title of Kiernan's major study on *A World History of Genocide and Extermination from Sparta to Darfur* underscores Arendt's concerns about the nature of the regimes unleashed upon the world in the last decade of the twentieth century. For the issue became and remains the struggle between totalitarian states and democratic regimes—and whether limits to state power can in fact hold off the power of maximum military might, backed by legal concentration of power.[23]

Kiernan's work, and those of his dedicated research associates, underscores the potential for totalitarian systems in small as well as large nations to fiercely struggle to retain power. Those with limited technologies no less than those of technologically sophisticated empire builders have resources, and are unafraid to use them. The merit of Kiernan's work, precisely because of the geo-political terrain that he covers, is to make it clear that totalitarianism may be the cunning "ism" of the Behemoth, but it is not therefore invincible or unstoppable. To be sure, the contradictions between behemoths become plain early on in the struggle for control. Arendt herself had little acquaintance with totalitarian designs in small, underdeveloped nations. As a result, she tacitly assumed that totalitarianism was a big power play and that only external military interventions could adequately prevent the expansion of such despotic killing regimes. This clearly is not the case. It is not the size of the nation embarking on authoritarianism, but the authoritarian drive that created the foundations of totalitarianism. The wreckage of Third World systems in less developed regions is a tragic reminder that it's not size but system that drives extreme despotism.

V.

In summary, it must be appreciated that totalitarianism is not simply an "ism" plucked from the metaphysical air by Arendt. Rather it came about through a deep understanding that something new came about as a result of the Europe of the Second World War. As with Hegel and Marx in the nineteenth century, the world of Nazism and Communism under Hitler and Stalin brought forth a diabolical "unity of opposites": two regimes bitterly at war with each other, with the exception of the 1939-1941 periods of what came to be known as the Molotov-Ribbentrop Europe, that yielded a bizarre and deadly "dialectical synthesis." The regimes of Germany and Russia displayed stunning similarities in political operations and goals that changed the face of "left" and "right" in reality if not always in rhetoric.

The two regimes had in common the following characteristics: (1) Unbridled nationalism that crushed any possibilities of pluralist expressions of differences. (2) A fusion of party and state operations symbolized by leadership figures with unquestioned dominance of both. (3) The establishment of concentration camps, or killing fields, in remote parts of their respective empires responsible for massive genocides. (4) Ethnic cleansing, with special identification of Jews in particular, as inherently enemies of the state fit for punishment, exile, and death. (5) Command and control by the state of all media outlets, educational institutions, and cultural artifacts or performances. (6) Conversion of science and technology into instruments of government mandate, often with perverse features, to service its goals. (7) State worship replaced religious affiliations, which completed the circle of nationalist fervor.

While the information on these features of totalitarianism were less well understood at the time Arendt was writing on the master theme of totalitarianism, and not each facet was covered with the thoroughness that current social and historical researches have made apparent, it was the crowning achievement of Arendt to have placed these various strands into some kind of cohesive framework that has come to be identified as totalitarianism. The fact that real differences existed between Nazism and Communism, such as the relevant importance of race and class, which have been pointed out on innumerable occasions by an endless stream of commentators may score minor points at Arendt's expense, they hardly dent the edifice she helped establish. For this was not simply an understanding of autocracy in its most brutal form, but by implication, helped to explain democracy in its most elemental form.

The work of the post-Arendt generation has shown that outright warfare between nations may not to be the best-case scenario for such struggles. Internal dissent, disaffection, and conflicts within hierarchies, continue unabashedly in much smaller nation totalitarian systems. Individuals do not own intellectual designs or paradigms. Frameworks emerge in the crucible of discourse, which in turn derive from shared experience in difficult and often hostile human climates. Such is the case with Arendt's notion of totalitarianism. The radical element was for her to encapsulate, in a single word, trends that evolved throughout the course of the twentieth century. The conservative element is to see this tendency for what it was worth, as a drive toward collectivism, away from individualism, and a denial of responsibility for governance. It was her suspicions of the behemoth that made her come close to the conservative vantage point; while it was her radicalism that made it possible for her to move beyond calls for liberalism and fatuous distinctions between totalitarian regimes. She championed legal remedies as a potential vehicle to confront the extremists, but not at the price of surrendering the power of weapons. She was in this closer to Hobbes than to Kant—and her critics in the world law and order held her accountable for being "hard" rather than wise.

There was something tough and gritty in both the persona and the writings of Arendt, and these were belatedly recognized by her critics and advocates, but all too rarely incorporated into their own thinking. Rather they too often preferred to see her as a political philosopher who lost her way, with an emphasis on the latter word, and not as a single-minded crusty advocate of the measured uses of power in a world of fanatics and ideologues. It is not that Arendt was a callous "realist" playing at power; rather, she was a thinker for whom the line between theory and practice was narrowed by those for whom theories were reduced to slogans and practices that were incorporated into the destruction of human souls. It was her unique capacity to assess prospects for democracy within a democratic area, not a democracy enfeebled by libertarian tendentious dogmas that resonate well to the ears but so poorly to the survival of bodies. In hard times, the world of ideas puts forth a hard thinker. In Arendt, there may be found awkward formulations, prosaic writing style, and unsteady images—but the end result is a monumental contribution to the world of political affairs, and in so doing to the world of real philosophical discoveries.

Notes

1. Hannah Arendt, *The Origins of Totalitarianism* (New York: Schocken Books, 2004).
2. Erving Goffman, Asylums: Essays on the Social Situation of Mental Patients and Other Inmates (Chicago: Aldine Publishing Company, 1970).
3. David Riesman in collaboration with Reuel Denney and Nathan Glazer, *The Lonely Crowd: A Study of the Changing American Character* (New Haven: Yale University Press, 1950); and again in *Faces in the Crowd: Individual Studies in Character and Politics* (New Haven: Yale University Press, 1952).

4. Karl Raimund Popper, *The Open Society and Its Enemies*, rev. ed. (Princeton: Princeton University Press, 1950).

5. Irving Louis Horowitz, *Radicalism and the Revolt against Reason: The Social Theories of Georges Sorel* (London: Routledge & Kegan Paul Publishers, 1961).

6. Irving Louis Horowitz, *C. Wright Mills: An American Utopian* (New York: Free Press, 1983).

7. Irving Louis Horowitz, *Taking Lives: State Power and Mass Murder*, 5th ed. (New Brunswick and London: Transaction Publishers, 2002). My own work is decidedly indebted to the formulations of Hannah Arendt.

8. Peter Watson, *The German Genius: Europe's Third Renaissance, the Second Scientific Revolution, and the Twentieth Century* (New York: HarperCollins Publishers, 2010), 720-724.

9. Michael Knox Beran, "Hannah Arendt in the Public Square: The Tyranny of the Social Imagination," in *Pathology of the Elites: How the Arrogant Classes Plan to Run Your Life* (Chicago: Ivan R. Dee, Publishers, 2010), 67-82.

10. Michael T. Florinsky, *Fascism and National Socialism: A Study of the Economic and Social Policies of the Totalitarian State* (New York: The Macmillan Company, 1938). Carlo Sforza, *The Totalitarian War and After: Personal Recollections and Political Considerations* (Chicago: University of Chicago Press, 1941).

11. Carl J. Friedrich, *Totalitarianism* (New York, N.Y.: Grosset & Dunlap, 1964).

12. Jean-François Revel, *The Totalitarian Temptation*, trans. David Hapgood (Garden City, New York: Doubleday, 1977).

13. Franz Borkenau, *The Totalitarian Enemy* (New York: AMS Press, 1982).

14. Abbott Gleason, *Totalitarianism: The Inner History of the Cold War* (New York: Oxford University Press, 1995); Ellen Frankel Paul, *Totalitarianism at the Crossroads: Studies in Social Philosophy and Policy* (New Brunswick and London: Transaction Publishers, 1990); and Michael Curtis, *Totalitarianism* (New Brunswick and London: Transaction Publishers, 1980).

15. Leonard Schapiro, *Totalitarianism* (New York: Praeger Publishers, 1972).

16. Irving Howe ed., *1984 Revisited: Totalitarianism in Our Century* (New York: Harper & Row, 1983).

17. Arthur Koestler, *Darkness at Noon* (New York: Modern Library, 1941).

18. Peter L. Berger, *The Capitalist Revolution: Fifty Propositions about Prosperity, Equality, and Liberty* (New York: Basic Books, 1986).

19. Michael Novak, *The Spirit of Democratic Capitalism* (New York: Simon and Schuster, 1982).

20. Timothy Snyder, *Bloodlands: Europe Between Hitler and Stalin* (New York: Basic Books, 2010).

21. Mark Mazower, *Hitler's Empire: How the Nazis Ruled Europe* (New York: The Penguin Press, 2008).

22. Marie Luise Knott ed., *Hannah Arendt and Gershom Scholem: Der Briefwechsel, 1939-1945* (Frankfurt-Berlin: Judischer Verlag/Suhrkamp, 2010). I am indebted to George Steiner's review essay called "Salvaged from Silence," *The Times Literary Supplement*, December 10, 2010, 11 for this insight.

23. Ben Kiernan, *Blood and Soil: A World History of Genocide and Extermination from Sparta to Darfur* (New Haven: Yale University Press, 2007).

Irving Louis Horowitz is Hannah Arendt University Professor Emeritus at Rutgers University and founding editor of *Society*. He serves as chairman and editorial director of Transaction Publishers. His is the author of numerous books including *Publishing as a Vocation: Studies of an Old Occupation in a New Technological Era*, *Taking Lives: Genocide and State Power* (now in its fifth edition) and most recently *Hannah Arendt: Radical Conservative*.

15

Max Gluckman, *The Politics of Law and Ritual in Tribal Society*

Sally Falk Moore

IN HIS AMBITIOUS and well-known book, *Politics, Law and Ritual in Tribal Society*, Max Gluckman (1911-1975) offers a succinct version of a lifetime of opinionated analysis. At the outset he explains to the reader that "custom" is "the focus of interest of all types of anthropology."[1] What about everything else that anthropologists observe? What about the great variety of topics that Gluckman himself writes about in his enormous list of publications? His statement about custom is an example of the persuasive way in which Gluckman frequently condensed his ideas in an easy-to-understand form. It was also a style that was easy to misunderstand. He reached for grand generalizations.

Some Basic Categories

As the content of *Politics, Law and Ritual in Tribal Society* itself shows, Gluckman was interested in much more than custom. His approach included a strong interest in economy and politics, and above all, in social relationships. As he says about the theoretical content of the book, "I have throughout concentrated on a single approach to the analysis of all action and belief: an approach from the context of social relations."[2] He sought to illumine problems of causality and meaning by looking at small-scale social relations and their large-scale social context. That was his mission as an interpreter of ethnographic data.

Politics, Law and Ritual in Tribal Society compares a number of societies, most of them African and most of them "tribal," which is to say, in their putatively pre-colonial tribal condition. The number is large. Before proceeding with his text, Gluckman lists about forty peoples whose practices he will analyze succinctly in the course of about 300 pages. The material is organized by theme. The ethnographic examples appear as brief illustrations of theoretical questions.

One such issue has to do with the apparent stability of certain tribal political structures despite periods of major political disorder. To elucidate this Gluckman draws a distinction between rebellion and revolution. Rebellions may depose a ruler, but they install another person to rule in the same manner, in the same kind of position. The basic organization of the society remains the same. There is simply a change of personnel. Revolutions, on the contrary, are more radical. They are attempts to change the social structure, not just to oust the incumbents in office. Gluckman's contention is that tribal societies do not have revolutions.

Gluckman thus examines tribal organizational structures and their response to serious disruption. He says of the book: "it is a statement of how one social anthropologist, working in the full tradition of the subject, sees the general problem of rule and disorder in social life."[3] The unfolding process of re-stabilization after disruption is his topic. It is described as it operates in the domain of politics, of law, and of ritual.

Implicit in the comparison of tribal peoples is the underlying assumption that "tribal" systems are distinct from "differentiated" societies in fundamental ways. These differences explain the particulars of their organizational response to threats of revolt or fission or other types of disorder. Gluckman conceived of tribal society as being economically egalitarian, producing for consumption, its rules and practices dominated by long-term, multiplex social relationships. What he meant by multiplex relationships (the term was his invention) was that in these small-scale societies, long-term relationships between the same persons were played out in many domains: the religious, the economic, the political, the domain of kinship, and so on. The prestige of leaders depended on the number of dependents or subjects they had, not on material wealth.

Differentiated, or modern society, in contrast, has a class structure, sharp distinctions of wealth, specialization in labor, production for the market, a money economy, and regional economic interdependence. In differentiated societies, impersonal economic transactions between strangers are a major activity, and the legal and regulatory system is dominated by this circumstance. Many economic transactions involve short-term, transitory social relationships.[4]

This binary scheme, tribal/differentiated, does not make room for "mixed" systems—social systems that had some of the characteristics of tribal structures and some of the traits of the differentiated type—nor does it accommodate other organizational frameworks. When anthropologists observed the largest number of African societies, it was during the late colonial period. By then many, if not all, were at least partially mixed systems. Gluckman himself said, "In the last

> The prestige of leaders depended on the number of dependents or subjects they had, not on material wealth.

century the highly differentiated relations of Western industrial society have been extended to most of the world's tribal societies."[5] But that knowledge did not keep him from trying to compare "tribal" systems in this book. There is an immense range of distinct ways of life described. He was making an effort to depict their differences in organization and to establish a catalogue of types.

For Gluckman, whose political sympathies were strongly anticolonial, there was always a tension in this project. The "tribal" type implied an "early" social system that was in some dimensions simpler and less developed than the "differentiated." Tribal societies had some characteristics in common with medieval Europe. There was an evolutionary flavor to that side of the story. Their exoticism was interesting.

But, on the other side, the respect that Gluckman had for Africans—for their standards of justice, for their legal logic, for their ways of addressing complex issues of morality, his sense that they were ready for independence from colonial rule—made him argue time and time again that many of their ideas were no different from European ones. His had a capacious conception of the world that accommodated the idea that there were certain universal forms of reasoning and certain values found in all human societies, despite their marked differences in other respects.

Academic Beginnings and First Fieldwork

Born in 1911 in South Africa to a Russian-Jewish family, Max Gluckman grew up intending to study law. His father was a lawyer and, starting in that direction, Gluckman began some formal legal training. However, when he reached the university he chose to specialize in anthropology instead. He went to the University of Witswatersrand, and studied with Winifred Hoernle and Isaac Shapera. His interest in Africa and Africans became a preoccupation and was to mark his lifelong career.

After his initial South African training he continued at Oxford on a Transvaal Rhodes Scholarship. Once in England, he sampled the views of all the great men of anthropology of the day. At Oxford he studied with and was greatly influenced by E. E. Evans-Pritchard. In London, he attended the famous seminars of Bronislaw Malinowski at the London School of Economics. But though Gluckman absorbed the perspective of Malinowski and Evans-Pritchard, and greatly respected them both, probably the greatest theoretical influence on him was the structural functionalism of A. R. Radcliffe Brown (1881-1955).

Radcliffe-Brown's theoretical frame conceived society as a coherent system of related customs and beliefs. According to his scheme, every culturally established custom was a contribution to the integrated life of the whole. The task of the anthropologist was essentially to describe the structural "whole" of any particular society, and then to explain by what logic a particular custom fit into the totality. He/she was to explain what "function" it had, the "function" defined as the contribution it made to the life of the whole. Radcliffe-Brown wrote, "The function of a particular social usage is the contribution it makes to the total social life as the functioning of the total social system."[6] "Following Durkheim and others, I would define the social function of a socially standardized mode of activity, or mode of thought, as its relation to the social structure to the existence and continuity of which it makes some contribution."[7] For Gluckman, "a standard mode of activity" could be redefined as "custom." This is the source of Gluckman's generalizations about the importance of custom to anthropological work.

A decade after Radcliffe-Brown's death, Gluckman wrote that, as Radcliffe-Brown did not have the personality to be as effective a fieldworker as Malinowski, it was no wonder that he devoted himself instead to the development of a grand theoretical scheme. Recognizing Radcliffe-Brown's shortcomings as a fieldworker did not prevent Gluckman from becoming a partial disciple of his theoretical approach; at least, for a while. Over time, in interactions with his students and professional colleagues, Gluckman could not but become increasingly involved in the innovations in theory and method and even of subject matter that left Radcliffe-Brown far behind. Many of these developments took place under his nose in projects he guided, and in his own seminar and department, often with his encouragement. But as *Politics, Law and Ritual in Tribal Society* shows, he had a tendency to revert to the tenets of structural functionalism when he was making total social comparisons.

Gluckman's own first fieldwork was conducted among the Zulu from 1936 to 1938. Out of this study he contributed a chapter on the Zulu to an important book by Fortes and Evans-Pritchard (1940) then current on African political systems.[8] The Fortes and Evans-Pritchard book divided the political dimensions of the societies they were examining into two categories: primitive states and stateless societies. Gluckman's chapter described two stages of the pre-colonial Zulu polity, depicting a coherent and self-stabilizing indigenous organization. However, unlike most of the other contributors to that volume, Gluckman made a point of including some pages about the subsequent colonial situation and the racial domination of the Zulu by whites.

Fifteen years later Gluckman, in *Politics, Law and Ritual in Tribal Society*, makes a much more nuanced classification of the range of states including "tribal states," large stratified kingdoms, and various partial combinations along the way. Gluckman was concerned with the fissiparous tendencies in decentralized polities, and tried to gauge what difference it made whether large populations were involved. He also asked whether there was economic interdependence among the geographical segments which might have constrained their tendency to rebel. He was looking for causality outside of the domain of custom.

Analyzing an Event

As has been suggested, despite his inclination to proceed from the basic idea of an overarching and integrated social system, Gluckman was frequently more interested in what might be called the "anti-systemic" domain, the elements, real or potential, of disruption and disorder in the putatively coherent unit. One can see evidence of this from the very beginning of his career, and in his first dazzlingly original contribution in the form of "situational analysis."

At about the time he wrote his chapter on the Zulu polity, Gluckman produced a detailed report of a colonial ceremony he had observed several years earlier.[9] His report described an event, the opening of a bridge in South Africa. The occasion brought together white colonial officials, missionaries, ordinary white citizens, and the Zulu king, chiefs, and Zulu commoners. In its approach this paper opened the door to some of the distinctive ideas and methods that later became part of the practice of the Manchester School. The article has often been reprinted and cited. Many years later, Don Handelman gave a succinct description of what took place, based on Gluckman's paper:

> As the cars of the Europeans approached the bridge, they were directed by Zulu in full war dress. The Europeans gathered on one side of the bridge, the Zulu on the other. The regent joined the Zulu, the European commissioner, the whites. The clan songs of the Zulu warriors were hailed by the regent, a Christian, and hymn singing (during which the warriors removed their head gear), led by a missionary, opened the ceremony. Europeans and the regent gave speeches thanking one another. The commissioner gave the Zulu Cattle to slaughter, so that they could pour the bile at the foot of the bridge to ensure safety and good fortune, and then cook and eat the meat. The Zulu warriors led the cars of the Europeans across the bridge to break the opening ribbon, after which the cars drove back to the European side. The Europeans retired to their shelter for tea and cakes, some of which the commissioner sent across the bridge to the regent. In turn, from amongst the Zulu, drinking beer and waiting for their meat to cook, the regent sent over four pots of brew. Though the Europeans left soon after, the Zulu gathered at the bridge for the rest of the day.[10]

Gluckman went on beyond his description to make what was called a "situational analysis" of this ceremony. He argued that one could see in it many of the complex social elements that appeared in

the larger South African society, seeing persons and groups in opposi-
tional but intersecting relationships. As Gluckman himself put it, "Social
situations are a large part of the raw material of the anthropologist.
They are events he observes, and from them and their interrelationships
in a particular society he abstracts the social structure, relationships,
institutions etc. of that society."[11] In a letter in 1940 to Clyde Mitchell,
Gluckman said, "the approach through situations is crucial."[12]

Directing a Research Institute

After his work on the Zulu, in 1939, Gluckman took a position
at the Rhodes-Livingstone Institute (RLI), a research institution, in
what was then Northern Rhodesia
(now Zambia). And in 1942, after
the suicide of Godfrey Wilson, the
director of the Institute, Gluckman
himself became the Institute's director. While there he began his own
major fieldwork on the Lozi and
Barotse of Central Africa. And, in
the milieu of the Institute, he also led
intensive, ongoing group discussions
with the anthropologists who were attached to the institution or
who passed through.[13] Also of considerable interest is Gluckman's
large-scale seven-year plan for the Rhodes-Livingstone Institute
which he prepared in 1945.[14]

> Gluckman outlined
> and achieved ways of
> supporting research.
> His was a lifetime
> commitment to the
> greater development of
> anthropology.

Gluckman starts his proposal by saying, "This plan for co-opera-
tive, co-ordinated, social research in British Central Africa is the
first plan of the kind in the British Empire. It aims to analyse the
organization of modern Central Africa and to show how selected
urban and tribal African Communities live within it."[15] What this
plan describes in thirty-one pages, is not only the detailed objectives
of the research, but it also indicates something about the funding
of the work. Funding for anthropological projects was very difficult
to come by at the time, but through the Institute and other connections Gluckman outlined and achieved ways of supporting the
research. His was a lifetime commitment to the greater development
of anthropology.

He conceived of the project as a team effort. This was an opportunity to do comparative work in a setting where the comparisons could be active and ongoing, with a continuous exchange of ideas and information among the researchers. Administrative problems in Africa were among the topics to be considered. Gluckman writes:

> We shall be investigating the attitudes of tribes to their Native authorities, the extent to which the people play Native authorities against British, the working of Native treasuries, etc. In selecting the areas for our sociological research, I did so in order to produce data on the comparative development of local government in tribes with different types of social structure and different histories of British administration and land policy.[16]

The project described is obviously a modern study of African peoples in the midst of colonial rule.

Gluckman insisted on independence from the colonial government. Anthropologists and sociologists were thus able to carry on their investigations.

Gluckman insisted on independence from the colonial government for the associated anthropologists and sociologists were thus able to carry on their investigations. He was hugely stimulated by the group with which he worked. He was excited by the ideas that flowed from the interaction he had organized and initiated. Among many other things the Rhodes-Livingston Institute was one of the places where the concept of the social network was used as a technique in fieldwork, since tracing the lives of urban Africans required new methods. Their way of life could not to be understood through the study of tribal custom. This was also where the idea of the extended case study got under way. In the RLI work Gluckman was as committed to looking at a modern Africa as to continuing his interest in what he termed "tribal" systems.

As his share of the RLI research, Gluckman did fieldwork among the Barotse/Lozi. Out of this project he published an enormous number of short monographs, chapters, papers and several books.[17] The best known of these are his two large books on Barotse law: *The Judicial Process Among the Barotse* (1955) and *The Ideas in Barotse Jurisprudence* (1965).

Court Cases in Africa

The *Judicial Process* examined and analyzed about sixty appellate cases that came before a court in the Lozi capital in the 1940s. Gluckman was the first anthropologist to listen to cases in an African court, take notes on them, and analyze them. That example of a new kind of fieldwork was remarkable and influential. The facts of the cases he heard are very interesting and one gets a clear idea of what seemed important to the disputants. But Gluckman was interested in more than the particular subject matter of local quarrels. He was interested in the total system of Lozi norms and in the logic of the judges.

There are many things about Gluckman's approach to the cases he heard that are not entirely satisfactory, and there are serious questions about the special circumstances of the historical moment in which the disputes came to court. It was a period during World War II when 60 to 70 percent of the male population was absent from the area, many of them working in the mines and 80 percent of the cases before the *kutas* (courts) were domestic relations cases.[18] No doubt the kind of cases that came to the court were considerably skewed by the demography of the moment.

As trials for witchcraft were prohibited by colonial law, Gluckman felt free to exclude witchcraft issues from his analysis. However the issue continued to be important outside the courts in the villages.[19] That meant that sometimes there were dimensions of the disputes that came to the court that were excluded from discussion, and that Gluckman could not consider when he was considering the ideas and logic of the judges.

Besides, what was "Barotse law" given that the Barotse were not one people, but an assemblage of about 300,000 people, divided into 25 tribes, ruled by one group, the Lozi? Could one assume that what was law for the Lozi was law for all the Barotse? Gluckman was stationed in the Lozi capital and what he heard were largely cases that concerned Lozi villagers.

There are also questions about the structure of the court itself given the conclusions to which Gluckman came about the reasoning behind the application of norms to cases. In the *kuta* (court) which

Gluckman attended, a group of judges heard cases together, and the judges, in other roles, also held administrative power. The judges in the court he attended were by no means always in agreement about who was right in any particular case. They gave their concluding opinions orally, in sequence, the most junior judge first, with the most senior title-holder giving the final and decisive verdict. Norms were not always explicitly mentioned.

At various points in late-colonial history various officials tried to make lists of the norms used in particular areas with the idea of eventually codifying them. They tried to elicit the rules by posing hypothetical cases. But this method was deeply flawed. Africans often replied that hypotheticals are empty of the very information that is needed for the kind of decision-making they practice. They explained that they cannot judge a case unless they know which particular parties were involved, all about the character of the persons in the dispute, and the history of the relationship between the parties.

Thus, the Barotse cases Gluckman describes are not always about selecting from a system of rules the ones that apply. They are often about which disputant is on the higher moral ground once their individual character is known and the transactional record as a whole is weighed. Gluckman's collection of actual cases that he heard was a far more revealing mode of reporting on the activities of the court than any previous effort to address local African law. But given the premises on which the court operated, his relentless search for underlying norms in each case was not altogether satisfactory.

There were other problems with Gluckman's legal interpretation. He was describing what he observed in a court in the 1940s, but he was also looking at its cases to find in them an "archaic" essence of the law. Confirming this explicitly, Gluckman said in *The Ideas in Barotse Jurisprudence* (1965) that in his Barotse work he had wanted to come as close as he could to providing the example of "pure archaic law" that Sir Henry Maine had called for.[20] How could the judicial reasoning of courts in the 1940s embody the archaic?

Gluckman resorted to several methods for reconciling the past and the present. He specified that the "judicial process," by which he meant a form of judicial reasoning, had not changed from the past.[21] He said, "I believe that my observations not only yield a valid analysis of judicial practice in Lozi courts at present, but also that this analysis gives, with reservations for the past made clear in the text, a true view of their judicial *process* in that past."[22] He acknowledged that there had been many changes in Lozi society. "These changes were so great that an entirely different social system has to be studied."[23] Nevertheless he felt able to reconstruct continuities in Lozi judicial process.

Other than the question of norms, what Gluckman tried to distill from the cases was the Lozi form of "judicial reasoning." What Gluckman meant by "the judicial process" was "a process of reasoning" by the judges, in which they "applied" concepts to cases.[24] He argued that despite many modern changes in Lozi/Barotse life, the judicial process was the same as it had been in the deep past. The timeless continuity of judicial logic was a necessary part of his theoretical construct, though of course, there were no records of the nature of reasoning in the past.

Part of Gluckman's interpretation of Lozi judicial thought was his idea that the Lozi used the concept of the "reasonable man" to determine whether the behavior of the disputing parties was or was not appropriate. Not satisfied to attribute this fellow to the Lozi alone, Gluckman said, "The reasonable man is recognized as the central figure in all developed systems of law."[25] Gluckman was trying to be true to Radcliffe-Brown's (1952) notion that behavior appropriate to a social position was universally the legally relevant standard of right-doing and wrong-doing. The reasonable man was the man who behaved correctly.

In Gluckman's *The Judicial Process Among the Barotse of Northern Rhodesia* (1955), the concept of a reasonable man as a legal standard could be presumed to be timeless and not special to any particular society or era. The judgment of what constituted reasonable behavior could allow for the exercise of judicial discretion. Was the reasonable man really an expressed Lozi idea, or was it a Gluckman idea? Gluckman's temporal and spatial double-think about judicial reasoning made the Lozi judges' logic apply equally to then and now, and whenever.

When Gluckman's says that Lozi concepts and logic were the same as "Western" law was he right? Certainly to the extent that he was speaking about their reasoning from general ideas to specific instances his argument is sound. But he is on less-firm ground when he talks about Lozi *legal concepts*: "The Lozi share most of these concepts with Western law."[26] This way of looking at the matter may have had something to do with his political position when the research was conducted (1940 to 1947) and when the book was written. It was a time when the demands of colonial states for independence were being heard more and more loudly. There were contrary voices in the metropole which declared that the Africans were not competent to handle their own affairs. Some of the intense interest Gluckman had in showing the nature of Lozi logic may have been his own way of declaring that the Lozi were as logical and as competent as their colonial rulers. Northern Rhodesia did not, in fact, achieve independence (as Zambia) until 1964.

An Evolutionary Approach to Legal Concepts

The second big Barotse book, *The Ideas in Barotse Jurisprudence* (1965), was quite different from *The Judicial Process Among the Barotse of Northern Rhodesia*. It was not a book about Lozi jurisprudential reasoning and its similarity to Western legal logic. On the contrary, it was a book that emphasized the *difference* between aspects of the substantive law of a tribal society and modern law. It was an attempt to illuminate Barotse ideas of power, property, contracts, injury, obligation, and debt. These are treated in a comparative context. Gluckman argued that in these matters Barotse law epitomizes an early stage of legal evolution. *The Ideas* connects Barotse' substantive legal ideas to the kind of society in which they lived. It reaches widely in its analogies to medieval European history, and to the ethnographies of other anthropologists. Gluckman speculates a good deal on the social structural causes and consequences that lie behind legal concepts.

The greater speculative freedom of *The Ideas* and the wide ranging content of *Politics, Law and Ritual in Tribal Society* may be attributable to a profound recasting of his own thought that Gluckman experienced. His "Introduction" to a collection of his essays published in 1963, *Order and Rebellion in Tribal Africa*, expresses very clearly the fundamental change in his own thinking:

I now abandon altogether the type of organic analogy for a social system with which Radcliffe-Brown worked, and which led me to speak of civil war as being necessary to maintain the system. Social systems are not nearly as integrated as organic systems, and the processes working within them are not as cyclical or repetitive as are those in organic systems. Moreover, social systems are open to the influences of changes in environment, and to changes due to relations with other social systems, as organic systems are not. I think therefore much more in terms of series of social processes, operating within an ecological setting and the bio-psychical framework of human life, as well as of the restriction and action of a technology and a culture. These are never perfectly adjusted; and hence processes do not cancel themselves out as in organic systems. We have, as Fortes and Firth have stressed, to think of a field of social action...The structure of such a field is much less rigid and self-consistent than it was thought to be by social anthropologists from the 1920s to about 1950.[27]

Yet in *Politics, Law and Ritual in Tribal Society*, Gluckman avoided the issue of internally-generated social structural change. He says, "The manner in which social anthropologists have analyzed radical social change lies outside the main scope of the present book...Every study of a particular tribe that I have cited in the course of this book, after analyzing the tribal equilibrium, considers the tribe's position since it came under European domination."[28] In short, the basic model Gluckman used again and again is of a tribal social order that coheres and is inherently stable. Social change is conceived of as being introduced from the outside by modern conditions, ways in which contact with modern societies impinged on African polities. It is as if, for the purposes of this book, most of the political systems of tribal societies were conceived as reconstructed in a pre-colonial form. Gluckman, to a great extent, still seemed attached to the structural functional model and to an idea of an indigenous system in equilibrium, operating as a self-replicating, organic whole. However radical the revisions of Gluckman's thought were in 1963, one can see a considerable residue of an earlier mode of analysis in *Politics, Law and Ritual in Tribal Society*. What he does very effectively in this volume is point to the sociological problems of explanation that fascinated him. His views on these issues are sometimes stated as speculations, but more often as conclusive arguments.

Constructing a New Department at Manchester

When Gluckman returned from his stay at the Rhodes-Livingstone Institute he taught for two years at Oxford but then moved on. In 1947 there was a major change in his life. He was invited to found a Department of Anthropology at Manchester University. He accepted. The Department grew and became influential in the academic world. Not only did it become a voice to be noted in the competition in England with Oxford and Cambridge, but it won a worldwide reputation.

A great deal of this repute was achieved through Gluckman's indefatigable efforts. To his students Gluckman was a remarkable teacher, though sometimes exasperating in his insistence on his own views. He was dedicated to anthropology, its theories, its personnel, its subjects, and its objects. He was also dedicated to the achievements of the local soccer team, Manchester United. He required his teaching staff members to accompany him to their games. This was only one of the ways in which he entered and dominated the lives of his associates in and out of the classroom. He showered them with appreciation when he saw that their work was distinguished. He helped them to get published and saw to it that they were introduced around, and that their work was presented to the various seminars in England. At Manchester, his many outstanding students and colleagues had his unqualified attention, sometimes more than they wanted. Over time the collective product was the launching of a variegated methodological and theoretical framework that came to be known as the "Manchester School."[29]

The Academic Legacy

In his academic career in and out of Manchester, Max Gluckman was a powerful influence; partly through his large production of books and articles, partly as a public intellectual, partly as a teacher who attracted and developed remarkable students, and partly as a uniquely commanding presence at scholarly meetings and seminars. He loved discussion and debate. His fascination with new ethnographic data was inexhaustible. He listened carefully. He was always intuitively making sociological comparisons, frequently reanalyzing material that caught his attention. He was also involved in lively public disagreements.

As is probably already evident, Gluckman had a striking personality. He was not a man who effaced himself. When he was in a room he made everyone aware of his presence. He never hesitated to give emphatic voice to his own opinions. He challenged others to reply. And they did. I remember one meeting many years ago when his analytic methods were vigorously attacked. He was criticized for using legal terms borrowed from English law to describe the legal ideas of an African people. As his critics went on and on about the uniqueness of culture and the inappropriateness of his applied translations, he bowed his large bald head and held it between his hands and closed his eyes as if he had a headache or were sleeping. But when it came his turn to speak, it was clear from his cogent and biting response that he had listened carefully to every word, and was not going to accept the argument and moreover had contempt for the lack of legal knowledge of those who offered it.

An appraisal of the more than eighty papers he published, books he wrote, the many that he edited, the visiting appointments he held, the academic distinctions he was awarded over his lifetime, would be too lengthy a project to undertake here. Just after he died someone at Manchester sent me a curriculum vitae for him. The publications are overwhelming in quantity, let alone the special lectures, the academic boards on which he sat and the like. As we have seen, he did research in Africa, and directed a great deal of contemporary study there. Late in his life he also organized a research project in Israel.

Gluckman was by no means exclusively interested in the "tribal." He not only wrote a number of books, academic and popular, he also edited many on thematic topics which interested him, often himself mustering the contributions of others. He wrote forewords to many other books, forewords that frequently included theoretical assessments of his own. He presented anthropology and Africa on the BBC. I will not try to summarize his voluminous record further, except to say that the energy and concentration involved in such continuous professional activity is astonishing. His was a gigantic presence on the anthropological horizon.

Given the structural functionalist point of view that underlay the ethnographic work of many British social anthropologists in the mid-twentieth century, one can see that even within that academic fashion Gluckman's interests were innovative. His approach included an emphasis on social divisiveness, on rebellion, on dispute, on social cleavage, on analyzing the elements of social situations, and extended cases. It is true that he did not turn this set of interests directly to the task of dismembering structural functionalism. That was an endeavor which his students and colleagues carried forward, arguing with Gluckman all the way.

> His intellectual struggle was to reconcile the idea of change, with the analytic dynamic of repetitive systems.

Gluckman was very much aware of Africa's history, but in *Politics, Law and Ritual in Tribal Society* he argues nevertheless that "[t]he concept of equilibrium in repetitive systems...covers complex processes of disturbance and readjustment."[30] For Gluckman, the underlying idea is that in the "tribal" form, he has been analyzing repetitive systems. The companion of this idea is that, "[a]nthropologists analyse a society as if it were in a state of equilibrium."[31] He was, of course, speaking of himself. Needless to say Gluckman's idea of equilibrium and his way of addressing change provoked many scholarly arguments, and did not clarify his analysis of "tribal" systems. His final chapter in *Politics, Law and Ritual in Tribal Society* is an intellectual struggle to reconcile the idea of change, with the analytic dynamic of repetitive systems which he used throughout the book.

There is no doubt that in Africa and elsewhere, the ways of life of past and existing local societies are sufficiently different from each other and from European and American ways to be of great comparative interest. Gluckman's was a grand try at the awesome problem of comparing so many peoples and problems in so little page-space. One need not accept all of Gluckman's premises to profit from his summaries of local culture and his fascination with political issues. But the reader of *Politics, Law and Ritual in Tribal Society* is nevertheless bound to start thinking critically for him- or herself about the profound theoretical and analytical questions it raises.

Notes

1.   Max Gluckman, *Politics, Law and Ritual in Tribal Society*, 3rd ed. (New Brunswick: AldineTransaction, 2011), xxiv.
2.   Gluckman, *Politics*, xxv.
3.   Gluckman, *Politics*, xxiv.
4.   See Gluckman, *Politics*, 81; and Max Gluckman, *The Ideas in Barotse Jurisprudence* (New Haven, CT: Yale University Press, 1965), 4-5.
5.   Gluckman, *Politics*, 81.
6.   Radcliffe-Brown, A. R. *Structure and Function in Primitive Society* (London: Cohen and West, 1952), 181.
7.   Radcliffe-Brown, *Structure and Function*, 200.
8.   For a discussion of the controversies surrounding this work see Joan Vincent, *Anthropology and Politics: Visions, Traditions and Trends* (Tucson: University of Arizona Press, 1990), 258-264.
9.   Max Gluckman, "Analysis of a Social Situation in Modern Zululand," *Bantu Studies* 14 (1940): 147-174.
10. Don Handelman, "The Extended Case," in *The Manchester School: Practice and Ethnographic Praxis in Anthropology*, T. M. S. Evens and D. Handelman, eds. (Oxford, UK: Berghahn Books, 2006), 97.
11. As quoted by Marian Kempny, "History of the Manchester 'School' and the Extended Case Method," in *The Manchester School: Practice and Ethnographic Praxis in Anthropology*, T. M. S. Evens and D. Handelman, eds. (Oxford, UK: Berghahn Books, 2006), 194.
12. As quoted in Kempny, "A History of the Manchester 'School'," 170.
13. A list of the many anthropologists who worked and studied at the Institute under Gluckman's directorship is available at http://en.wikipedia.org/wiki/Manchester_school_(anthropology).
14. The full text of the plan is found in the photo essay on the Manchester School by Wim van Binsbergen. Available at http://www.shikanda.net/ethnicity/illustrations_manch/manchest.htm
15. *Seven Year Research Plan of the Rhodes Livingston Institute of Social Studies in British Central Africa*, 1945. Available at http://www.shikanda.net/ethnicity/illustrations_manch/seven_year_plan_2.pdf.
16. *Seven Year Research* Plan, 22.
17. For a few of these see Gluckman, *Economy of the Central Barotse Plain* (Livingstone, Northern Rhodesia: Rhodes-Livingstone Institute, 1941); *Essays on Lozi Land and Royal Property* (Livingstone, Northern Rhodesia: Rhodes-Livingstone Paper No. 10, 1943); and "The Lozi of Barotseland in Northern Rhodesia," in *Seven Tribes of British Central Africa*. 2nd ed., E. Colson and M. Gluckman, eds. (Manchester, UK: Manchester University Press, 1951).
18. Gluckman, Essays on Lozi Land, 46; and *The Judicial Process Among the Barotse of Northern Rhodesia* (Manchester, UK: Manchester University Press, 1955), 65.
19. Gluckman, *The Judicial Process*, 97, 218.
20. Sir Henry Maine, *Ancient Law* (London: John Murray, 1894), 258-259.
21. Gluckman, *Economy of the Central Barotse Plain*, 32-33.
22. Gluckman, *The Judicial Process*, 32; emphasis in original.
23. Gluckman, *Economy of the Central Barotse Plain*, 2-3.
24. Gluckman, *The Judicial Process*, 218, 323-326).
25. Gluckman, *The Judicial Process*, 83.
26. Gluckman, *The Judicial Process*, 365.
27. Max Gluckman, *Order and Rebellion in Tribal Africa* (London: Cohen and West, 1963), 38-39.
28. Gluckman, *Politics*, 285.
29. See T. M. S. Evens and Don Handelman, eds. *The Manchester School: Practice and Ethnographic Praxis in Anthropology* (Oxford, UK: Berghahn Books, 2006).

30. Gluckman, *Politics*, 282.
31. Gluckman, *Politics*, 279.

References

Evens, T. M. S., and Don Handelman, eds. *The Manchester School: Practice and Ethnographic Praxis in Anthropology.* Oxford, UK: Berghahn Books, 2006.

Fortes, M. and E. E. Evans-Prichard, eds. *African Political Systems.* Oxford University Press, 1940.

Gluckman, Max. "Analysis of a Social Situation in Modern Zululand." *Bantu Studies* 14 (1940): 147-174.

_____. *Economy of the Central Barotse Plain.* Livingstone, Northern Rhodesia: Rhodes-Livingstone Institute, 1941.

_____. *Essays on Lozi Land and Royal Property.* Livingstone, Northern Rhodesia: Rhodes-Livingston Paper No. 10, 1943.

_____. *Seven Year Research Plan of the Rhodes Livingston Institute of Social Studies in British Central Africa.* 1945. Available at http://www.shikanda.net/ethnicity/illustrations_manch/seven_year_plan_2.pdf.

_____. "The Lozi of Barotseland in Northern Rhodesia." In *Seven Tribes of British Central Africa.* 2nd ed. Edited by E. Colson and M. Gluckman. Manchester, UK: Manchester University Press, 1951.

_____. *The Judicial Process Among the Barotse of Northern Rhodesia.* Manchester, UK: Manchester University Press, 1955.

_____. *Order and Rebellion in Tribal Africa.* London: Cohen and West, 1963.

_____. *The Ideas in Barotse Jurisprudence.* New Haven, CT: Yale University Press, 1965.

Handelman, Don. "The Extended Case." In *The Manchester School: Practice and Ethnographic Praxis in Anthropology.* Edited by T. M. S. Evens and D. Handelman. Oxford, UK: Berghahn Books, 2006.

Kempny, Marian. "History of the Manchester 'School' and the Extended-Case Method." In *The Manchester School: Practice and Ethnographic Praxis in Anthropology.* Edited by T. M. S. Evens and D. Handelman. Oxford, UK: Berghahn Books, 2006.

Maine, Sir Henry. *Ancient Law.* London: John Murray, 1894.

Moore, Sally Falk. "Archaic Law and Modern Times on the Zambezi." In *Cross Examinations: Essays in Memory of Max Gluckman.* Edited by P. H. Gulliver. Leiden, The Netherlands: E. J. Brill, 1978.

Radcliffe-Brown, A. R. *Structure and Function in Primitive Society.* London: Cohen and West, 1952.

Vincent, Joan. *Anthropology and Politics: Visions, Traditions and Trends.* Tucson: University of Arizona Press, 1990.

Sally Falk Moore is professor of anthropology emerita at Harvard University and affiliated professor at Harvard Law School. A specialist in legal and political anthropology, she has done fieldwork in East Africa and consulting in West Africa. Her books include *Law as Process, Social Facts and Fabrications; "Customary" Law on Kilimanjaro, 1880-1980; Anthropology and Africa*; and *Law and Anthropology: A Reader.*